THE
HORSE AND
BUGGY DOCTOR

THE
HORSE AND
BUGGY DOCTOR

by

ARTHUR E. HERTZLER, M.D.

UNIVERSITY OF NEBRASKA PRESS   LINCOLN

First Bison Book printing: June 1970
Second Bison Book printing: July 1971

Bison Book edition reprinted from the first edition of 1938 by arrangement
with The Hertzler Research Foundation.

CONTENTS

FOREWORD

WHEN I WAS ASKED TO WRITE THE FOREWORD FOR THE EDITION OF this great book commemorating its author's one-hundredth birthday, it struck me as being quite an honor, and indeed it is, but somehow incongruous. For a fictional physician who "practiced" at a time when the art was only emerging from the barber shop, to introduce the reader to a book authored by one of the finest practitioners of real-life medicine would, it seemed to me, put me in the position of being presumptuous. My second thought was, "I'll have to read the book again." Have to read the book again? It was like the first time. I couldn't put it down. Most new readers will have that experience. Thousands who had the experience when the book was first published in 1938 will have it again.

Before proceeding I will explain who I am. This is necessary because I know that the grandchildren of the grandchildren of readers today will read this great piece of American literature, but the transient fame of the vehicle that has made me known will have faded entirely. My name is Milburn Stone. I am an actor. I was born near Burrton, Kansas, a small town ten miles from Halstead, Kansas, near which Dr. Arthur E. Hertzler lived and practiced, and where he built his great hospital.

FOREWORD

Dr. Hertzler was a practicing young physician when I was born. I do not remember the first time I ever saw him any more than I remember when I was first aware of the Kansas sun, the wind, or the endless wheat fields. In the land of my childhood, Dr. Hertzler was part of the environment.

Fifteen years ago a network television show titled "Gunsmoke" was first presented to the viewers of America. It has at times been the most popular and highly rated program in the early electronic age, and for a decade and a half I have been privileged to play the role of Doc Adams, a crusty old physician of the 1870s in Dodge City, Kansas. I am often asked if the memory of Dr. Hertzler and his work has influenced my portrayal of the old frontier medico. Such queries are indeed flattering, but since "Gunsmoke" has always tried for a documentary flavor of the period, I have resisted any suggestions that would have had me playing "Doc Adams, Microbe Hunter of the High Plains" or "Doc Adams, Pioneer Prairie Surgeon." I hope I have managed to portray Doc as the extractor of lead from losers in shooting contests, comfortor of the worried and bereaved, and occasionally someone who says to Matt Dillon, "Sorry, Matt, there ain't a thing I can do for him." In my copy of *The Horse and Buggy Doctor*, there is an artist's sketch of young Dr. Hertzler walking down a country road, carrying a bag in each hand. On his face is the suggestion of a kindly, knowing smile. I remember him that way. To me he looked sad—with a twinkle. He was homely and tall like Abraham Lincoln was homely and tall. I have been told he could be gruff and tough at times. Although I never saw this side to him, I do not doubt it. Add these warm recollections to the fact that I am at least six inches shorter than Dr. Hertzler was—no, I could not play Dr. Adams like that.

It is this honesty that gives me some sense of safety from possible retribution, for I feel certain that Dr. Hertzler was invited into heaven, where he can spend his time watching baseball

FOREWORD

games and sharpening his championship skill with a target pistol.
Yet, he may have been offered an option. Perhaps, having con-
quered Kansas winters, he may have challenged hell. Possibly he
is riding around that region in a battered old buggy drawn by
an unpredictable horse, soothing the fevered inhabitants and
calling the attention of Satan and his staff to the stupidity of
attempting to standardize everything.

I don't know where I'll be going. I figure my ticket is punched
but I don't know my destination. Wherever it is, I do not want
to face the scorn of Dr. Hertzler. I don't want him to have any
criticism for the way I portrayed a Kansas country doctor, a role
he created and played to perfection throughout his entire life.
It's all in the book. Read it.

MILBURN STONE

PREFACE

LET THIS SCREED BE A WARNING TO ALL THOSE WHO FEEL AN urge to take up a pencil. It began innocently enough. My kid daughter, a trained nurse, being possessed of a small son, desired to know something of my early life so that she might institute prophylactic proceedings before it was too late.

I chanced to tell a publisher friend, as an excuse for the delay in more important writing, what I was doing. At once he began his seductive procedures. He wanted to see what I had written. The argument presented was that there should be a record of the old country doctor by one of the species. Admitted. I prepared to write one anonymously. Rejected, because it might cast suspicion on some innocent colleague. Unanswerable. I started to write in the abstract, but it sounded like a sermon or a newspaper editorial. Terrible. Concrete cases had to be inserted to give point. I was urged to make it more and more personal. I protested modestly. A lifelong friend countered that it was a fine time to profess modesty after one had taken a bath in a glass bathroom located on Main Street. The argument was unanswerable.

I had to sacrifice my better judgment in telling the story as an individual. To write a life story when one is still in the height, or depth, of one's life work is, to say the least, premature. But it is not individual, because the same account might have been written by countless thousands of old country doctors with, of course, personal variations. Therefore it is in no sense an auto-biography. It is a history of my own times. It is personal only as far as is necessary in order to give it point. I have put down the facts as they unfolded themselves, as far as the material made it possible to do so. It is not an autobiography in that I have carefully avoided revealing my own philosophy of life, though I may seem to have done so. The facts presented are general, not personal, and can be defended on scientific grounds. A doctor of medicine may think one thing and feel another. It takes both thought and feeling to make his philosophy of life. The first he develops; the other is largely hereditary.

A. E. H.

THE
HORSE AND
BUGGY DOCTOR

CHAPTER

1 _____

"PROTECT US, O GOD, FROM DIPHTHERIA!" THESE RINGING WORDS uttered by my father at morning prayers were my first introduction to the tragedy of diseases. The atmosphere in our home that morning was tense. Father and mother ate no breakfast, and we children, not knowing why, left the large platter of fried mush, which usually quickly disappeared, practically untouched. Soon father left home dressed in his Sunday clothes. Mother, pale and silent, continued to walk the floor, wringing her hands and going to the window now and then to look down the road. I followed and looked up and down the road too, but saw nothing. Some hours later a long line of teams came slowly down that road. Driving the lead team, a strange one, was my father, and beside him sat a man I did not know. In the bed of the farm wagon were three oblong boxes. Following were spring wagons, farm wagons, and a large number of men on horseback. Questions directed to my mother brought no answer. Father returned home after many hours and cryptically anounced as he came in the door: "Five more." Mother sank into a chair and covered her face with her apron.

As days wore on I learned that the wagon had borne the coffins containing the bodies of three of my playmates. Five more followed in quick succession. Eight of the nine children in that one family died of diphtheria in ten days. There remained only a baby of nine months. The mother took to carrying this child constantly even while she did the farm housework. Clutched to her mother's breast, this child seemed inordinately wide-eyed as though affected by the silent grief which surrounded her. I used to steal away without knowing why and visit this home. There was something fascinatingly tragic about it. Watching that mother, I was learning then, though I did not know it, that it is not the dying but the living who suffer.

Only slightly less terrible was the havoc wrought by diphtheria in other families. I know of several cemeteries which contain four or five graves made within a week or two. In fact, there were few families in those days which had not suffered from this devastating disease. In my early practice a family history usually revealed that some member had died of one of the infectious diseases of childhood, of which diphtheria was the chief.

The reign of terror during a diphtheria epidemic brings out a trait common to the entire human race: when confronted with unknown perils people seek aid from some Supreme Being. Prayers for protection literally filled the air in those days of doom. There was no appeal to the science of medicine because there was none. The prayers were all abstract supplications; no one prayed that the doctors might find a remedy. No one thought of this possibility. The pious may believe that these prayers were answered through the instrumentality of doctors after a remedy was discovered. Nothing better illustrates the passive reliance on an unseen being than the text chosen by the ministers who preached the funeral sermons of these young victims: "The Lord giveth and the Lord taketh away." It also shows the universal tendency to place the blame for disaster beyond the pale of our own efforts.

In order to appreciate the distance medical science has traveled, let us picture the course of a typical case of diphtheria fifty years ago. The child is dumpy, listless and feverish. It may or may not complain of sore throat, for diphtheria is much less likely than tonsillitis to produce local symptoms. The membrane more or less covers the tonsils and the adjacent regions of the pharynx, even into the nose. The pulse rate becomes rapid, even running, and thready until it is uncountable. In some cases the membrane extends to the nose; one detects this extension by the appearance of obstructed nasal breathing. These cases die of toxemia, the effect of the poison produced by the bacteria. This caused the death of approximately a fourth of the patients about the sixth day. Sometimes the patient seemed better on the fourth and fifth day and the parents became hopeful. The doctor, noting the obstructed nasal breathing, knew those hopes were unfounded. Shall he tell the parents now that the child is doomed or shall he wait a few days, letting them hope until the blow falls?

More dramatic still were those cases in which the disease began in the larynx or extended to it from above. The membrane gradually clogs the lumen of the windpipe. The child, fevered and delirious, becomes bluer and bluer as the windpipe fills up. He is too busy breathing to cry. The appearance of the deeply blue face is made more terrible by the bulging, unseeing eyes. The head and shoulders pull back, the hands twitch. Then the entire body relaxes and the face becomes less livid. The child is dead. I sat through such a terrible night once, inactive—just once.

Nor was diphtheria the only disease of bygone days that decimated, even several times plus, many families. Scarlet fever swept entire neighborhoods, destroying many children directly or indirectly by involvement of the kidneys or by brain infection due to the invasion of the middle ears. The latter complication when it did not kill often resulted in deaf-mutism. Scarlet fever is as infectious as diphtheria but much less fatal.

3

It ran its course in a week or ten days, and death from collapse, though not common, sometimes occurred.

Measles, though less fatal than diphtheria or scarlet fever, added its quota to the casualty list of childhood. Of all diseases it is the one most readily disseminated. If housing facilities were poor, pneumonia was a frequent complication which resulted fatally in many cases and in many more left constitutional defects. I had experience enough with this disease in my early years of practice.

Since measles is much more fatal in adults than in children, mothers were anxious that their offspring should have the disease in childhood. My mother sent me, when I was nine years old, to play with a neighbor boy who had the disease. We played dominoes several hours but I took nothing. This is inexplicable because, as already mentioned, measles is the most readily spread of all infectious diseases.

Smallpox was the only infectious disease which the profession knew how to combat. Vaccination was already known and practiced in a crude sort of way. Because of this crudeness infections sometimes resulted, giving rise to skepticism as to the value of the preventative. Instead of using "points" as is done now, the vaccination was done from patient to candidate. A healthy child who had been vaccinated and had a good "take" was selected and the children to be vaccinated were lined up before the donor. The doctor scratched a little place on the skin on the upper arm until the blood began to ooze and then, dipping the lancet into the pus of the lesion on the arm of the inoculated child, rubbed it over the denuded area of the candidate's arm.

Then, even as now, tuberculosis was the great and universal scourge. Here also the etiology was unknown and it was generally considered a constitutional disease with the local lesion as secondary. This was the status when I was a child. The incipient stages of the disease were mistaken for the precursors.

MEDICINE AS IT WAS IN MY BOYHOOD

Anemia, for example, particularly when associated with suppression of menses, was supposed to lead to tuberculosis. The fact was that the tuberculosis was already present and these obvious states were the result of the disease instead of antecedents. I recall a young girl who, following baptism by immersion, died a few months later of galloping consumption. The scoffers attributed the tuberculosis to the exposure. There is no doubt in my mind now, as I recall her pale thin body, that she already presented an advanced stage of the disease before undergoing the exposure. The exposure merely added a terminal pneumonia.

The prejudices of the time regarded the spread of disease as inevitable. The occurrence of these diseases was believed to be the expression of the Divine will. Mere native ignorance, unsupported by some such thought, would not have been sufficient to blind generations to the fact that tuberculosis spread from individual to individual. The havoc it wrought is well illustrated by the mournful annals of one of our neighbor families. This family lost eight of nine children from tuberculosis in the course of eight years. The children sickened in turn and after a year or two died. I visited this home once in company with my father. The mother and three children who were bedfast with the terminal stages of the disease were all cooped up in a small three-room shack. The unaffected members of the family played about at will.

One member of this family taught our rural school. I can still hear his typical phthisical cough. He coughed all day long expectorating promiscuously about the floor. I remember that he once coughed in my face as he violently shook me for not knowing the answer to the problem, "How much is seven times eight?" I remember the smell of his breath. I know now he had a cavity in his lungs with mixed infection. He died before the school term was half over, from a hemorrhage which fortunately for us children did not occur in the schoolroom. Because of the number of sick members in the family, the youngest boy, a mere child, was given to an aunt to rear. He escaped the disease and is still living. Such instances should have quickly enlightened the laity, certainly the medical profession, as to the importance of isolation, yet it escaped the notice of everybody, including the doctors.

In those early days the chief difficulty in controlling disease was due to the fact that its bacterial causes were not recognized. Hence there was no effort at prevention by quarantine. The season of the year, atmospheric conditions and what not— at least something beyond the control of man—were believed to be causes. The frequency of complications was due to the poor housing conditions. The sick child became chilled and inflammation of the kidneys developed or ear infections followed.

Diseases that were not epidemic fared no better in the hands of the old doctor. Acute abdominal infections went unrecognized until the terminal stages after general inflammation had been established; and the infection being general, a general term was applied. A definite diagnosis was not made in such cases until the peritonitis had spread all over the abdomen. Hence the term "inflammation of the bowels" was used, but it was the covering of the bowels that was involved: to wit, the peritoneum. In those days autopsies were not permitted, as they were considered sacrilegious. No one wanted to enter the pearly gates carrying a miscellaneous lot of his viscera in a basket. The consequences were that in many cases doctors did not make a diagnosis even after death and so repeated their errors throughout generations, even centuries.

Operations in rural districts, even for the simplest of lesions, were practically unknown. In those days all wounds suppurated. It was the common practice for the surgeons in that day to operate garbed in the Prince Albert coat then regarded as the only fitting garment for the professional man. The cuff was turned up by the more fastidious. In the first operation I witnessed the surgeon threaded the needles with silk and then stuck them in the lapel of his coat so as to have them readily accessible when needed. He held the knife in his teeth when not in actual use.

It is, therefore, easy to understand why all wounds suppurated. Injuries which today seem comparatively trivial were treated by amputation. I remember a lacerated hand treated by amputation, and a simple compound fracture of the tibia likewise amputated, and in the mid-thigh at that. In fact, it was a general rule in compound fractures to amputate, and injuries to the larger joints invariably were subjected to this procedure. The reason for such radical measures was that because of suppuration the surgeon, usually called from a distance, found amputation the most practical measure. There was no one present to care for the wound. The experience was that if amputation was not done death from infection would most likely follow, an end not obviated, however, in many cases by amputation, because the wound made by the amputation often became infected and killed the patient. The vessels were tied by silk threads cut long so that they could be pulled out after the end of the vessel sloughed off: that is, if the patient did not die of secondary hemorrhage.

Operations for abdominal affections were almost unheard of in those days. When removal of the lesion required an abdominal incision, death from peritonitis almost invariably followed. Ovarian cysts and myomas of the uterus were treated expectantly. Expectant treatment, I may add, is treatment which one does not even expect to be efficient. The doctor employing expectant treatment has only the satisfaction of knowing that he is doing nothing injurious—a merit, it may be added, that is today sometimes overlooked.

Many operations now done daily in every hospital were then unheard of. For instance, operation for goiter had been done only in a few isolated instances. In fact, goiters were regarded merely as deformities which caused no trouble unless they attained excessive size. When patients died from heart failure this was regarded not as a concomitant but as a separate disease. Prostatic obstructions were treated by catheterization until the patient died of ascending kidney infection, which usually required about two years. This is called palliative treatment and consists in alleviating as much as possible the suffering of the patient until he dies. Palliative treatment, in contrast with expectant, consists in doing something which temporarily helps but does not cure.

Anesthesia was known in that early day, ether coming into use in 1846, and chloroform in 1872. However, in country practice in the repair of wounds involving the suturing of skin, it was seldom resorted to. The doctor just sewed the lacerations. This was a good time to get a line-up on the patient's general view of life. Some drank whisky, some cursed, some prayed, some did all three. But the doctors worked fast in order to reduce the period of pain. The first laceration of the scalp I ever saw was managed by simply tying small strands of hair across the wound. Very simple, and, in this case, very effective. Happily, those with bald heads were too smart to invite trouble which might result in lacerations of the scalp.

When no anesthetic was available speed was the mark of a good surgeon. One surgeon in the Civil War did a thigh amputation in forty seconds. Time was called when the surgeon started the incision and again when the severed limb hit the floor. Of course, this included only the cutting of the soft parts and the sawing of the bone. The ligation of the vessels had to be done later, but this time was not counted in clocking the operation because this was relatively painless: that is, if the surgeon avoided ligating a nerve with the vessel.

Even such simple things as strangulated hernias went unrelieved by operation. My grandfather died of this condition.

MEDICINE AS IT WAS IN MY BOYHOOD

I can still hear his continued vomiting for the ten days he lived.

The foregoing is a brief survey of the state of medical science and practice in my childhood. As I look back on those days, in the light of my present knowledge, I can scarcely think of a single disease that the doctors actually cured during those early years of my memory. The possible exceptions were malaria and the itch. Doctors knew how to relieve suffering, set bones, sew up cuts and open boils on small boys. Perhaps the greatest service the old doctor rendered was in the case of childbirth. I have never known a doctor to refuse a call in these cases even though the response required endless physical discomfort, even risk to life. The doctor was eagerly awaited when disaster came. He did his best.

CHAPTER

2 _____

THE MOST ENCOURAGING SIGN THAT THE HUMAN RACE MAY ultimately achieve a Christian civilization is to be found in the changing attitude toward children. Quality is receiving attention, something that does not worry the lower animals and that is relatively new among civilized races. Many now realize that children, having been born without their consent, have some rights which parents must respect. It has become quite generally recognized that parenthood carries some responsibility. There would be no excuse to drag forth a description of the conditions of the past were it not that this concept is not generally recognized, not even in the next block. Yet in the history of progress in the attitude toward children we find encouragement for the hope of further advance in the future.

The old and the new ideas loom large in the life of every practicing physician. There are still neglected children who are duplicating the childhood which was the common lot half a century ago. One has only to look around the corner to find the old conditions existing today but little changed. This state is the concern of civilization in general. "Bring the little children unto me" has sounded down the avenues of time for two thousand years. Yet even today the admonition falls on unhearing ears. It was an expression of affection and carried no mathematical implications.

The childhood of sixty years ago was essentially one of neglect. It was due not to a lack of parental affection, but to the customs of the times. One heard the expressions "Spare the rod and spoil the child" or "Lick hell out of them and larn them," or "Lam them and make them tough." These expressions, though having a different ecclesiastic touch, led to the same result. It made them tough or broke their spirits. To the child these quotations had an equally ecclesiastic sound as they were stored in our subconscious selves. To cause a child to obey because he loves his parents is a new thought in our civilization, a thought grasped after only two thousand years of alleged Christian civilization.

This is not the place to examine too closely the reasons for the disregard of the rights of the child. Children played a useful economic part in the struggle for existence, to which end everything was sacrificed. The child as such had no inherent rights. Having produced him, the parents' obligations were fulfilled. His presence in the scheme of things was almost wholly economic and he was levied on at the earliest possible period figured in terms of usefulness. This concept, admirable as a general proposition, was the subject of common abuse. Minor ailments did not absolve the child from his labors. Unless the child was obviously acutely ill no attention was paid to his complaints. Many diseases, insidious in their beginning, caused no distress, hence they passed without recognition, and being unrecognized were ignored. Only when death threatened was the doctor appealed to for help.

The child once born had the choice of dying or fighting for his life, and circumstances largely decided which would be his portion. Broadly speaking, the fittest survived; the weakling had no chance. This attitude is not so neglectful as it sounds. Parents learned that to call a doctor then available was likely to end only in expense. My first experience with a doctor, before my recollection, resulted in the prognosis that I would die before morning. He added, so it is related, "Too bad, he is such a smart-looking boy." I have always cherished this generous opinion because, so far as I know, he is the only person ever to make this keen observation.

It must be remembered that those were the days of the pioneer. It was a case of "root hog or die" for the grown-ups as well as the children. Children merely took up the burden; it was a family affair. This was the spirit which built the nation.

Childish wants as we recognize them now were ignored in that day. The child made his own playthings and his play was the anticipation of the things to come. He made wooden guns and rode stick horses after imaginary enemies. The only gesture toward childish desires was an orange and a few sticks of candy at the church Christmas tree. This state was not a total loss. The child of that day learned many things. He learned to shift for himself, found his own amusements and learned to wriggle out of his predicaments. Every boy had a knife and could make willow whistles in time almost to signalize the appearance of his first pair of pants.

I recall with interest my first day in school. I had been taught to read at home by my sister. On that first day in school I carved, in the soft-pine homemade desk, the date, Nov. 26, 1877, in figures nearly two inches high. This meant that a boy seven and a half years old had a knife sufficiently keen of edge to enable him to do such things and that he was capable of using it. It also indicates a keen sense of opportunity which could be acquired only by practice. I got roundly thrashed for my efforts. I still regard that as a very fine achievement for the first day in school. Few boys of this age today could duplicate it. It involved the care of tools, mechanical ability to execute a thing visualized. Not the least was the capacity to take a licking without hollering. There is my whole life experience in miniature literally covered on my first day in school.

The teaching of the country schools in that day was limited to the three R's—reading, 'riting and 'rithmetic. The student supplemented this in many ways, improvising things to play with, hunting and trapping of game and fighting: all things that laid a foundation for his future endeavors, for indeed life is made up of just those things—hunting for something, getting hold of it and then fighting to keep it. The acquisition of these talents anticipated by half a century the income taxes.

On the first day of school the teachers regularly brought either a strap or a yardstick and as a preliminary explained its uses. The pupils being always anxious to please, it was a contest to see who would be the first to excite a demonstration. The weather was cold and each student was encased in many layers of clothing, so that the measure of the degree of punishment had to be judged by the sound made by contact of the instrument on the unruly student. If the time and location of the application of the instrument of torture could be predetermined we augmented our clothing by placing our copy books where they would do the most good. The presence of these books produced a resounding smack when struck, which brought a satisfied look to the teacher's face and, it may be added, to the face of the pupil.

One of the most beneficent practices of modern times is the study of the unusual child. In the old days any unusual trait was ascribed to the work of the devil. Of course there were no school nurses in that day, and no doctors capable of discovering the defects in children. My experience was a replica of that related by the distinguished Sir James Mackenzie. He records that he, being nearsighted, was forthwith catalogued as "dumb," a verdict which he accepted without protest. More than this he does not reveal. In my case, being unable to see what was written on the blackboard, my ignorance was ascribed to inattention and

I was soundly whipped, that being the one remedy administered for all derelictions of omission and commission. These whippings made me resentful and then it was necessary to lick me for pure orneriness. If these were not justified it was no fault of mine, for I applied all my ingenuity and energy to achieve the distinction of being the orneriest kid in semicaptivity. Some of my achievements along this line exhibited a lurking talent that turned useful in later years. The chief ones were in the abstract: to keep one's mouth shut when in trouble and to figure consequences before one starts, valuable fundamental training for a surgeon.

Lest these escapades be imagined worse than they were, a few may be mentioned. Most of them had a background of devilment rather than meanness, at least from my point of view. For instance, we had a yarn ball which we were wont to toss to one another while school was in session. These looping Texas leaguers of course were tossed when the teacher was not supposed to be looking; but now and then she caught a glimpse of the ball, though it was always a case of now you see it, now you don't— a sort of shell game. The teacher had tried for a long time to get hold of that ball. One day I tied a string to it and rolled it beneath the seat to the front of the room. She spied the ball and got up to retrieve it, remarking, "Now at last I've got it." She did not see the attached string. As she stooped to grasp the ball I gave the string a little pull and she found her hand grasping nothing. The ball had disappeared again. Careful inquiry on her part disclosed the fact that no one had seen any ball at any time in any place. She compromised by licking all of us. She did not notice a hole in the floor. By guiding contraband articles down this hole, we could put them temporarily out of circulation. By crawling under the schoolhouse we could retrieve the hidden articles.

I was engaged one day in a rather nonscholastic occupation. In fact, I was making a box out of paper in which I intended to inclose a newborn mouse so that I could toss it across the aisle to a young lady friend. The teacher remarked, "Since you are such a little baby, always playing, I shall have to hold you on my lap." She took me on her lap and I at once put my arm around her neck and buried my face in her slatted chest. She yelped, "You impudent thing," and gave me a violent shove which sent me sprawling on the floor ten feet away. Then I went back to the job of incasing the mouse. But I had learned a new word—"impudent." I had never heard of a dictionary and I had to construct a meaning for myself. It is interesting to note that the young lady who received the mouse just giggled with glee. The teacher, attracted by this sudden individual merriment, hastened back to discover the cause of it. In answer to the teacher's question as to the reason for the hilarity, my friend replied simply, "Nothing." She had deftly slipped the little mouse up the sleeve of her dress.

These escapades are related in the first person. This is an act of generosity. My playmates did their just share in furnishing amusement for the teacher. Putting a rooster and a dead cat in the teacher's desk was none of my doing, though I got licked on both occasions.

The teacher, a large angular lady of decidedly mature years, declared that ours was the orneriest school she had ever taught and refused reemployment. A large truculent male was then employed who declared he could break any school. We found in the morning of his first day a paper nailed on the door naming eighteen things we must not do. He explained them in detail, which was quite a help. They ranged all the way from plain and fancy whispering to fighting in class. That first day, we succeeded in breaking all his rules but one. There were just too many of them. That was the busiest day I ever spent in school.

Sometimes our activities were distinctly disciplinary. We discovered that sometimes teachers needed instruction. This same teacher had the habit of taking a nap immediately after school was taken up after the noon recess. He would place his feet on his desk and go peacefully to sleep. Now it was obvious to us that this was not a gentlemanly thing to do, there being young ladies present. We held a conference and it was easy to decide the proper remedial procedure, but there were no volunteers. So we drew straws. I got the short straw. To fulfill my obligation, I stuck a pin through a piece of cardboard and at the proper moment crept up to his desk and deftly slid this implement on the part of the chair for the moment not used, but which would have been occupied by his legs had he been a gentleman. After the usual interval he began to rub his eyes and gradually to pull his feet off the desk. As his feet hit the floor he let out a yell, jumped into the air and with both hands sought the implement of torture. He was very, very angry; in fact, he was boiling mad. Each student was quizzed in turn as to the events of the past half hour. Everyone, boy and girl, had been busy studying, a previously unheard of thing, and had seen nothing. He decided to lick the whole school. Several of the students were grown ladies, with big brothers at home, it may be added, so he decided to postpone chastisement. He never put his feet on the desk again nor took a noonday nap, hoping, I presume, sometime to see all the students simultaneously in the act of studying their lessons. Needless to say, he never did.

One playful trick was in vogue during that time. A boy would fasten a pin in the toe of his boot and, so armed, gently jab a fellow student in the seat: that is, the boy sitting in the seat ahead or several seats ahead. In retaliation the jabbed one would "sock" the jabber. If the wrong party was suspected it called for a settlement after school. I understand such things are no longer thought to be proper in well-regulated schools.

Some of our stunts do not admit of classification. It depends on the point of view. I had made a wooden monkey which, if the string was pulled on, would jig its arms and legs, a really clever piece of work for a ten-year-old boy to construct with nothing but a pocketknife to work with. My young lady friend suggested it would be fun for me to pin it on the teacher's coattail. Since she had rescued me from trouble by hiding the mouse I felt I was indebted to her. I figured that the best time to accomplish this was when he came to put coal in the stove. He evidently suspected something, for he stooped low so that he could see between his legs and thus saw me in the act of attaching my monkey to his coat. He got up, gripped me by the neck and shook me until we were both exhausted. And he confiscated the monkey. The young lady said she was sorry she had made the suggestion and this was ample reward; I had received sympathetic understanding from a young lady.

These examples suffice to show how our book learning was supplemented by other activities which had their disciplinary value. I fail to understand why parents nowadays make such a fuss when their sons get whipped in school. If one knows how to take thrashings they may be made positively entertaining. The technic in taking a licking is to wholly relax. It is difficult to apply the rod with one hand while the other is occupied in holding the recipient in the upright position. I have been getting lickings all my life and the same technic applies. Just relax; the other party is doing all the work. Don't holler; watch your chance.

Playing hooky was frequently indulged in; the free time was usually devoted to hunting rabbits or going skating. Nowadays parents haul their children around to show them the sights. We did our own exploring. The teacher was prone to accept any excuse one offered for his absences, being thankful apparently for an occasional day of comparative peace. I learn from a grandson that the term "hooky" has been eliminated from the school's vocabulary, it being replaced by the less obnoxious term "absenting oneself" or something like that. Thus does civilization advance.

Fights on the school grounds were a frequent occurrence. It was everybody for himself. It was no concern of the teacher. When I was nine years old a big visiting bully caught me by the hands and, swinging me about his head, threw me some distance on the frozen ground. I was stunned for a moment but was able to walk home. I was sick for some weeks, unconscious or in delirium which the doctor called malaria. In harmony with this diagnosis I was prescribed quinine "as much as would stick on the end of a knife." This, of course, was deposited on the tongue. After I regained complete consciousness I conceived the notion of depositing the drug in the middle of a spoonful of applesauce and then gulping the whole. It worked. This was in anticipation of the gelatin capsule.

What happened to my brain from that injury is clear enough now. I was able to walk home a mile and a half but then came the darkness, certain evidence of a delayed brain hemorrhage. In the days of twilight, as I recovered from my injury, there was plenty of time to do a lot of thinking. I realized that my frail body was no match for those better endowed with physical strength and ever thence I knew how to supplement my natural weapons with what the occasion offered. Self-protection at any cost became my motto. I recall some years later a bully who had poked and boxed me for some months. I beat him up. After he regained consciousness he became my best friend and appointed himself a committee of one to see that I was not imposed upon by other ambitious youths. The resolution made while recovering from the head injury had an astonishing aftereffect when I was eleven years old. During the summer months it was the habit of German families to send their children to private schools. The teacher this summer, a red-headed preacher, was, I think, the meanest man I ever met. One day I stepped on a piece of glass, receiving a nasty wound. The last exercise of the day was the spelling class when we all stood along the wall. My injured foot pained severely when it hung down. To remedy this I hooked my toe on a window ledge just behind me. Noticing my position, this teacher angrily commanded me to put my foot down. I explained that I had injured my foot and by holding it up it lessened the pain, and put my foot on the window ledge again. He was in the habit of carrying a cane hooked over his arm when he walked the streets. It was as large as a man's finger. He came charging toward me with this cane drawn back. I had in my hand a large double slate. Before he had time to strike me with the cane I cracked him over the temple with the edge of this slate with every ounce of strength I had. He spun around and forgot what he started to do. I regard this as an excellent example of the old dictum that if one must fight, start early, said to be regarded as excellent tactics by military men.

That was a terrible thing to do but I even yet look back on it with a degree of satisfaction because it showed that I had something in me of the born surgeon—the ability to act quickly, accurately and energetically. I had had an experience with this same teacher some time earlier. One of the boys, much stronger and older than I, had placed some horse dung in my dinner bucket, which meant that I would have no dinner. I landed on this lad with fury and proved to the satisfaction of both that an early start and speed give startling results. The blubbering bully went to the teacher. Documentary evidence aplenty was written on his face that he actually had been injured. Being teacher's pet, without a moment's hesitation or an attempt to find out the cause of the row the teacher beat me with that cane. That was the only whipping I ever got that really hurt. It hurt some physically but worse mentally. The other whippings I had received had always been preceded by some devilment, either on my own part or one of my pals. The injustice of this one tormented me, and was enhanced in the evening when I noticed several black and blue streaks on my shoulder extending back and downward—I never knew how far, for I could not see and I said nothing about it to anyone. As the stripes turned green I saw green, but when they turned yellow I most emphatically did not. I concluded if he ever charged me with that cane he would get all I had of whatever I could get hold of. It just happened to be a slate. Here is where the relation to surgery came in. A surgeon thinks over his problem and makes up his mind what he will do in certain emergencies. He must stand his ground no matter what happens. He cannot run. I have never had to hesitate at the operating table. This is sufficient to show that not all useful knowledge learned in the classroom is didactic. It is pleasant to recall that that same preacher was chased out of town just three weeks later for whipping his little daughter.

Just what changed my disposition after the brain hemorrhage above related I have often pondered since I have had the chance to see many head injuries. There remained after I recovered a resolve to give no quarter and to ask no help. I had the feeling that I had no friends and that in the future I would have to depend on my own efforts in defending myself. I recall the bitterness I felt against our Sunday-school teacher as I was recovering. He had told us if we just tried to do right everything would be all right. That had seemed to me to be a fine thing and I resolved to do right. With experience the whole thing fell down and I was now resentful toward Sunday-school teaching. A little tiger was born within me. He has been a fairly decent tiger as tigers go but still a tiger. I have had to slap him in the face many times but he has not always obeyed. I acquired a small muzzle-loading pistol at this time. Ever after I was an ardent pistol shot. In time I acquired my share of national medals and for a time held a record. There has been throughout my life a subconscious something which whispered, "If you must, you can." I still have at hand an impressive array of artillery which whispers the same words. I never had an aggressive fight in my boyhood but I never turned back to foe. That injury changed something.

The following year we got as teacher the sweetest little lady we had ever seen. She brought no whip but simply announced that her name was Lilly and we were not to call her teacher. She was a lily and no one would ever have thought of painting her in the hope of improvement. All devilishness vanished and not one of us ever did a single thing to annoy her. She weighed scarce a hundred pounds and we saw to it that a path was broken through the snow for her each morning. This quiet little lady subdued us with kindness after daily lickings had failed to make any impressions whatever. It must have been the element of surprise. Not one of us had ever been subjected to that sort of thing. We all loved her but I am sure none of us had ever heard the word "love," except when the preacher asked us if we loved Jesus, which inquiry conveyed no meaning to us.

Other experiences changed my childish mind. My family were Mennonites, a denomination which has for creed a Christian altruism, and my grandfather was the preacher, a typical kindly old pioneer to whom preaching was an avocation. He worked during the week and preached three hours each Sunday without compensation. When I was six years old, at the urgence of a brother my father seceded from this church and joined another which had for creed, save your soul even if you have to lie to achieve this end. This new church had regular preachers. The first one we had was eighteen years old and had attended school for six months. I remember his first visit well. He asked me if I loved Jesus, and if all was well with my soul, and at that instant kicked my pup who had come up to see what it was all about. In fact, the dog knew as much about the answers to the questions as I did. The best way to alienate a boy is to kick his dog. I hated the sight of him ever after.

We were afflicted with this sort of moral guardian as long as we lived in that community. There was one exception. This minister told us Bible stories and was apparently indifferent to the state of our souls—at least he never made inquiry. Aside from this one man, all the preachers excited in me an antagonism that has remained a subconscious influence even to the present day, being augmented as it was from time to time.

But the clergy had broader activities. In some way I acquired a copy, minus one cover, of Dr. Foote's *Family Physician*. A minister discovered me in the act of reading it and promptly with his own hands consigned it to the flames. The reason for this summary cremation I learned just recently was that it mentioned that there were two sexes, male and female, a thing which, of course, was unsuspected by a farmer's boy. This same minister discovered that my brother and I had a set of dominoes. These also he consigned to the flames, explaining to my father that the next step would be a euchre deck. That was a bright idea. We promptly acquired a deck from an uncle who taught us to play. With this euchre deck brother and I used to sit in the back seat at revival services and never miss a hand. This would have been impossible with dominoes. At sixteen I beat the county champion, and after that I did not touch a card for twenty years. Also I got a copy of Miss Mulock's *John Halifax, Gentleman*. This was burned because it was a novel. Then followed a period of reading the wildest of ten-cent redbacks. These really *were* wild. To the reading of these I ascribe an early baldness. Thus the clergy contributed to the broadening of my education.

About this time I learned the delights of reading a book at one sitting. The first book I read was *Peck's Bad Boy*. A neighbor had a visitor who carried a copy. I was told I might borrow it if I brought it back on my way to school. I finished it just at breakfast time. It was disappointing. There was nothing new in it. The next was a *Life of Garfield*. A visiting uncle had a copy and as he was leaving the next day I had but the night for the reading of it. I read all night and finished it by schooltime. I was much inspired by it, not knowing anything about politics. These were the first books I had ever seen except ecclesiastic works and the experience of reading them taught me the delights of a book spree. I still delight in them.

When I was twelve years old I quit the little red schoolhouse and began to attend the school of our nearest town. My girl friend of the mouse episode had started to attend this school and advised that I do likewise. As in the case of the monkey I heeded her advice but with happier results. I shall never forget that first day. I wore a suit of clothes my mother had made; bless her memory, she did her best, but they were made to fit an imaginary son. Because of the long and muddy road I had to walk night and morning it was necessary that I wear heavy boots. I had to stuff my pants into the tops of these boots, because they were too narrow and short to go over the top. This had the advantage of concealing their inadequate length. Worst of all, an accident with a loose nail in my saddle had made it necessary to put a patch on my pants, so placed that while it did not disturb my view it was a source of amusement to others. As I stalked into the schoolroom on the first day, clattering with my heavy boots, a shout of derision went up from the assembled students. I was at once nicknamed "Boots." The pants were blue jeans, the patch yellow, and this combination brought forth the artistic efforts of a number of students. Those first few weeks were the most humiliating of my life.

An occurrence of this time shows something of the school discipline of those days. A student sitting just behind me amused himself by putting sundry articles down the back of my neck, bugs preferred. It suddenly occurred to me one day that there had been enough of that. I swung a vicious left to the tip of his jaw and he went sprawling into the aisle. The teacher calmly remarked, "Harry, it serves you right, you had it coming for a month." Hazing, as I understand it, is now done only in first-rate colleges and then only when the odds are at least forty to one. In my day it was boy for boy. Thus does education advance.

It was impossible for me to start to school until the corn was husked. This meant that the school had been going for two months when I began and it was necessary for me to work both ways, to cover what the class had gone over and also to do the work of the class day by day. The class in arithmetic was in the midst of cube root. I knew nothing of square root. I discovered then what I had not known existed, a friend. A girl several years older than I, the belle of the town, one of the most beautiful girls I have ever seen, took me in charge and helped me with the lessons that had already been covered. I can see yet the look of amazement on the faces of those boys who had taunted me, when this charming girl sat beside me, her arm placed gently on my shoulder while she helped me with the bygone lessons. Nobody but a woman can figure out why this wonderful girl should take under her protecting wing an apparently hopeless derelict. All I could do to express my appreciation was to lead the whole pack before the year ended, not only in arithmetic but the algebra that followed. I am sure on resurrection morn I shall see that wonderful Cora, but the rising sun, I fear, will be partly obstructed by that yellow patch which I never had a chance to view in all its glory.

During these years my education was supplemented in another direction. When nine years old I had begun taking my part in milking cows. Two events stand out. Once a cow stepped on my bare foot, tearing the nail completely off my big toe. I distinctly remember that in conversation with that cow I for the first time in my life got my ecclesiastical vocabulary mixed in. One never knows his latent talent until some impressive event calls it forth. Another time in kicking me the old cow's foot became engaged in the pocket of my stout homemade jacket. She nearly shook the daylights out of me. My father was present and I did not emit a sound, showing that circumstances may suppress a very impressive talent.

There was always farm work to do in addition to the chores.

I PREPARE TO STUDY MEDICINE

When I was eleven I started to plow corn. At twelve I took my regular place plowing ten hours a day. I had for my team an old mare and her cantankerous colt. This added to my labors because the colt wanted to go every place but straight down the row, and watching him and the plow also doubled my labor. Tall and frail of body, I am still haunted by these long cruel days. I can say with Horace Mann that I was rocked in the cradle of toil and she rocked me too hard. At this time came an experience that left me changed. Toward the end of a long hot day my tired muscles became so painful it seemed that I could not take another step. I knelt beside the plow and prayed for strength to finish the day. It didn't do a bit of good. Somehow the abstract teaching of Sunday school when subjected to a concrete test had failed again. I felt that I had been fooled. It may be remarked that to plow ten acres in a day is regarded as a good ten hours' work. Those who are handy with a pencil will readily discover that this requires walking just twenty miles. Even today at the end of a long day in the clinic this old pain in my legs comes to remind me of the days long gone by.

During the less strenuous seasons of the year there was time for diversions. Breaking colts to ride and running impromptu races present the most pleasant memories. Picking up a watermelon off the ground without leaving the saddle was a stunt that my attenuated nether extremities made possible to achieve with ease. Being thrown off a horse was just a part of the game. Going hunting at night for imaginary 'coons was a pleasant diversion. The only result usually was a roast of a "borrowed" chicken. Half burned and half raw, they were delicious. We anticipated many of the stunts the Boy Scouts do now. The vast number of mischievous things we did are long since lost in the advance of civilization but even so they had an educative value, though one possessed of grandsons cannot regard them as suitable experiences for record.

The town school I attended had no regular course. Every

student took what suited his fancy, no matter what the order. If he made it, well and good; if not, he did not. After four years, having covered every course the school had to offer, I sought out an academy in a neighboring town. I had an uncle living in the town where this academy was located. This uncle, the village blacksmith, learning that I was an omnivorous reader and not much of a farmer, suggested that I come and live with him and attend the academy located across the street from his shop. In exchange for board I was to milk the cows, tend the horses and flatten out iron in the blacksmith shop with a sixteen-pound sledge hammer. A new world loomed in the offing.

After the corn was husked I sought this new world. One morning when the lady principal passed the blacksmith shop my uncle hailed her and presented me as a prospective sponge which it was hoped might absorb knowledge. She smiled most graciously. That is, at the time I thought she smiled. Thinking it over in later years I concluded she just laughed. Most certainly the students laughed. What else could one expect? I was six feet two inches tall, weighed one hundred and forty pounds and was decked out in cheap hand-me-down clothes such as might be had in a village store of that day. No wonder some boys develop an inferiority complex which they must battle the rest of their lives. Six inches more of pants might have changed my whole life.

Entering school six weeks after the term had begun, I was under a considerable handicap. I had not only to prepare the lesson of the day but had also to make up what the class had already covered. Mathematics was no task, but Latin was something different. When I first recited *amo, amas, amat* I am sure it was the most embarrassing moment of my life. I knew nothing about love in English, to say nothing about it in Latin. The girls in the class all giggled, as girls sometimes will, even today. Also I learned that a straight line is the shortest distance between two points. This impressed me as utterly silly. I had already demonstrated this fact, in the course of farm labors, whenever the dinner bell rang.

The course of study in those days consisted chiefly of Latin, Greek, mathematics and English. The second year I anticipated a late start and got a Greek grammar during the summer and learned the alphabet and the declensions by copying them on a card and nailing this on the back end of the walking cultivator. My team, consisting of the old mama horse and her perverse three-year-old son, above mentioned, no doubt learned the declensions as I recited to them. I also practiced writing the letters. When I had written my first exercise on the blackboard after I entered school the teacher gave a howl of delight, declaring that he had never known a beginner to write the Greek letters so well. Had he seen our farmstead covered with Greek letters he would have thought he was visiting a fraternity neighborhood.

All I remember about Greek is that you learn one verb, all the rest are irregular, that Darius had three huge sons and that buzzard meat tastes like venison, only sweeter. Nevertheless were I to begin the study of medicine again I should choose the same courses in Latin and Greek as a preliminary. For though, like Shakespeare, I had small Latin and less Greek, they made medical terminology more interesting and intelligible, and when I began the study of medicine I recognized the derivation of new words as I came across them in my reading. During examinations and recitations if one was a bit shy on knowledge one could start by giving the derivation of the word while he collected his wits, if any. This also impressed the professor, particularly if that worthy lacked such knowledge himself. If one knows the structure of a word he can make a pretty good stall at making a recitation, good say for a five. I tried this bluff on an instructor one day, who unbeknown to me had once been a professor of Greek. But in general it worked very well. I would not imply that a resort to this means was often necessary in my case, but there was a satisfaction in possessing the knowledge, like a spare dollar in one's pocket. Aside from its practical value, I am sure this slight knowledge of the basic languages has made the reading of medicine more pleasurable throughout life.

Languages have always been an impossible field for me. The fortieth chapter of Caesar is said to have a principal verb. Maybe so, but I never succeeded in locating it. I built sextants whereby I measured the height of a church steeple from the sidewalk two blocks away, and the width of the river from a bank. This was accepted in lieu of the elusive verb.

The first two years I worked for my board. A part of my duty was to keep the fire going under a molasses vat. I used such occasions to study astronomy. By the aid of a lantern I studied the stellar maps and by simply turning on my back I sought the counterpart in the heavens. In this way I developed a really good knowledge of celestial geography.

Working for my board became too strenuous so that I sought to board myself. A number of bushels of potatoes were taken to my room in the fall. Each week end I walked home some seven miles and carried back a bag of bread. In those days no one knew anything about calories and vitamins but I learned that a bread and potato diet was insufficient, month in and month out, for a growing boy—at least I know it now.

To go hungry is not so bad at the time; the pangs of hunger are not so keen to a boy as a real healthy appetite. Possibly those so zealous to feed the heathen while they neglect the child next door know this. It is not the tragedies of childhood that hurt so much as the memory of them in later years. The child has no means of comparison; as far as he knows his is the experience of all, the inevitable thing of life. The pain does not come then.

Struggling for an education on a bread and potato diet, I

did not suffer from a sense of a lack of proper nutrition but from a feeling of utter exhaustion. I had no knowledge of dietetics. The bitterness came later when I came to realize that it was needless, being ecclesiastic and in no wise ignorance. Needless, because the religion of that day taught that for a boy to secure an education was for him to travel the broad road to hell and the best way to keep him from traveling that road was to starve him out of school. Starve and be damned, the best way to make a boy fight is to starve him. Starve him thoroughly enough, and long enough, and he will fight the devil and his cohorts to his dying day. A stunted development, the ill health it brings, stays throughout the years to haunt him and to embitter him when he comes to realize the needless cruelty of it all. Fearing that education was the road to hell, in their zeal to save me from a hell in the hereafter they made one for me in my young boyhood.

Despite these experiences, the essays I was required to write were all of a humorous turn. So much so that my teacher regarded this as my most promising field and suggested that I prepare myself for a literary career. Had he known that I intended to study medicine he would have found additional evidence that I was a born humorist. Unfortunately I have never been able to distinguish between humor and silliness, or wisecracking as it is called now.

Four years in the academy equaled what is about the first two years of the colleges of today. Better training in literature than most college graduates (three years of English composition and rhetoric—our English teacher was a Canadian who had the idea that English was a good language to learn); mathematics as far as differential calculus; German, mostly grammar and time spent in the utterly futile attempt to read Wallenstein and several other works of the same kind—everything except what I would need in the future. I never could understand poetry or drama even in English and the German was a nightmare.

I learned many fundamental facts in those four years but I missed my education. The social contacts the student makes are as valuable as the knowledge gained. Because of my ill-fitting clothes and utter lack of any training, the social life was largely closed to me—at least I thought it was. The better families treated me decently as far as the front gate. I did essay once to take a little lady named Flossie to view the digging of an artesian well in process a few miles in the country. Her mother took one look at me and delivered herself of the following oration: to wit, "Scat." That experience was very humiliating. For the most part, as it appears to me now, it was largely imaginary, a manifestation of an inferiority complex developed through the years.

I graduated from the academy at nineteen years of age. The graduating scene has left two events in my mind. The graduates were expected to select a motto. Mine was "Never be late to a meal." This suggestion excited no great enthusiasm but I have lived up to it, which is more than those can say who selected more high-sounding ones, such as "Step by step we reach the heights." The other was still a matter of clothes. One was supposed to wear a cutaway coat at graduation. Because of my great height the tails of my coat but grudgingly covered the seat of my pants and the buttons on the back found a resting place somewhere between the shoulder blades and my hips, just where I never found out. The suit cost twelve dollars. I was cheated. Though this ensemble was excruciatingly funny—nothing so funny ever appeared on a vaudeville stage—nobody laughed.

My oration was on "What of the Future?" The principal, being familiar with my struggles, was most kind to me, reciting some of my original achievements in mathematics; and, knowing the needlessness of my struggles, he said a number of things only he and my father understood. The assembled crowd somehow fell in line with this kindly feeling. The adieus from all and sundry were most cordial, something wholly new in my experience. The cordial farewells were augmented by the old minister of the local church who told my father that he was glad to have me as a member of his church—I had joined unknown to my father.

On the way home my father said Christianity was only indirectly related to the church. Churches could be good or bad. If good people made them up, they were good; if bad, the church was bad. He realized then that the church which had engendered in him the fear that education was pernicious was a bad church. I could have told him that ten years earlier.

Had I had those four years to live over again the bitterness which attended them would have been obviated. Perhaps if my clothes had fit, Flossie's mother would not have chased me off— she was a noble, gentle soul—and I might have been saved one of the bitterest experiences of life.

I had seen a fine transplanted Christian New England community. But I also learned that to enjoy the Christian benefits to the full extent one's pants must fit. The scars our souls receive in our childhood remain in our subconscious selves and all our philosophy and learning will not eradicate them. Unbidden they rise to the surface at the most inopportune times to haunt us the remainder of our lives.

I left school June 18, 1890, a very much confused and bewildered boy.

CHAPTER

3 ⸺⸺⸺⸺

IT IS DIFFICULT TO REALIZE THE POSITION OF THE COUNTRY BOY of fifty years ago bitten by an ambition to enter the medical profession. It was generally believed by the laity in our community that all the lawyers and two-thirds of the doctors went to hell. The third saved were homeopaths with beards. Most of the doctors of that day were addicted to liquor, smoked pipes and did not go to church. I knew full well that any mention of my ambitions would bring on a storm of protest. My father believed, with Mr. Tulliver, that all lawyers were created for and by the devil and that approximately all doctors were parasites of society. He cannot be blamed for his uncomplimentary opinion of doctors because the small fortune he spent for alleged medical skill for members of his family netted just about nothing. How he came to his conclusions about lawyers I never made out, unless it was just plain instinct. I have no brief for the lawyers. But doctors are now accorded a better prospect of escaping an unhappy destination. At least only the clergy still harbor any apprehension and the obvious futility of doing anything about it seems to discourage them. It never did cause the doctors any concern. Some of the more unregenerate among us would even prefer to be in hell with the babies than in heaven with the criminals, for all executed culprits profess assurance of salvation before they take their last drop.

I STUDY MEDICINE

Clergymen in those days often chose their profession because of a desire to save the world. It is a noble urge. Doctors of medicine also occasionally profess altruistic motives, but I never knew one who amounted to anything making any such pretensions. These gentlemen talk much of their "noble calling." Any calling is noble in exactly the proportion that nobility is brought to it, as for instance carpentering. Most people who amount to anything start and go at high speed wherever they find themselves. They start in a certain direction because of associations or circumstances.

In the passing years I have looked over my classes and wondered why they chose to study medicine. In many cases there seems to be no obvious reason. In most students there seems to be a desire to insure themselves throughout life of a more or less certain supply of bacon and eggs. With some it is the ambition to follow in their father's footsteps—a fine reason for them and a great satisfaction to the fathers. Sometimes mother is the first to think of a profession for her son, particularly if she has found her own life not exactly satisfactory, she has a desire for her son to achieve a height not obvious in pop's career.

In my case there was no excuse nor even any thought of where the study of medicine would lead; I am by no means clear on that point even now. When I was four years old I began playing with bottles and carefully observing the manner of the doctors on their numerous visits to my mother. Why I got this notion into my head is as inexplicable as many other notions that have since entered the same head. There had never been a doctor in our family, only farmers and mechanics, some of whom preached on Sunday. I was excluded from such an avocation because of an incoordination of my ecclesiastic terminology. Whatever may have been the motivating factor, I never gave a thought to doing anything else than doctoring folks.

Certainly there was nothing obviously attractive so far as was visible to me about the practice of medicine. All I had observed about sick people was tragic, little calculated to attract anyone to elect such a hopeless combat with disease as one's life work. Certainly I had no way of learning anything about the life of a doctor. I eagerly watched the doctors in those days as they passed along the road on their visits to their patients. I visioned perhaps that somewhere someone was anxiously waiting, because in the frequent visits to my mother, from the time the messenger started for the doctor until he arrived we watched the road. He was kind and sympathetic to her, which appealed to me. He seemed anxious to be of service to her. I did not know that he had little else to offer.

Most of the doctors of that day had drugstores and wore whiskers and examined patients as they were seated beside the counter in view of other customers, and loafers. That is to say, the patient's tongues were looked at, and the more thorough, if they had a watch, counted their pulses; then medicines were handed out from the stock on the shelves. For example, when I was a boy I had repeated attacks of severe pains in my back which radiated to the groin. My father took me to see one of these drugstore doctors. After the doctor heard the story he stroked his long gray beard, looked at me for a moment over his glasses and, turning to my father, delivered himself of the following: "Dan, he yust grow too fast." That was fine logic, because I had certainly done all that; but the diagnosis was wrong—after a number of months I passed a kidney stone.

Most of the doctors had never attended a medical school. Most of them had "read medicine" with some active doctor but many just bought a book. Not all doctors, however, were unschooled. We had one man in our town who had been to medical school— that is, to Keokuk Medical College—spending there two years of five months each. He had the reputation of being a very fine doctor if one could find him sober. It seemed that it was the generally accepted opinion in that day that drunken doctors were very capable if sober. Just how this conclusion was arrived at in the case of our doctor I do not know, for he never was sober. But he had an office. I was burning with a desire to see the interior of the office of a doctor who was educated and did not have a drugstore. His side line was trying to put the distilleries out of business. This is a charitable estimate because from all one could see it was the practice of medicine that was the side line, since this employed his time only intermittently. There seemed no chance to inspect his office because my family patronized only homeopaths with drugstores and whiskers. I had no closer contact with this educated doctor than seeing him drive, or rather being hauled by his weary ponies, over muddy or frozen roads, for he was always slumped in the seat of the buggy, the team seeming to know where the sick person lived.

One day I got a bright idea. I would boldly go to his office and have a tooth pulled. I had no defective teeth but I had more good ones than I needed, at least I did not need them so much as I needed to know what the inside of a doctor's office looked like. No medical procedure I have met since has required so much courage as did the opening of that office door. I entered. The doctor was slumped in a chair at his desk. I do not know what awakened him unless it was the knocking of my knees. At any rate, he roused enough to say, "Boy, what t'hell you want?" "Tooth pulled," I stammered. He selected a forceps, from a pile of dirty instruments lying on a table and approached me. "Sit down. Vich one?" I indicated the first upper right molar, that being the most accessible to my trembling right digit. He made one awkward jab and the tooth was out. "Spit in basin," was his direction as he slumped in his chair again. It took plenty of time for the bleeding to cease so that in the meantime I could take a careful inventory of the office. First of all on a shelf above his desk were more books than I believed existed—eight of them, five big ones and three little ones. An old couch, three chairs, a small table on which lay a great variety of inexpressibly dirty instruments, including the one he had used to pull my tooth, then his desk and a big chair in which he sat, made up the furniture of the room.

Why I was not sufficiently disgusted with this ensemble to abandon the thought of studying medicine I do not know. Perhaps it was because he lived for his patients, like all country doctors. He had few social contacts. He joined the lodge but seldom attended. He fought mud and snow until he was exhausted, and then he took a nip of whisky to give him strength; when the weather was good he took a nip in anticipation of mud and snow. It was the same from year's end to year's end. On one dark night his team dumped him in the creek and he got pneumonia and died. The concourse in the lobby of the postoffice agreed it was too bad, for he was a good doctor—when he was sober.

Funny how the children and the old ladies loved him—he knew the safe ages. They put him in a box and carried him to the village church. The minister made an eloquent discourse on the virtues of temperance. I suggested to my father that the reason they took him into the church was to make sure he was really dead; if not, he would jump out of the box and flee. Father said that was no way to talk of sacred things. I still do not see the justice of the reprimand.

Then they took him to the graveyard—it wasn't a cemetery then, and his lodge made funny motions; there they covered him up. He was home at last to stay, with many of his patients who had preceded him. Finally, those who had neglected ever to remember him in a remunerative way while he was alive donated a dollar each to pay the undertaker for his trouble. The preacher got nothing; he was well repaid by the chance to preach a temperance sermon. Yet with this hardy man a spirit died, the spirit of service, a service done without thought of reward either here or hereafter. Whether or not he was a good doctor when sober, somehow the children came to him and he loved them. It is always safe to love little children. Drunk or sober, he knew that much. To my small mind there was something heroic about him. He was not afraid of mud, high water or the devil.

This is the first mention I have ever made of what came of that tooth. It has always seemed to me that that was a silly adventure. In fact, I still feel sheepish about it after more than fifty years. Rather a big price—fifty cents and a tooth—to pay just for the privilege of taking a hurried look at the interior of an "educated" doctor's office. I remember distinctly how I got all that money. Chickens were wont to lay eggs a long way from the henhouse. I acquired these by none too honorable means, put them in my pants pocket and transported them to the grocer. It required several months to accumulate all that money.

When about fifteen years of age, I noticed in the *Toledo Blade* an advertisement of the Pulte Medical College of Toledo, Ohio, which stated they would send a catalogue on request. I requested. The catalogue said that a reading and writing knowledge of English was required for entrance to the college, also a certificate of good moral character from one's clergyman, also a fee of one hundred dollars. I noted, in the list of the faculty, the names of those occupying the top of the page had A.M., M.D., after their names. I knew what M.D. meant but the A.M. was a mystery. At any rate I resolved to get an A.M., whatever that was, because, of course, I had resolved to go to the top.

At any rate, all I lacked was the letter from a cleric and a hundred dollars. I did not consider that one would need to eat and, as I learned by experience before my education was completed, the usual custom of eating three times a day is really a habit which can be largely modified if necessary. My star had risen. I at last had found out how doctors were made.

At about the age of ten years my medical education began. As previously related I secured a copy of Dr. Foote's *Family*

Physician, which I read again and again. Though but a child, I learned the description of many diseases, notably diphtheria and the itch. When I learned what diseases someone in the neighborhood had or died of, I hastily read it up in my book.

In my twelfth year we studied Steele's *Physiology* in the country school. I committed the book to memory almost word for word. Because of my spare physical build I was able to identify most of the bones mentioned in the book. Here budded my skepticism of recorded medical opinion. This book stated that the capacity of the human stomach was three pints. I easily demonstrated that in so far as I was concerned this was a gross underestimate. I was later able to harmonize this difference of opinion. The stomach of a diseased person is contracted and rigid and in this condition holds about three pints, but a boy's stomach is capable of expansion far beyond the capacity of a cadaveric stomach.

Fifty years ago, when I first planned to study medicine, most medical schools required for graduation an attendance at two courses of lectures of five months each as above noted. All the lectures were given to the whole school at the same time, so that the student heard the same lectures twice, one each year. It was a pastime for the second-year men to tell the first-year men what jokes were due the next lecture. This tended to keep the boys awake so as not to miss the story. A lecture, it may be explained, consisted of a vocal effort by the professor for the duration, or endurance, of practically an hour. An hour in those old days was a long time for the lecturer when he had little to say and was confronted by several hundred wild-eyed critical yokels. In order not too greatly to exhaust the students, many stories were interpolated. These not only revived some of the students to consciousness but also enabled the lecturer to fill up such gaps as might exist in his knowledge of the subject. For instance, a lecturer on anatomy held at arm's length a bone from a skull. In a high-pitched oratorical voice he delivered himself of the following: "Gentlemen, this is a sphenoid bone. Damn the sphenoid bone." Having thus expressed his opinion of the value of a knowledge of this particular bone, he threw it back into the box. Thus ended the study of a very complicated structure.

When I began my medical teaching more than thirty-five years ago I learned the difficulties attending the lecturing to students. It was a ticklish business, because in those days if students did not like an uninteresting teacher they hooted him; and if he did not take the hint, they shied tin cans and rubber shoes at him. Then the trustees had to elect another "professor." It may be explained that many schools of that day were so-called proprietary schools: that is, private schools which were dependent for overhead expenses on the fees the students paid. Teachers could be had for the asking but to expel a student meant the loss of his tuition. It is too bad that the custom of chasing dumb instructors has fallen into disuse. Certainly the need for such measures still exists. Even today when I see an instructor dully quizzing from a ponderous tome I feel that the old boys had the right idea.

As a preliminary to entering a medical school the prospective doctor in those days began by "reading medicine" with an established practitioner called a preceptor. One drove his horse, cleaned the office and in general performed the labor of janitor and nurse. I recall an amusing incident of that time. A town boy I knew had started to read medicine with a doctor. He had been serving the doctor just three weeks when he delivered himself of the following: "Hell, if I hadda knowed a feller had to git up every night I would never have started to learn doctoring." That sentence tells everything.

In turn for the services rendered by the "student" the doctor allowed the fledgling to read his books and to see patients with him: that is, he was allowed to see the patient if the disease afflicted those parts that normally protruded from the patient's clothes. Thus I saw a senile gangrene of the foot in a man nearly eighty years old. Some preceptors even guided the student in his reading. The association with a preceptor was valuable, therefore, according to the man to whom one might be attached and to one's diligence. My preceptor required me to commit a good share of Gray's *Anatomy* to memory, regularly assigning me ten pages which I recited to him. I walked seven miles each week in order to make these recitations. This memory work was a great help after I entered medical school. I have always remembered my old preceptor with a great deal of affection. He was a fine Christian gentleman, with a New England brogue and training and general outlook on life.

I made my first clinical diagnosis during this period. A man aged seventy-six fell off the porch steps and dislocated his hip, so it was reported. My preceptor, together with his colleague, was to journey thither to relieve the afflicted. I was invited to accompany them. A pulley was screwed into a log in the ceiling and one in the floor. A rope was passed through these. The patient was laid on a straw mattress on the floor between the pulleys. I noted the leg was some four inches shorter than its fellow and the foot fell unrestrained outward. I cautiously sidled up to my preceptor and said that the leg lay just like a picture in his surgery book which was labeled "Fracture of the Neck of the Femur." He withdrew, together with his colleague, to the porch. Presently they came back, looked at the leg again and without a word returned the patient to his bed. It really was a fracture of the neck of the femur. In a week the man was dead. On the way back to town my preceptor remarked: "Boy, you have a doctor's eye." That man was really smart.

After the student had served his preliminary year "reading" with a preceptor he was ready to enter a school. The candidate was supposed to be able to read the English language and be of good moral character. Needless to say, only a clergyman was capable of passing on the moral character of the prospective student. I have forgotten how or if I obtained such a certificate. Possibly my preceptor performed this function, because he was superintendent of the Sunday school and sometimes substituted for the regular minister.

The first order of business was to select a medical school. I chose Northwestern University, on the advice of my preceptor, because the entrance requirements were relatively high—that is to say, the equivalent of a high-school course—and the medical course required attendance for three years of seven months each. The course was graded, classes being taught separately so that one advanced from year to year. Of course, all schools do so now but Dr. Davis, the dean, got the idea first and it found practical expression in Northwestern. It was a happy choice. The faculty contained a number of medical men of the first rank in professional knowledge, coupled with high character, things essential to the making of a good teacher. Also valuable, it may be added, to keep the students in the straight and narrow way while they are attending school. Dr. Davis was a teetotaler against everything except hard work. Getting "stewed" was not the respectable thing then that it is now. If a student got drunk and Dr. Davis found it out, that was the last of Mr. Student. Of course, the doctor did not learn all that was going on. We had some students in those days from Milwaukee.

A summary of the teaching as it was offered to us is of historic interest. The modern student will compare it with his own experiences with a sense of satisfaction to himself no doubt.

All teaching, save chemistry, was done entirely by men in active practice. Our school had but two full-time men, the professor of chemistry and the janitor. Of necessity, therefore, instruction in the scientific branches was for the most part very meager. For instance, the slides in histopathology, which were prepared for us, I reckon, by the janitor, rivaled in thickness and translucency a restaurant beefsteak. One advantage of this was that the student could not see enough to permit him to embarrass the teacher by asking any pertinent or impertinent questions. I remember well my slides of small round-celled sarcoma. It was shaped like the state of Texas and was a deep mahogany brown. I could always identify it by its shape and got a ten for so doing at examination. Not a single cell was recognizable.

We committed to memory Schaefer's *Histology* and Delafield and Prudden's *Pathology*. It was just like learning the irregular Greek verbs, plain hard memory work. We were quizzed so often that we really remembered the text, and by comparing the cuts we got a fair knowledge of the subject. This method of teaching has its advantages. One really learned a little about the subject, which served as a foundation for further acquisition of facts. It seems to me that teachers now fail to recognize that in order to reason one must have facts. Facts are not congenital; one must gather them. Furthermore, in the dawn of time memory was started first; reason came after. We learn to practice medicine in the same order.

Chemistry was well taught by the redoubtable John Harper Long, "Johnnie Hydrogen" to us. Most of us were handicapped by a lack of a preliminary course in chemistry, but that made no difference to the aforesaid professor. His chief delight was in "flunking" as many as possible and his capacity along this line was agonizing. This course corresponded to the dreaded "P.Chem." of the student of today. The laboratory work in this course was adequate, considering the times.

Anatomy was taught by young surgeons. We had to commit most of Gray's *Anatomy* to memory, so that we could recite it like a devout man saying his prayers. The nearer one could come to repeating the book verbatim the better student was he. Having done much of this memory work during my preceptor year, I found this easy sledding. Then, as now, in the classroom but little attention was paid to the differentiation between the important and unimportant. We learned what was in the book. For instance, the trifacial nerve had something like forty-five branches in the classroom, while in the dissecting room it had only three; so far as I am concerned it never has had a greater number, though I once taught anatomy.

In the dissecting rooms matters were different. Here we learned chiefly those things which would be needed in practice, because the young surgeons who taught us knew what structures were of practical importance and stressed them. We learned the anatomy about the windpipe, so that if we had quickly to do a tracheotomy for diphtheria we would not have to look it up in a book. Likewise, the inguinal canal was carefully dissected and demonstrated, because we might be called upon to care for a strangulated hernia, sometimes between days, without notice. The result was that we learned only the practical things, but we learned these well. We came out of school with a pretty clear idea of where not to cut. On the whole, anatomy was better taught then than now, at least in so far as it relates to the practice of medicine. Of course, we lost the mental development which attends the dissection of tadpoles and dogfish, which privilege the students of today enjoy or, perhaps better said, are compelled to endure.

The dissecting room in our day was a mess. The preservation of material was then not understood, certainly not by our custodian. Many a properly raised young man blew his first tobacco smoke across the dissecting tables. Tradition had established that it was impossible to endure the odors of the dissecting room unless one smoked. I chose the lesser odor and did not smoke.

Curiosity brought many visitors to the dissecting room. The policeman on our beat was greeted by a shower of whatever happened to be at hand on the occasion of his visit. He had been called several times to quell class riots and we were all anxious to do him honor. One evening a number of students from the theological department paid us a visit. To them, medical students were a terrible lot of rowdies. They all wore Prince Albert coats and many of them received, in their tail pockets, free donations of the various available appendages. They probably thought no better of us after this experience. As a matter of fact, the cultural standing of the medics was not very highly regarded in the university as a whole. Once in a get-together parade on the campus the pharmacy boys hired an Italian with his hand organ and monkey to lead the concourse just ahead of the president. Without any inquiry whatever it was concluded that the medics were responsible and the president came to the city the next day and told us collectively that we were a lousy bunch not fit to mingle in civilized society.

The practical branches were taught by men of the highest attainments in active practice. The teaching was chiefly by lectures followed by frequent quizzes. The student took notes at these lectures and then committed them to memory. We really committed these notes to memory. We formed groups of students, usually about ten, called a quiz class, who met frequently and recited to each other. The fraternities functioned as groups in a like manner. The result of this frequent quizzing was that we knew a few facts thoroughly. I still have my old notebooks and I could pass an examination on them without notice. That is to say, I still know as much as I did when I graduated and that is a lot more than most doctors can say.

The lectures were given in amphitheaters in which the seats were arranged in an angle of about forty-five degrees. The students amused themselves by "passing up" their fellows. The technic was as follows: Two students sitting just back of the victim selected would pass their hands under his arms and raise him up. Then another pair of students in the seat above assumed the burden. By these successive efforts the victim soon found himself at the topmost row of the amphitheater. The members of the class not so engaged supplied the music, rendering effectively such tunes as "There is a hole in the bottom of the sea" or "The girl I left behind me." What these efforts lacked in melodiousness was made up in enthusiasm.

Teaching by lectures had the advantage over the study of ponderous textbooks in that the lecturer was able to stress the important points as these had been emphasized to him in actual practice. Fortunately the number of instructors was small, sixteen in all. Old Alma Mater now has something like four hundred. The thought of it makes one shudder. This increase is accounted for in large part, however, by the fact that instruction is now given to small groups while in our day one lecturer addressed the entire class. In great part, also, the addition in number of teachers is required because of the increase in the number of subjects now being taught. This is particularly true of the laboratory branches. For instance, we had a few lectures in the young science of bacteriology but no laboratory work whatever. Nowadays many small courses are given, too numerous to mention, and too brief to make it possible for the student to learn anything worth while about them. I presume these subjects might be called "cultural," because they cannot possibly do more than acquaint the student with the fact that there is such a subject. It does have the value that in case any student should become interested in it any time in the future he will know there is such a thing. Such superficial courses only detract from the things worth while. The latest of these courses is medical sociology. The next course, I predict, will be a course in medical hemstitching or doily making. These courses will be valuable in enabling the doctor to contact the neglected ladies. This statement is not made in derision. It is evidence of the foresightedness of those professors of Greek who outlined the medical course as it is taught today.

One reason the medical lecture has gone out of style is that there are no longer lecturers of the old type; researchers are seldom eloquent speakers. Since most researchers wear spectacles, that is another handicap. Spectacles, like false teeth, are likely to become disarranged if the lecturer reaches flights of oratory. It has been demonstrated that the wearing of glasses is compatible with the relatively machinelike tasks of playing second base, but an orator wearing glasses is unthinkable. Also, those accustomed to hairsplitting reasoning are usually deadly as speakers. This is not said in disparagement. To be oratorical it is necessary to deal only with the most superficial of facts, if any, as the politicians abundantly demonstrate, while the researcher must weigh each bit of evidence carefully. I give place to no man in the appreciation of the medical researcher but his problems are not for the medical student. Researchers should be quarantined both for their own good and for the good of the student. I speak sympathetically because I have dabbled in the border lines myself, but I have never mentioned them to my students. The fact should be recognized that the average doctor never does catch up with what the researcher is doing. We doctors should be spared the agony of the scientific delivery room and should be allowed to hold the baby only after the nurse has him all polished up and dressed.

A good teacher should have some outstanding characteristics. Two of our teachers in particular had this desirable attribute.

Jaggard, professor of obstetrics, spoke very slowly, almost dictated, so that a rapid writer could take down his words almost verbatim. We were required to commit his words to memory, and that really meant committing them to memory so that the points could be presented in the order in which they were given in the lecture. One had to know thoroughly every lecture at all times, for he was likely to quiz on lectures given months before, without notice, and woe be unto him who was not prepared. There was no forgiveness there. I can pass Jaggard's examination today, so thoroughly were the lectures made a part of me, though I have not seen a newborn baby for more than thirty years.

I STUDY MEDICINE

Jaggard also had the ability to impress us in both word and deed with the seriousness of the professional responsibility. "Think first always," he insisted, "what harm the treatment may do." "Regard the information imparted by the patient as sacred," was another dictum. He was wont to illustrate this by placing a pencil on the desk before the students. "You know it—that's one." Obviously so, as one looked at the pencil. "Your patient knows it," placing another pencil beside the first— "that's two." That also seemed obvious. "Now you tell your wife"—placing another pencil beside the other two. "Now how many know it?" The quizzed student, viewing the row of three pencils, stated, naturally, that now three would possess the facts. "No," he would roar, "that is one hundred and eleven." He wanted to tell us that the confidences of the patients are sacred. That is a good example of hammering home a point.

Another incident may be mentioned. A delivery conducted before the class resulted in a stillborn baby. He turned to the class. "We must pause to think that our lack of skill may have deprived the world of a future Lincoln," he dramatically remarked. Since the demised infant was a colored female child the point lost something of its dramatic effect. But this interpretation is the product of after-years. At the time, we boys were tremendously impressed by the almost superhuman earnestness of the man. It has taken me a lifetime to see the humor of the situation.

The other notable teacher was Fenger. A native of Denmark, his use of the English language was never good. When he became particularly aggravated, because of the lack of the right word, he would sometimes say, "Tam the English language." Because of his troubles with our language his lectures were difficult to follow, but despite this he was an impressive teacher. His distinct value was due to the fact that he was a master of surgical pathology. He frequently stated that the only way to learn surgery was "to beat a path from the operating room to the laboratory" and to learn pathology you must "look through your microscope every day of your life." Fenger's outstanding characteristic was his thoroughness. I remember one tumor from which he had taken tissue from twelve different areas. "Now I know what is in this tumor?" he inquired. A student pointed at naturally assented. He fairly shouted, "No. I know only what is in those twelve places." If pathologists could just remember that what they diagnose from a slide represents only a small area, much useless generalization would be spared and many errors would be kept out of the literature.

Fenger insisted that every bit of tissue removed at operation must be examined microscopically. One time when the object of operation was tuberculosis of the lymph glands of the neck the assistant, tiring of examining the same sort of tissue day after day, cast the specimens away. The next week Dr. Fenger asked to see the slides. The assistant replied that they were not finished. He hoped that the professor certainly would forget about them in another week. Not so. As he hove into sight the next week the first words were: "Where are those slides?" The assistant, despairing of his ever forgetting about them, confessed that the tissue had been lost. Dr. Fenger dropped the instrument bags he was carrying, his normally livid face became a bluish red and he burst forth: "Tam it t'hell a thousand times. How you learn surgery if you throw the material away?" From then he got going good on the necessity of studying surgical material. No one could escape appreciation of surgical pathology after sitting at his feet for several years.

Dr. Fenger had an amusing way of expressing disgust. "Tam" was the only expletive used but he used it in multiples according to the degree of irritation. The estimate was carefully made. For instance, one day in walking across the operating room his foot thrust against an object. His face grew livid and he blurted out, "Tam it a thousand times." Then, turning to his assistant, he asked, "What was that?" The assistant replied that it was only a block of wood used to elevate the table. "Oh," he added soothingly, "only ten times." The first morning he was to operate in Mercy Hospital his assistant teasingly remarked that he would not be allowed to swear in the Sisters' Hospital. After a moment's thought he replied, "So? I swear then in Danish," that being his native language.

Despite his oddities I have always counted Professor Fenger as one of my greatest teachers. The lasting influence of the man is what made him a great teacher. Work without ceasing, run from the operating room to the laboratory and back again, beat a path between the two. That was his message as it was his example.

Most people believe that surgical pathology is synonymous with the pathology of surgical specimens. Nothing is farther from the truth. Surgical pathology includes the disease from its beginning, often long before the disease comes to the attention of the surgeon or even the patient. He must be able to visualize the development of the disease from the beginning. It begins with a human being and ends with a human being. Why did we let him die? More knowledge and we will see the lesion earlier and with our trusty scalpel intercept the ravages of the disease. That is the spirit of surgical pathology. The surgeon approximates the limit of his powers only after he has seen many cases and compared them in detail. He sees the disease in the clinic; its appearance as it is seen in the gross at the operating table comes next. This he can recognize only after he has followed many similar cases to the laboratory. Only in the last step comes the microscopic examination. The greater the experience in the operating room the less need for laboratory examination. This is what Fenger meant when he said a surgeon must needs look through his microscope every day.

The preliminary factors as revealed in the clinic are not accessible to the pathologist in his laboratory. He sees only one part of the picture. He does not see a human being. Tumors might as well be bugs or plants or rocks as far as he is concerned. Surgical pathology as it is in most hospitals today is cold, lifeless, utterly useless. The pathologist looks at the slides, mumbles two paragraphs to his stenographer—twelve lines each, the one having to do with the gross appearance, the other with the microscopic findings. The lower line contains the conclusions. The surgeon reads it and can tell from this line if the lesion was malignant or not. This report is attached to the patient's chart and the people who regulate our hospitals say, "Well done, good and faithful servant." Utterly useless, a travesty on science, mockery to the human beings who look to us for help for themselves and for their children. It makes me mad.

It makes me mad because it made Fenger mad. No one in my acquaintance could emphasize these facts so well as did he. His insistence on the value of a study of surgical pathology day in and day out is the most valuable thing I ever learned from any teacher. It is the greatest disappointment of my life that I have been utterly unable to transmit this teaching to my students.

To surgeons the value of the study of material obtained at operation is unrecognized, ignored. At most, to the vast majority of surgeons it seems to be like their religion—the value is assented to but the practice of it is ignored. Yet there is a subconscious recognition of its value, because they pretend to have it when they have it not. To say the least, those surgeons who do not study their tissue lose all the fun. While a good surgical pathologist is able to anticipate the microscopic picture, tissue in hand, yet there are surprises and one always feels a sense of anticipation as he approaches the study of the slide, much as one does, say, in picking up a hand in a card game.

The clinical facilities at Northwestern in our time, in comparison to present-day medical schools, were pitiably inadequate. Sure enough, we had dispensary clinics, much as we have today, and they were run as they are today, usually by young men just one jump ahead of the students they taught. Dispensary clinics were supplemented by the college clinics, and by clinics in several hospitals, held by the regular staff. Ward study of patients was instituted in Mercy Hospital in our senior year. Students were consigned patients and were expected to take a history, make the examination and then tell the professor all about it when he made his rounds the next day. This part of my education came to pot. I was assigned a large Hibernian policeman. I approached him and informed him that he was assigned me for examination. With an oath he chased me out of the ward. I was too overcome to tell the professor why I had not examined the patient assigned me, so he docked me ten per cent on the final examination.

Then as now operative clinics were given a prominent place in the curriculum. These were really shows or rest periods for us students. All we saw were the backs of the professor and his assistants. But the nurses were well worth looking at, so what we missed in surgery we made up in the study of art. Of course, the inevitable result was that some of the students married nurses, or nurses married medical students, as the case may be, even as it is today.

What a student learns in major surgical clinics is negligible and the time might better be devoted to problems within his range. I have never yet been able to understand why undergraduates are exposed to clinics in major surgery, or why they should even be required to learn more than just something of their nature. Before these operations become of importance to them a long apprenticeship is, or should be, required. For instance, I learned in school all the little details in the technic of abdominal hysterectomy, but no one thought to tell me not to molest the little boils which sometimes form in the upper lip.

We worked as hard as students do now. The student today is curious to know what we did with so few things known in the whole range of medicine to learn about. I sometimes wonder about it too. We were occupied with the things which pertain to practice. If one knows thoroughly the facts about a disease through the simple act of memory, he has gone a long way toward recognizing it when he sees it in practice, though he never saw such a condition during his school course. As I look back it is interesting to note how easy it was to recognize a disease one had never seen, such as appendicitis, or a gallstone attack, when one met his first case at the bedside, even if he had no more than book knowledge.

There were not so many theories as there are now; even so, we learned many things that never have been true and learned about diseases one never has seen, such as yaws, beriberi and Chinese itch. The result was that we knew at least the common points of diseases met with in everyday practice. The most illuminating truism was expressed by Murphy: "In order to practice medicine, you do not need to know much, but you must know that little well." If the young men knew how little we old duffers know today, they would scoff at us more than they do. I was impressed by this recently in looking over the questions of the National Board. At the same time, at least three-fourths of the knowledge therein asked for is useless as far as the practice of the healing art is concerned.

What is more, we learned well the palliative measures necessary to make the patient comfortable until the diagnosis was made or, as was perhaps more often the case, until the patient spontaneously recovered. But this condition exists today. The saving of life is the chief function of the doctor, let us admit, but it is a function he performs only now and then. It is the relief of pain that chiefly interests the patient, and skill along this line is the big factor in the life of the man in general practice. It is not scientific to treat symptoms, hence it is not taught in the schools.

I was fortunate enough to spend the vacation between my junior and senior years with a country doctor of large practice. I learned here what to do to relieve the patient of his distress. There is a tendency now for some schools to farm out students at this stage to men in active practice. This certainly is an excellent idea.

It is interesting to consider the attainments of the student of our day, when he emerged from school, as compared with the young man of today. After all, we were much the same breed. The student now, of course, knows a little about many things undreamed of in the days of long ago. But of common diseases we had more fundamental facts ground into us than the student of today. We knew drugs better and we knew their application for the relief of symptoms even though we did not know their action on pink bullfrogs.

After all the practice of medicine is an art, no matter how profound the scientific knowledge. We can learn a lot about how doctors are educated by studying dogs. The pup sniffs and recognizes a smell. He goes to see what it comes from. By gosh, there is a rabbit! After he does this a few times he knows that that smell indicates the presence of a rabbit. He does not go to discover from what the smell comes. He knows before he starts that there is a rabbit there. Much of the practice of medicine is like that. The doctor learns by the feel of a belly that there is inflammation inside. His reasoning is just as profound as the dog's; it is knowledge arrived at in the same way. Seeing things of like nature repeatedly is the basis of the healing art. Herein the experienced practitioner may outclass his better educated but less experienced colleague. Teachers should recognize the limitations of the comprehension of the student so as not to confuse him with irrelevant and immaterial data by quoting the contrary opinions of a number of authors on subjects about which nobody knows anything. They should avoid the rare conditions which the student will probably never meet in his own practice. The most common thing must be stressed. For example, suppose a mule were a disease, as he sometimes is a pest. One would know, of course, that he is likely to kick. The good lecturer would emphasize the well-known fact that a mule will kick, not may or can, but will. In his quizzes he would ask, what does a mule do? The simple answer "Kick" would be good for a ten. When the student met a mule in practice it would at once come to his mind that the object before him will kick. That is practical medicine.

Not so the research-minded teacher. A bare mention of the fact that mules have been known to kick suffices for him. Most likely he has never seen a mule except in a museum. In fact he is bored by the mere mention of it, it is so obvious. Everybody knows it, so why mention it—except of course the student who is destined to have to do with mules may not know it. With a mere mention of the fact that a mule has been known to kick the lecturer passes on at once to say that the mule may also bite; he then proceeds to cite instances in which it is alleged that a mule did bite—say in the Garden of Eden a mule is alleged to have bitten a blind boy as recorded in the *Jerusalem Medical Gazette*, vol. 76, 1128 B.C. Then of course there would be the need of quoting someone with the contrary opinion, that it was not a mule but an ass and that the ass, not the boy, was blind and furthermore it was the boy who bit the beast, not the beast the boy. The end result would be that the student would forget the opening statement, that the mule is a kicking animal, and when he met such a brute, while trying to recall the name of the man who reported that a mule bit a blind boy, he would be kicked into the next county by the mule. Of course there is nothing more interesting than to try to figure out the psychology of a mule, as revealed in his habits, but this is pure science.

The practice nowadays is to make a diagnosis and if the disease is self-limited to turn the patient over to the tender mercy of the nurses—or the mercy of tender nurses, which is not the same thing. That may be scientific, of course, but not exactly humane. The patient will get well just as fast without suffering, so why let him suffer just because we do not know the action of drugs that will give him relief? We knew how to relieve the various pains, because experience had proved that such and such a drug would relieve that particular kind of pain, though we never had a course in laboratory pharmacology. Nowadays if the drug in question does not have a certain action in the experimental laboratory no scientifically trained young doctor would use it. The use of potassium iodide, for instance, is taboo in the treatment of asthma because it seems to have no effect on asthma in bullfrogs, though experience has abundantly proved it relieves asthma in wheezy old men.

The pity of it is that this waning interest in the pain the individual is momentarily interested in has given the various cults their chance. When we were children and had a hurt we ran to Mother to have her rub it. After a time the pain ceased, which increased our faith in Mother's rubbing. Sometimes Mother would kiss the hurt place if conveniently located. Here is a grand possibility for the development of another cult, or has it already been included in the repertoire of some of those we now have? Far be it from me to cast any insinuations; but it is generally recognized that the handsomer the man the better quack he makes, which suggests that a possible osculatory contact may lurk in the subconscious background. That quacks are usually prepossessing and handsome is universally recognized and not a product of my own limited observations. Someone may counter that the only reason that most of us are regular doctors is that we are too unattractive to be quacks. What I am attempting to express is that many pains are temporary, ephemeral and not serious, and the object to be sought is to arrange things so that this short interval may be spent as pleasantly as possible. We only regard with envy those who can accomplish this without drugs. It is permissible to note that some of the drugless healers are just now making an awful furor because narcotic permits are denied them. Certainly no one is so dull as to miss the humor of it. Real pain does not yield to incantation. Pain due to organic disease requires morphine—and the quacks know this as well as we do.

The important thing is that the suffering patient wants action. Whether there is any sense in what is being done to him is quite beside the point. He wants someone else to be interested in his pain, too. He indicates that right here is his pain and he becomes impatient if his doctor with apparent lack of interest ignores that little spot and orders a blood count, a Wasser-mann and a chemical examination of this or that.

Whether one gives the patient something, or rubs the sore spot or puts something on may be immaterial, because sooner or later his pain ceases or else he dies. Doctors when they get sick, as is generally recognized, howl louder than the common run and are just as much interested in their own private pain, the interest in which completely overshadows their scientific training. Furthermore, their credulity prompts them to credit the measure being used, at the time the pain disappears, with securing relief and, if they live, for curing the disease. That is the way most of us got our reputation, if any, let it be admitted. Not what we did but what the patient believes we did is what counts.

These somewhat facetious remarks must not overshadow the fact that the ability of the doctor is measured by his capacity to properly evaluate the trivial and the serious. He must be able to gauge the degree and meaning of pain, when to wait, when to act swiftly.

It is always well occasionally to take off our intellectual topper and study innovations. There may be some reason for their being innovations. The homeopaths taught us a couple of generations ago that utterly actionless drugs were often followed by relief of pain. That was a fact, because their drugs were wholly impotent. Their theory was that by diluting a drug the potency was increased. Therefore, if you diluted a drug ten times it was ten times as strong. Silly, of course, as time has proved. Nobody believes it now. Then why did it go over? Simply because their medicines, being sugar of milk, tasted like sugar of milk and the children cried for them. Most ailments got well just as fast on such measures as they did on nux vomica and tincture of chloride of iron, the giving of which made it necessary to lasso and hogtie the youthful candidate.

In the cults of the present day we have the same problem. Even a pet pig likes to have its belly rubbed. Why should it not have an equally salutary effect on the humans who have even more impressionable minds? The effect is sometimes salutary enough to be expressed in terms of encomiums and cash. The important point for the medical student to remember is that because his patient is relieved of his pain it does not follow that his ministrations had anything to do with the results. It may be shrewd to fool the patient, but no doctor but a fool would fool himself. If he does, some fatal disease may slip up on him and kill his patient. To rub a tummy for a lady who is mad at Papa is one thing; to rub the same region for a patient with a perforated appendix is something quite different.

We laugh at the tom-toms of the Indian but they had their place, and we should not fail to recognize their modern prototype even if it is we who are beating the tom-toms, and the best of us are engaged more or less in the pastime. Medicine as well as quackery has indulged in much drum beating and chanting. It is well for us to exercise occasional introspection. It is well for every doctor to take a little time out now and then and try to discover what is science and what is hokum. Though one may be conscientious in his acts, it still may be hokum. I once subjected myself to the greatest vicissitudes in reaching a long series of pneumonia patients and I believed I was instrumental in saving many lives, but the remedies I gave them had nothing to do with their recovery. I know this now full well, but not then. This goes to show that if one is dumb enough one may dispense hokum and be perfectly honest in so doing.

This digression illustrates the many things, most of which were valuable in practice, the old doctors taught us which the modern student does not hear from his vastly more learned full-time professor.

Whatever our qualifications and our limitations at the end of our course of study may have been, we were granted diplomas which indicated to the anxious public that we were qualified to practice the healing art. In giving them the faculty neither laughed nor wept, so that it is likely they shared our delusions—which is just another indication of the truth of the fact above noted. Whether this self-deception was ever lifted from the faculty, the students each in due time, I am sure, came to realize the fallacy and have, I hope, devoted themselves assiduously to remedying it.

What our teachers bequeathed us was, let us admit, but little knowledge. They gave us abundantly the will to do, to strive unceasingly. Were I to live my life over again I should want the old teachers back. They were as unstandardized as a bunch of bronchos, but each had his merit, the product of his own experience. Even now, despite our standardized profession, each doctor expresses his own individuality, the product of his own efforts in the assiduous application of what little brains the fates gave him. The doctor that faces the patient is the product of his own individuality which expresses itself in human understanding, in scientific knowledge, and the art of its application. To socialize medicine is to remove the human touch, to suppress this individualizing of the doctor, it makes of the patient just a case, just as a sick horse is not a patient but a case.

Even though the scholastic requirements for the practice of medicine fifty years ago were not very high they were higher than the public demanded; it is so even today. In fact the public demands nothing except the privilege of patronizing quacks and cults. Higher medical standards are entirely the work of doctors themselves conscious of their limitations. For proof of the public attitude witness the various cults permitted by law, that is public opinion, to practice the healing art, or perhaps it were better to say, the "heeling" art, since the end sought is financial and to be opulent is, in the vernacular of the prairie states, to be "well heeled."

Let it be repeated here that the advance in medical requirements has been autonomous action by the medical profession, and not in response to public demand. So far as the public demand is concerned the world might still be enjoying all the infectious diseases in their pristine glory and laudable pus might inundate the earth. The public, taken on the whole, still occupies itself enthusiastically with placing obstructions in the path of progress. Once in a while a "malefactor of great wealth" gives the whole process a boost. It would not be a great exaggeration to say the Rockefellers have done more for medical education than all the rest of the laymen since the beginning of time. That may be an exaggeration but it will do until someone comes along with figures. It illustrates the point I wish to make.

It may be remarked in passing that the doctors are sometimes called silly because they spend their lives inventing ways of controlling disease, thereby lessening their business. That is a stupid view. By preventing the epidemics we keep the kids alive until they reach old age, opulence, and achieve rheumatism and high blood pressure. One rheumatic patient will produce more revenue than a whole epidemic of measles. I can prove it by my books.

But there is a more intimate reason why we try to advance medical knowledge. Perhaps I am revealing a professional secret when I admit that doctors sometimes make mistakes. Even though we bury them, as we are facetiously accused of doing, that does not blot them from memory. A catastrophe, whether preventable or not, sticks in the unfortunate Aesculapian's memory, or wherever it is such things stick. They hurt and they hurt terribly, and we really want to avoid a repetition. Sometimes I think that whoever it was that calculated three score and ten was about all anyone could endure of this life must have had doctors in mind. For by the time a doctor reaches that age his mind is so full of tragic memories that the limit of endurance is just about reached. He forgets his successes, as things normally expected of him; but the tragedies, like Banquo's ghost, will not down. The unexplained infection, the heart block, the thrombosis, to mention only a few, lurk constantly in the background of memory. And what is more disturbing still, they also lurk just around the corner as imminent possibilities. Such things are a constant incentive to higher education, and spur on the hunt for new facts which will protect us from past errors. We doctors wear poker faces, or at least are accused of doing so, while dispensing our opinion, in which we do not differ from lawyers and preachers. We do so because we so often have our errors thrust upon us. The patient has the last guess; if he dies he is dead. Besides if we told all we knew there would be scandals, fugitives and murders. When the doctor says nothing it is a cause for thanksgiving. When we assume a jocular vein it may not be very deep. My father once said that we are given a sense of humor that we may cloak our grief.

CHAPTER

4 _____

COUNTRY PRACTICE WAS SO CALLED BECAUSE IT WAS JUST THAT. The patients lived in the country and it was necessary for the doctor to drive out into the country to visit them. The doctors, for the most part, lived in the villages but the village inhabitants formed only a very small part of the doctor's practice. There was but little office practice because patients were treated with the simple remedies at home unless or until the state of the disease seemed to be threatening or the pain became too great to bear.

Country practice, therefore, naturally divided itself into two divisions, first that of transportation, the act of conducting oneself to the bedside of the patient; second, what one did after he arrived at the bedside of the patient.

The means of transportation at the beginning of any practice was preferred in the order named: horse or team and buggy; horse and road cart, a two-wheeled vehicle with a simple and very hard board seat on which no cushion could be fastened; horseback; and finally just plain everyday walking it or pedaling a lowly bicycle. The bicycle was fine when roads were good and the distance not too great but I never could suppress an inferiority complex while riding one. A long-legged man never can look professional riding a bicycle. Therefore after I began to get some consultation practice this means of transportation was abandoned.

Naturally most of the sicknesses occurred when the weather was inclement, either very hot or very cold and stormy and the roads indescribably bad; in fact there were no roads. At such seasons I sometimes spent the greater part of the twenty-four hours in the buggy. Sometimes in the spring and fall when the weather was fine there might not be a country call for a week or even longer. When the roads were good the population suddenly became provokingly healthy. Not only was country driving time-consuming and fatiguing but at times it became exceedingly inconvenient. But we accepted it as part of the job. It was this phase of the work, it may be noted, that made many young men shun country practice. Being inured to such things by life on the farm and being delighted to earn enough to eat with a fair degree of regularity, I accepted the conditions with eagerness.

The present automobile speed gives one a very poor idea of the trials of travel by team. Nowadays the country doctor whizzes into the country at reckless speed and comes back faster. Doctors are notorious speed fiends. I recently rode with a doctor at a speed of seventy-five miles an hour on a road that averaged seven curves a mile. The reason? None whatever—it is just the small-boy hangover. It is a trite question when one sees a speeder, even a doctor, to ask what he will do with the few minutes saved by the excessive speed. The answer is the same in all cases—nothing. It was even so in the horse and buggy days. Some doctors dashed about with fine teams with much show. In such cases one could be sure that he was not going very far and for no great purpose. Such things did not fool the public for very long. Some other doctor who had preceded him in the community and employed the same antics, having proved unreliable after a time, the public remembered and classed the newcomer in the same category. It is interesting to note how the psychology of a man could be judged by the way he held the lines. A friend of mine, a most excellent horseman, used to remark to me that I did not drive; I just herded the horses along. That was exactly correct, but long drives do not permit driving a team.

Generally a speed of seven miles an hour was good time for a team in cold weather and good roads. In muddy roads, when a horse cannot exceed a walk, three miles an hour is average time. A mule will walk unmolested two and a half miles an hour, if urged he reduces this to two miles and if urged too strongly he may stop entirely and look back over his shoulder to inquire what you are going to do about it. This is one of those questions the form of which carries its own answer: to wit, nothing. On the whole, the mule was the most reliable means of transportation available. The great drawback of mule transportation, as I remember it, was that it was so undignified. For the consulting doctor to arrive drawn by a span of unwilling mules was a very bad start as far as dignity was concerned. Be it remembered that dignity is a very important item to a young doctor—observe nowadays the hospital interns, magnificent, all decked out in white; but after one is established he acts naturally. But even then dignity had on occasion to give way to dependability. Though the mule occasionally backfires he does not run out of gas—no dead batteries, no flat tires. But one must learn to respect his individuality. Some of them have the disposition of a prima donna, and if their feelings are hurt they may repudiate their contract. I remember one eleven-mile trip into the country, which required five hours with a span of mules hitched to an improvised sled. This trip is ever memorable because as I entered the house the patient called from an adjoining room: "Doc, you are too late." As indeed I was. Perforated appendix was the answer.

The buggy used by doctors was a single-seated four-wheeled vehicle to which one or two horses were attached. The buggy was preferred to a road cart and was used whenever the condition of the roads permitted. It was more comfortable and one could wrap himself up to greater advantage as a protection against wind, rain and snow. When the roads were extremely muddy the road cart had its advantages. The pull on the horse was considerably less and one could dodge in and out and past mudholes and it was easier to cross fields because one could make short turns. Besides, if one upset it was easy to right the vehicle again.

The use of the road cart had the advantage that one could, in a measure, protect himself; but the seat was a board affair and uncomfortable at best. The chief disadvantage, however, was their insecurity. A sudden lurch of the horse might cause distressing disarrangements of the passenger. For instance, I once rode dozing slumped over in a cart when a large dog attacked my horse. He raised up and gave a sudden lunge forward in an effort to strike the dog. Unwarned and unprepared, this precipitated me completely behind the cart and I found myself sitting flat in the road. Fortunately this unexpected event so surprised the dog that he took to his heels. Had he attacked me, I would have been at a serious disadvantage. Bronchos were seldom hitched to a road cart. They had a way of tying themselves into a knot only to appear outside the shafts and not infrequently wrong end to. One of these little rascals I once had must have had Quaker blood, for as soon as hitched she would lie down and one had to wait until the spirit moved her; but when it did move her she jumped up and started off on a dead run and it was not easy to stick to the smooth board seat. Horseback riding was resorted to only when there were no roads, a condition rare in prairie countries. A road cart permits the use of a lap robe, which is impossible on horseback because the broncho also has ideas of dignity. These animals, it may be mentioned, had a constitutional aversion to much-petticoated ladies and a doctor trying to protect his legs by a blanket was classed in this

64

group, so that the pony precipitated him with promptness and precision. When approaching these sad-eyed rascals, I could imagine them humming to themselves the tune of the lovelorn: "Juanita, I feel that we must part."

The buggy seat was usually from thirty to thirty-six inches long, suitable for seating two persons. This was all right as a seat but it made rather a short bed, particularly for a person afflicted as I am with excessive longitudinality. This made it necessary for me to stick my feet and legs through the top bows into the adjacent atmosphere when in a recumbent position. This was not exactly a graceful pose but sleep thus obtained was better than none. Dignity obviously is less important at night when everybody else is asleep. Of course, in the out trip one could not sleep for long because the team had to be guided in the proper direction, but on the return trip the team could be depended on to go directly home—that is, some teams. My own horse, after he had been to a place a time or two, could be depended upon to go there unguided and he invariably returned home directly but in his own sweet time, which consisted in making about four or five miles an hour with some stops interposed for viewing the scenery or visiting with a wayside horse. When he stopped, it invariably wakened me and a jerk of the lines started him off at once, sometimes on a dead run for a short distance.

Livery teams were undependable. They were contrary as a species and could not be depended upon to return home unguided. A good many times such a team wandered off and I wakened to find myself in unknown surroundings. On clear nights the North Star gave me the direction and the Santa Fe railway track furnished a guide east and west. One drove until this was reached and then turned right or left as the case might be. On cloudy nights nothing remained but to find a farmhouse and inquire one's way. Usually the bellowing of dogs indicated the location of a house long before it came into view, but those same dogs prevented an approach to the house and it was sometimes difficult to raise the occupant. A bark from the Colt six-shooter invariably got response, albeit sometimes the resident appeared with shotgun in hand to inquire as to the cause of the unseemly disturbance. Once convinced that it was a doctor, help was certain, even to the extent of riding with the doctor to locate a little-used road.

Some teams also had a habit of locating a haystack on the prairie and peacefully feeding themselves until urged on. It was aggravating to wake up when one should be home or on the way to another call, only to find his team peacefully eating hay miles from home, not rarely in a strange environment.

Doctors being dependable drivers, the livery man gave them teams which were unsafe for inexperienced drivers. Moreover, each team had its own specialty in cussedness and one was somewhat prepared for coming events if he knew the team. The two chief specialties were running away and kicking the driver out of the buggy if anything went wrong. Dogs were the common excuse for running away. Most farmsteads had two or three dogs which on long nights were glad to find a belated team to chase purely as a matter of diversion. In such cases one would wake up only to find his team wildly tearing down the road or across the prairie.

Mustang ponies, much used in my time, were the runaway specialists. They were durable, so that they would jog along at a moderate trot hours without end. They were unsuitable because of their size when the road was muddy or the snow deep. The kickers were usually horses bred for carriage service; but having flunked in their examinations for this service they were consigned to work in a livery stable. Fortunately, only one horse at a time would kick. In such event one slid to the side of the seat opposite the kicking horse and could thus dodge the flying hoofs—that is, generally. Only once I was too slow and got an injury resulting in a dislocated cartilage of one of my knees,

The Stork
When the horses and mules gave out the country doctor walked.

from the result of which I have never recovered. This knee would be a serious handicap to a pious person.

If two occupied the buggy the problem was more complicated. One day while I was driving a notoriously kicking horse the neck-yoke strap broke, but instead of running as a team would naturally do under such circumstances, the horse stopped, humped up his back and started to kick. My assistant was driving and I was peacefully dozing, but the slight jerk caused by the breaking of the strap wakened me enough to enable me to sense the importance of the humping back of the kicking specialist. The rear curtain being rolled up, with one leap I landed in the road behind the buggy—and landed on my feet. This feat has always given me pleasant memories, for I believe if I had not lived a generation too soon I might have achieved fame on the basketball court.

Next to the bad roads dogs were the common pest. Every farmyard had several, at least one of which was a big Newfoundland. Sometimes these dogs lay in wait along the side of the road. The team, sensing this, might turn sharply around, threatening to upset the buggy or take off across an adjoining field. Others would dash out of the barnyard, causing the team to go down the road on the dead run. If the frightened team ran straight ahead, leading the dogs, there was no difficulty; but if the dogs outdistanced the team and jumped at the noses of the horses and they swerved too sharply, the buggy was upset and then there was pandemonium right; or even if the team took across an adjacent field they might encounter farm machinery or ditches of unpleasant depth. It was necessary to educate the dogs. Some of them would take the hint if a carefully placed bullet were planted at their heels. The more persistent had to be treated more roughly. Three of this species chased me one night when my assistant was driving. The next day there was one. Some dogs bear a charmed life. One large Newfoundland dog was an example of this. Despite his size and despite my careful work with both revolver and carbine, this dog died of old age.

One dog presented an unusual problem. He was a very large brindle dog who acquired the ability to jump on the side of a horse and grab the check ring and hang on. A big dog hanging on the harness, of course, excited the horse to frantic efforts. A bouncing buggy and a plunging horse with a dog hanging on him presented a mark that even a revolver expert dare not risk. Try as I might, I could not get a shot at that dog before he landed on the horse. One fine Sunday afternoon, having a driver and armed with a carbine, I was looking for him. There he was standing some twenty feet from the kitchen door inspecting the weather, not at all interested in doctors and their horses. I was a bit peeved at this unseemly indifference, so I got out of the buggy and lay down in the grass and with a nice elbow rest planted a carbine bullet behind his front legs. Illegal, of course, but I failed to find a statute granting permission to any brindle dog to scare the daylights out of a sleepy doctor's team. At any rate a doctor often must operate in the face of a doubtful prognosis.

When afoot these big dogs sometimes were a real menace. One night when I was walking down a road a dog, known throughout the neighborhood as dangerous, came tearing out and made a dive for my throat. I parried his dive with the instrument bag I was carrying and as he started to fall backward I placed a bullet in his chest, from my six-shooter, shooting from my hip. That was fast and fine shooting and no audience to acclaim it.

But there was a lighter vein. When the roads were good I occupied my time by reading or by shooting at wayside objects or jack rabbits. I was then interested in biology and read most of Lubbock's books and really learned Flower's *Osteology of the Mammalia* while riding the long weary hours. Bones of all sorts of animals were plentiful and my buggy contained a fair-sized museum of comparative osteology. Insects and butterflies were collected as occasion required. I got what I then considered a fair reading knowledge of French by study done wholly in the buggy. What I then thought was a fair reading knowledge is right. I learned later, when I had the advantages of a native tutor, that one can never learn French sitting down, one hand occupied with holding the lines. The reason is the same as why a one-armed man never makes a good clothing salesman.

Reading was interspersed with shooting with both six-shooter and Winchester. Fence posts furnished the usual mark as the team jogged along. I have fired as many as five hundred rounds on a single trip. Jack rabbits, prairie dogs and owls furnished variation. I had a friend, an excellent rifle shot, who used to pair with me on some of these trips. I would shoot under a jack rabbit with my 40-82, throwing him a yard in the air. He lit running and my friend would shoot him on the run with a small rifle.

Such diversions lessened very much the tedium of reading on long trips. Much of my reading was so done, not a good thing for the eyes, and this practice much aggravated my hereditary migraine.

Usually driving was just plain wearisome work, but trials and even dangers sometimes attended these country drives. A few specific instances may be mentioned in illustration. One night I had to cross a considerable stream which had a low water bridge. As I crossed on the out trip the water was just flowing over the floor of the bridge. When I returned, after several hours, the bridge was no longer visible but I estimated the water had risen only about a foot, which would permit easy crossing. But my horse had other ideas. He positively refused even to approach the water, so I turned, or rather he turned, around and came home by a circuitous route. Some days later an occurrence in a neighboring town caused me to go and inspect that bridge. It was gone. The occurrence just referred to befell a young doctor who tried to cross a bridge that was not there and he was drowned. This same horse of mine saved me on two other occasions. One of them occurred in one of my first trips when roads were strange to me. The water was even with the bridge but the approach on the opposite side was under water. I urged my horse to go through but he refused, so I backed off the bridge and sought another road. After the flood subsided I chanced to cross the bridge and discovered that the approach was eight feet below the level of the bridge. Had I tried to cross this flood it would certainly have been disastrous. I am a most excellent wader but eight feet is a bit beyond my capacity.

Dog trainers have a saying that in order to train a dog one must know more than the dog. In order to drive a horse in dangerous situations one must know more than the horse. I soon learned that in intelligence in dangerous situations my horse knew more than I and I always deferred to his judgment. One night he jumped a washout of a bridge approach which was fully six feet wide and fifteen feet deep. He cleared it together with the front wheels of the buggy but the hind wheels fell into the water; yet he dragged the wheels to safety after they had fallen some distance in the water. On a pitch-dark night finding myself in a buggy horizontal to the earth's surface nearly scared the daylights out of me. My patient lived a very short distance from the bridge and his father had expected to warn me not to cross. He had intended to guard the bridge with a lantern but I came sooner than expected.

My patient on this occasion was a small boy with an abscess in his neck. Obviously it needed opening. I placed my instrument bag on the table and proceeded to inspect its contents. I went to sleep while doing so—it must have been but momentarily; I closed my bag and went back to town, by another road, needless to mention. When I awoke the next morning I remembered that I had not opened that abscess. I hastened back to do the necessary operation. The family thought that after looking in my bag I found I lacked the necessary instruments and had gone back to town after them. They did not realize that I had gone to sleep. This instance illustrates the placidity of a weary country doctor. Within fifteen minutes after being frightened stiff by the fall of the hind part of the buggy into the water, I went to sleep hunting for instruments with which to open an abscess.

Speaking of nice peaceful slumber, an incident occurs to my mind. One nice moonlit night I got a call to the outskirts of the town. It could not have been more than six blocks from home, because that was as far as the town extended. I thought I would walk rather than trouble to hitch up my horse. After walking a few blocks I got so sleepy I just had to sit down for a rest. That was about eleven o'clock. I sat down in a nice place under a tree which shaded me from the brilliant full moon. I woke up at three the next morning and I had entirely forgotten where I had started for, so I had to return home. The call was not repeated and as nobody died in that neighborhood I concluded the patient had not been very sick. This occurrence is interesting in that it shows how a weary brain refuses to take even the impression of a sick call.

One of the most peculiar feelings I ever had occurred one night when I was awakened out of a nice sleep by a peculiar jerk of the buggy. I awoke with a start and my team was gone. There I sat in a buggy on a snow-covered prairie apparently without a team. The fact was, of course, that the team had run into a snow-filled ditch; once in, the loose snow covered them completely and they were quite invisible to sleepy eyes. It was necessary to take my shovel and dig away the snow, unhitch the team, push the buggy away from the ditch, hitch up again and start in a different direction. Which direction to go was the problem. One might find other and deeper ditches. In such cases an experienced driver knows just exactly which way to go. He goes back from whence he came. Snow makes this possible but on dark muddy nights one did not know from whence he came any more than where he was going. One had on such occasion to fall back on the Cartesian philosophy: namely, "I think, therefore I am," but this gives no information as to where one is or how long he will be. Descartes evidently was writing in his library. Had he been lost out on a prairie he would have written: "I can't think and I do not know where I am."

On this particular occasion I had slept so long that the team had lost its way and I was completely lost. Nothing was in sight except a wide level expanse of snow and I had no idea where there might be other ditches. I was scared. The glare of the moon on the snow made snow-covered buildings poorly visible. But I followed the golden rule of the prairies—when in doubt, trust to the horse. That worked out well in this case and after traveling several miles I got my bearings and could start out anew. I was five miles off the road that led to my patient.

I learned to take these mishaps as just one of those things incident to country practice. In fact, I got a peculiar thrill out of battling the elements when nobody else was abroad and no one thought the doctor could make it. Thus conceit doth make fools of us all, but if misinterpreted by the public it also makes heroes. My people thought I was brave; I thought so too then, but now I know it was plain dumb. In fact, it is a question whether heroes are not just plain fools who got the breaks. I have no specific instance in mind.

If the roads were fenced and drifted full of snow one just cut the wires and took out across the field, and after the drift was passed cut his way back into the road again. I recall with great satisfaction that no farmer complained if an embattled doctor cut his way out of a difficult situation. He repaired the fence with the satisfaction of knowing that it is an incident in the common fellowship of man. Some neighbor needed help and got it, theoretically at least.

I may mention incidentally that when the snow was deep, a scoop shovel, wire cutters and a hammer were as much a part of my equipment as was my Colt six-shooter and medicine and instrument bags.

One of the most perplexing situations I ever found myself in was one night I awakened to find my team following the bed of a dry stream. Kansas, I may say, has many streams, just in case it should rain. These "streams," except on rare occasions, are without water. The ditch was scarcely wider than the buggy and nearly as high as the buggy top. It was evident that I was headed up a stream and consequently that conditions ahead were worse. I unhitched the team and by partly upending the buggy succeeded in turning it. There was just enough space to get the team past the buggy. After driving a number of miles I came to where a road crossed and I was enabled to follow the trail. I was completely lost and do not know to this day where I was.

On the trip that resulted in the incident just mentioned I had been to a town forty miles distant. A number of times I had made the twenty-hour round trip to this town. I would drive my team part way, get a new team for the balance of the way and on my return get my own team and drive home again. One of these trips was made because the patient, so I had been informed by telegram, was bleeding, the patient thought seriously; but all that was the matter was a dinky little cervical polyp as large as a lead pencil and an inch long. Fortunately, one's services were measured by the patient's notion of its seriousness and not by what the doctor accomplished viewed from a medical stand-point.

One of my most exciting trips was made one day when I had a drive of some twenty-odd miles to make in the face of a driving blizzard. The sleety snow was driven almost parallel into the faces of the horses as well as my own. I was driving a big powerful team known to have a will of its own. From the start the team objected to facing the storm and at every crossroad or driveway they made a bolt for it. I had to drive with a tight line to keep them going ahead. The farther we went the higher the wind raged and the more obstreperous the team became. I had repeatedly to belabor them with the whip to keep them going more or less straight ahead. After some twenty miles of this they became completely frantic. I belabored them in my most energetic vein. I had a lighted lantern between my feet under the lap robe as a means of keeping warm. While my attention was given to the team, this lantern broke and ignited the lap robe. The team was plunging desperately. At just this time we came to a driveway to a farmhouse. They dashed down the lane on a dead run. I tried to give attention to both the lantern and the team, doing a poor job of both. As the team entered the barnyard, fortunately the farmer was there and grabbed the team. I jumped out of the buggy with the flaming lap robe and the still burning lantern without its globe. The barn was a large one with a driveway in the middle. The door was open and had the team not been stopped by the farmer they would most certainly have gone in there with results not difficult to imagine. Fortunately the fire was immediately extinguished and the team calmed, at least in a measure. The skin on my legs healed after a number of weeks but my pants and the lap robe never did. However, I eventually got to my destination and I recall with pleasure that my presence was really urgently needed and I was able to render the much-needed aid. The patient had a chest full of pus.

My closest call had nothing directly to do with the practice of medicine but with a horse with a mind far ahead of his time. This horse had a mania for trying to beat a train to a crossing. One very cold day I was returning to town and had to pass a mill which obstructed the view of a railroad track. As we emerged from behind the obstruction he spied the on-coming train. My hands were encased in heavy fur mittens. As he lunged for a start the lines slipped from my hands. Quickly throwing off my mittens I caught one line with both hands and pulled with all my might. I succeeded in jerking him parallel with the track just as the engine whizzed by. The engineer told me afterwards that he could have caught the horse by the ears. The car step missed the buggy wheel by a bare six inches. The smallest fraction of a second and this screed would have terminated with this paragraph. This horse had certainly saved my life on three occasions but for some perverse reason tried to commit a suicide pact like those one reads of in the papers. This could not have been his intention, however, because he was a boy horse.

The doctor was often inconvenienced by being given the wrong direction by some excited person. My most notable experience with wrong directions was as follows: I was told to go to a certain town forty miles distant, then eight miles east and then eight miles south. I did so but when I arrived in that neighborhood no one knew the parties. I suspected the nature of the mistake. I retraced eight miles and found a small country store still open though it was eleven o'clock at night. No one knew such a party, in fact knew of no one sick. Then a little girl about eight years old, sitting unobserved in a corner, gave me the proper directions. The child had heard her mother and some neighbors discussing the serious sickness of some acquaintance. Let those who will scoff at women's clubs—they were called quiltings in those days. Had it not been for the gossip of her elders this little girl would not have known of the illness of the neighbor. At any rate I found the place all right, a very sick man and a very anxious family. As it was I arrived only in time to predict that he would be dead before morning. Of course having been unable to be of any service I was not entitled to any pay. This was one of my first trips in an automobile—that is if the old chain-drive Cadillac was an automobile. The chain broke eight times on this trip. But the trip was made in record time, one hundred and twenty miles in fifteen hours. I paid the car owner eight dollars for making the trip.

I GO TO THE PATIENT

Speaking of friends in need, here is my prize recollection: One night I drove into the livery stable and called for a fresh team. It was just midnight. I had been on the road on the average of some sixteen hours a day for weeks. I spied the boy's bunk. An irresistible desire seized me. I do not know just how I got on the cot. When I awoke to my horror I found it was four o'clock. The office door was closed. I opened it and there sat the livery boy in a chair in the driveway. As introduction, without turning his head he said: "Say, Doc, I lied for you. Mr. X and Mr. Y were here looking for you. I told them you hadn't got back yet. I thought that if their folks was worse off than you, they's dead anyhow and don't need no doctor." He gave me the directions for the calls and hitched up a fresh team for me. I relate this instance with satisfaction, for it shows that concern for the doctor sometimes came from unexpected sources.

Our weary labors endeared us to our patients and even to the livery boys. We got credit for doing our best. I look back on those days without bitterness. For all the weary toil, I did but little real service as I recall now. But I relieved suffering and relieved the worries of the family. I did what I was given credit for doing, the best I knew how. I always recall, when I think of those old days, an incident which occurred about that time. A person by the name of Jim Barrett was an undesirable citizen and the sheriff shot him. His friends buried him, and on a plain board, placed at the head of the grave, these words were scrawled: "Jim, he done his damndest; angels could do no more." No country doctor desires a more eloquent epitaph.

One summer I was attending a series of typhoid patients and had been on the road almost constantly for many weeks. All the sleep I had for six days I got in the buggy. I did not even have my shoes off during this time. The weather was very hot and when the time finally came when I could take my shoes off, my socks had so intimately attached themselves to the skin of my feet that they had literally to be peeled off. The next morning my feet were so swollen I had to go about my work wearing bedroom slippers. That was the most arduous week I ever spent in my life.

A I look back over the old casebooks I wonder now just how much real good I did. Certainly the medicines I dispensed were merely symbols of good intentions. The friends of the patient felt better when I called but the muttering patients were often oblivious to the presence of the doctor. Cold-sponging a patient back to consciousness was a long weary task, but pleased the friends. Whether we did good or harm by keeping the temperature down it is impossible to say. I do know that hours of sponging a delirious patient was a terrible ordeal to the doctor who had not seen his bed literally for days.

In those days there were no telephones. Neighbors knew by grapevine messages when the doctor had been called to one of their number and if members of their families needed a doctor they hung a sheet at some conspicuous object. If it was at night a lantern was hung up. I knew these signals and answered the call. I remember that on one trip I visited seven patients in addition to the one for whom I was originally called.

Many of these families are still grateful. That close contact made the closest of friends. I sometimes think I would like to end my medical career amidst these intimate contacts. They answered the age-old question of the affirmative: "We are our brother's keeper."

These memories of neighborly kindness are the most pleasurable in my experience. Many times these side calls disclosed nothing serious. Sickness in the neighborhood, particularly if of an infectious nature, made other families apprehensive and the least evidence of sickness caused them to seek advice. Often when epidemics, notably measles, started from a school the entire neighborhood was likely to have one or more patients afflicted with the disease.

Ordinarily a doctor was not called for such simple diseases

unless complications were feared. The patients were put to bed and covered up well, but when the eruption began to fade and the little patients had many areas which all needed immediate attention the bedclothes became disarranged and many developed bronchitis or pneumonia.

The foregoing presents a few of the high lights of country driving. By far the greater part of it was hitch up, plug along the roads, make a call, plug back again at the same old weary pace. Get stuck in the mud, get out somehow, meet a snow-drift, shovel out or cut the fence and drive around the obstruction. The countryside was always willing to render aid to a distressed doctor. They repaired their fences which had been cut, without grumbling. If one horse became exhausted they were willing to offer their services and teams without question. It was a fine lesson in the brotherhood of man, in those old days; but there was but little actual medical service, viewed in our present state of advancement. Being dumb is not painful if one does not realize it.

We knew nothing of the more abundant life and took all these things as a matter of course. If a patient needed help all the neighbors were ready to lend a willing hand. Whether it meant a general gathering to husk his corn crop, or sitting up all night playing nurse it made no difference. Changing hot applications was usually assigned the women and many of these showed marked skill and understanding. The obvious willingness to do their best in large measure compensated for lack of skill in technical detail.

It was aggravating to make a long trip only to find a petulant female at the end of the trip, not sick but mad. I had a good many such cases. These were almost without exception dead-heads. They complained usually of headaches and they surely gave the doctor one. He was out his time, the price of a team, a nice warm sleep and his temper was utterly ruined. The memory of one of these still makes me boil with indignation. The call came while I was in a night sweat incident to tuberculosis. I expostulated with the messenger, explaining that it would be dangerous for me to go out in my condition on a cold night and urged him to call another doctor. He said their regular doctor was not at home. So I bundled up the best I could. When I arrived at the house all was dark. I beat on the door. In fact, I kicked the door in. The husband came rushing then and explained that his wife had had a pain but now was quietly sleeping. She certainly was if my belaboring of the door did not waken her. But she woke after I got into the house. She never could eat backbone and sauerkraut without getting stomach distress from it, she explained. Their regular doctor was at home all right but he suggested to the messenger, who had called on him first, to go jump in the river. He knew the patient's stunts and also knew they were cheerful and voluntary deadheads.

There is a limit to all things. As already noted, I was fighting an epidemic of typhoid fever during the summer. I had been feeling bad, finding driving progressively more exhausting, totally lacking in appetite. One day when driving through a patch of weeds a plow hidden in the undergrowth so engaged itself in the wheel of the buggy that it upset. The effort to right the buggy quite exhausted me. I sat down on the offending plow and while so doing I inspected my distended and sensitive abdomen and found to my amazement the most gorgeous array of rose spots. These spots are positive evidence of typhoid fever. I took my temperature. It was 104.6°. I drove my horse to the stable and went to bed and sent word to those patients whom I had been attending that they must seek other medical help. The date, I learn now from consulting my old casebook, was August 22, 1897.

It is interesting to note what far-reaching effect some instances in life may have. While sick with the typhoid fever, well into the third week, I got a sudden severe pain in the right groin, a perforation of a typhoid ulcer. There could be no doubt of that. I was alone; no one within call. Though I was at that time a consistent member of the Methodist Church, as consistent as a hard-working country doctor could be, not a single "brother" showed hide nor hair during my weeks in bed. I did not give church or the future a single fleeting thought. I thought only of the little insurance I had with which to provide for my little girl, that and nothing more. After I recovered from the typhoid fever I reasoned thus. If one, when looking across the River Styx, thinks nothing of his church but much of life insurance for the little girl, one's future conduct seems very simply charted. I have not been to church since but have bought a lot of insurance for the little girl and those who later joined her.

As intimated, one naturally asks in afterthought if any real service was rendered to repay for those arduous trips. That is difficult to say. As I look over my casebooks of forty years ago I can form some notion on this point and will discuss it further in the next chapter. The people thought I did and at the time I was quite sure on that point. I was very serious in those days and prided myself on my reputation among my patients that literally "hell and high water" never stopped the young doctor when he started on a call. These were the happiest days of my life. I prided myself on my capacity to endure fatigue and then when I got home there was a black-eyed little girl to greet me. It is amazing what a stimulus a little mite of a human can be. She would need educating some day.

With the coming of the automobile new problems presented themselves to the country doctor. For a number of years they were too expensive and too unreliable to make them practical for the doctor's country driving. Besides, the roads were such that they could be used only during several months of the year. Many country doctors, however, provided themselves with the early models. For absorption of all spare money these were rivaled only by the private hospital. Having the latter, I had to deny myself the automobile even after they came in quite general use by my colleagues.

For those who did not drive one, automobiles were an unmitigated nuisance and often provided even dangerous situations. A team became frightened at dogs and attempted to run away, as already mentioned, but they retained some sense. After the dogs ceased their chasing, either because of fatigue or the bark of a six-shooter, the team calmed down and could be controlled usually in a quarter or half a mile. When the automobile began to invade the road it was quite a different matter. The team was frightened at the dogs; sometimes, indeed, it seemed to me they used the dogs just as an excuse for the exhibition of pure cussedness. But when they met the unknown gas wagon they were not frightened but utterly terror-stricken. They became uncontrollable, would turn back, upsetting the buggy, disregarded fences and ran wildly or kicked their way loose if their escape was obstructed. At night the flickering acetylene light added to their terror. One could see the light for long distances and one had to drive into a farmyard or into a field and wait until the apparition had passed. This required aggravating periods of waiting until the car wheezed slowly past. Not uncommonly the car was stopped for repairs, in which event one had to detour. In the daytime some teams after a time became sufficiently accustomed to the cars that they would permit them to pass; but at night, never. An unpleasant by-product was that one did not dare to go to sleep in the buggy for fear that a car might appear. Fortunately, when the roads were muddy and the travel with a team was slowest one had no need to fear a car.

After cars became more practical I had assistants to do the local country driving and they wheezed along in the uncertain automobile. But I saw aplenty of it when the circle of my activities became greater and the automobile rides became supplementary to a train ride. Its disposition to cut all sorts of antics often worked hardships when one was anxious to reach a certain place in order to have daylight in which to perform an operation, if such should be needed, and that usually was the purpose of the trip. Thus I once was obliged to drain a gall bladder by the aid of a coal-oil lamp and a flashlight because of six tire punctures on a sixty-mile trip.

Another incident comes to mind. I was traveling some distance to operate on a case of acute appendicitis before nightfall. There were only dirt roads and on a long stretch of road the only track was on the left side of the road. This was occupied by a large furniture truck. I honked and honked with one of the old rubber-bulb honkers. The driver had all the impudence of the early truck driver and made no move to allow me to pass. I took one crack at his left rear tire with my six-shooter and he turned sharply to the right and stopped. I also stopped and introduced myself, explaining that I would be at a certain place for the next several hours and if he desired to make conversation to please call. He did not appear. Also I got my appendix by daylight.

The old chain drive was a common source of annoyance. I have been wakened many times out of an uncertain slumber by the rattle of the chain. The common plague was, of course, a flat tire; once six flats, in a journey of fifty miles, caused me to miss my train by some three hours. The driver in those days did not change tires, he removed it, patched the hole, and put it on again, a time-consuming procedure to the inexpert. In the daytime it was not so bad, for I could spend my time reading or shooting at any convenient object with my six-shooter. Once this had a ludicrous result. The driver, busy with removing the tire, had not noticed my preparations for indulgence in a little marksmanship and dashed wildly for cover at the first bark of the forty-five. I had some trouble convincing him that he was not the object of my efforts, otherwise he would be dead.

During those years I gained an affection for the old Model T.

They always got you there and brought you back, even though you were thoroughly battered and worn out during the process. If the tires failed they were simply removed and the journey completed on the rim. Two or three hundred miles over rough roads in a Model T just about exhausted everything there was to exhaust in the human form but one got there.

Cars were not inclosed then and the early ones had no tops, many not even a windshield. One such trip stands in my memory. The prairie was putting on a good sample of a blizzard. The snow and sleet fell or traveled almost parallel. The wind was in the northwest and that was the direction of our journey, seventy-five miles of it. The car had neither fenders, top nor windshield. The temperature was considerably below zero. Despite blankets, lap robes and all that, it was bitter cold and there was the cheering prediction by some of the old-timers that we would never make it. There were no places to stop and had anything gone wrong with the car the prediction held out to us presented a considerable probability of being correct. One cheerful old chap, who had formerly lived in my home town, remarked, "All hell won't stop Doc but, by crickey, I'm afeard he may land there tonight." During the course of the trip we came across a herd of cattle, some lying down, some standing rump to the storm. After we had missed a few by a narrow margin I admonished my driver to slow down. His reply was: "Doc, the gas won't shut off and I can't get at the brakes." His feet were bundled in the remains of an ancient buffalo robe, so that the pedals were out of his reach. We made the seventy-five miles in three and one-half hours. I met the doctor at this town and proceeded sixteen miles farther where I found a brain abscess which was successfully drained as I shall discuss in a subsequent chapter. One soon forgot a trip if there was something one could do at the journey's end.

Fortunately the automobiles of that day did not possess sufficient speed to cause any very serious accidents. They upset and had to be righted, but there was seldom competition for possession of any particular part of the road; consequently collisions did not occur. Of course, there were farm wagons and livestock to give a fair chance for a collision. I remember once my assistant was traveling at a high speed of about twenty miles an hour. Topless and windshieldless, the car rattled along over the rough road, rocking me peacefully to sleep. I was half reclining. The car hit the rear end of a farm wagon loaded with wheat. I took a complete somersault, landing on my feet some distance ahead of the car, hands still in my pockets. That was a rude awakening and a long journey. My old assistant still believes his fortune would be made if he had a movie of that experience.

More amusing to me was an experience of one of my assistants. He was bowling along in the small hours of the night. A mule was lying in the middle of the road unobserved by my assistant and, I presume, my assistant unobserved by the mule— at least there was no mutual recognition. The front wheel of the old Maxwell passed over the animal but the hind one did not. The result was that the mule was weighted down by the car and could not get up. It made too big a bump to get the car off and some farmers had to be summoned to help extract the animal, none the worse for the experience. My assistant had a sense of humor, so did the neighbors and so no doubt did the mule so that a pleasant time was had by all, as the country newspapers are prone to describe a social event which goes off without a fight, or even with.

The automobiles of those days were, as we know now, unbelievably unreliable. To make a trip without a mishap was an event to be remembered. Of course, with the roads of that day even the car of the present would have its troubles. The annoyances of those trips were more aggravating than the trials of country driving.

Arduous as were some of the horse and buggy trips, and many

auto trips, many of the travels by rail really tried the soul, or whatever it is that gets mad at delays. Usually trips were combinations, train trip part way and auto or team the rest. Team and auto trips commonly involved but a part of a day, while the train trips often involved several days. As my acquaintance with doctors increased, the sphere of my activity widened. Many successive nights were, on frequent occasions, spent on the train. My peak was twenty-six nights in the month of January, 1916. That was too much.

Because many, in fact most, of my calls came from small towns, it was necessary to ride local trains or small branch lines. The trains were made up of "shoebox" coaches. One of these, the "peanut special" which many Missourians will recognize, was a fair example. On one of the trains I used to ride the conductor smoked a long curved stem pipe while collecting fares. This perhaps will place the train better than anything else I might say. I learned to know many of the train crews. Some of them would slow their trains through my small-town destination, where the train was not scheduled to stop. It would slow down to four or five miles an hour, permitting me to hop off. Sometimes the train would be moving faster than I had calculated and I got a few bad falls, once lacerating my hand on the cindered right of way, which seriously handicapped me for the operation I was required to perform, but usually I escaped unhurt. The horses I rode as a youngster taught me how to roll rather than try to catch myself, wherein lies the art of falling. The train men were kind to me and I learned to have great admiration for them. I count many of these railroad men among my best friends. Somehow we seem to speak the same language.

I recall two incidents. One night a bunch of boys were having a high time in the smoker. Along about midnight the brakemen came in and told the bunch, with the vehemence only a brakeman can express, that Doc was in No. 1 and he needed

Sweet rest, balmy sleep. Sometimes for many nights the buggy was the doctor's only couch.

rest. The other incident paid me the highest compliment I have ever received. I got on the train farther west than my usual place of catching the train. The brakeman said: "I see Doc got on the train. Kinda off his beat." The porter confirmed the statement. The brakeman added, "It will be a sad day in Kansas when Doc fails to answer 'present.'"

The bane of railway travel was late trains. One train which I rode regularly once a week, old Number 8, to my teaching job was frequently three or four hours late. This was not only annoying but interfered seriously with my schedule of work. The two most annoying trips still pester my memory. Once I was to catch a train at a small station which kept no night agent. The day agent gave me a lantern and told me to flag the eleven-twenty train. The date sticks to me, November 16, 1908. The depot had no fire and the night was cold. I kept warm the best I could by placing the lantern on the floor and making a canopy over it with my overcoat. The train did not come hour after hour. At 4:00 A.M. a headlight showed up. It was a freight. The irate fireman told me my train was in a wreck and would be along in an hour. After two hours another headlight hove into sight. This proved to be a wreck train which had attended the hapless passenger train for which I was waiting. Just as day was beginning to dawn my train came in. I was so disgusted I threw the lantern as far as I could into a patch of dead sunflowers. That was a long night.

Another notable ride was no fault of the train. I was called to stop at a way station—Waldeck was its name, cursed be its memory. The caller said he would meet the 1:30 A.M. train. I got off on time but there was no one to meet me. The depot was locked, no house in sight and the snow deep. I had no idea of where my patient lived nor how far nor even in what direction to go to find a house. In order to keep warm I beat a path around the little depot, chasing an imaginary person who would give a doctor a call and then not keep his date. After three hours my patient's father appeared with the apology that the patient's pain had eased and everybody went to sleep. The patient had had a pain the nature of which I never made out. But I had a pain located exactly in the middle of my neck, the precise nature of which I set forth with vehemence and great detail. Of course, I never got any fee for my trouble. That kind of people never pay.

I made use of my time as much as possible during the long train waits. I usually had some medical journals or books and usually a copy of Shakespeare. That was in the days before I learned the time-consuming capacity of detective mysteries. I did much of my writing on the train, and in the depot waits, so that the time was not lost; but, of course, the conditions for labor were not ideal. For instance, the first chapter in Volume I of my *Case Histories* was begun at 2:00 A.M. in Emporia, on two cups of Fred Harvey coffee, continued on Number 8 and finished in my office at 9:00 A.M. Save for the first page, it was printed just as written first draft. I still believe that it is a good example of first-draft copy.

My early trips were made in the smoking car because of the expense of a Pullman berth. I preferred the smoker to the chair car. There was less conversation. One funny incident comes to memory. I got on a train about midnight. All seats were filled except one beside a young traveling man. When I awoke in the morning the car was empty except the seat in which the traveling man and I were joined. The other passengers were track laborers and had all gotten off about three in the morning.

After I became able to ride the Pullmans I did not mind travel. The car was a sort of home to me. I knew the porters and they saw to it that I was properly cared for. Of course, there were annoyances. One night an old German couple occupied a berth next to mine. They kept up an incessant chatter. The porter explained that I occupied the berth next to theirs and needed sleep. They then began to chatter louder than ever, wondering where the doctor might be going. Another old pair who were to get off at three A.M., not trusting the porter, had brought along an alarm clock. They had set it for two o'clock, so they would have plenty of time before they reached their stop.

My prize laugh came with the following incident. Every berth of the Pullman was occupied. The loudest snorer I ever heard was going his best—snoring bits of grand opera or something. As eloquent snorers sometimes will, he occasionally held his breath for variable intervals. Once he had been silent for an unusually long time when he burst out with a loud blast as if to make up for lost time. Some wag shouted: "Hot dawg, I hoped the son of a gun was dead!" There were loud catcalls and laughter from every berth of that car.

The history of my travels would not be complete without a note about the old country hotels. They were nearly always of wooden construction and resembled what would now be called a rooming house but written, of course, without quotation marks. They might be divided into two general classes, first and second, that is without and with bedbugs.

The office of these hotels had a big red stove and a table for the use of traveling men for correspondence or card playing. At night after the table was no longer in use the proprietor placed a lantern on the table and retired. A late "guest" who knew the ropes knew that this meant that there was a room available. He took this lantern and ascended the steps and proceeded to find an open door. That was his room. This worked very well in winter time but in summer occupants regularly left the doors of their rooms open to admit the breeze (if any) and he had to inspect each room in turn until he found one unoccupied. The modest man looked at the clothes on the chair rather than at the bed to see if the room was occupied or not.

After finding one's room an inspection was necessary for

bugs in summer and for bed covers in winter. All rooms were unheated and, coming in from a cold drive, the covers were always inadequate. So the doctor laid his overcoat on top and crawled beneath the covers. In most cases the only thing to be decided was whether or not he should take off his shoes. If there was frost on the sheets naturally he left his shoes on. If one had to depart in the morning before the proprietor arose one took the lantern back to the office and placed a quarter or half a dollar under it and the transaction was closed. The proprietor knew then that he had a patron—especially if the guest slept with his shoes on.

At this late date I can regard with equanimity the runaway teams, the dogs, the ditches and streams and the snowdrifts, but the old country hotels rankle me still. I recall particularly a part of a night I spent in the worst hotel in my experience, after a five-hour ride behind a span of unwilling mules in a sleet storm over rough frozen roads. One window light of my room was broken and the defect repaired with a bundle of rags. There were but few covers. Damp from the ride, I was nearly frozen. The temperature outside was away below zero and the room appeared even colder. I did not remove my overcoat but lay down and pulled the frosted musty covers over me.

It may be interpolated here that all old timers knew the heat-retaining value of a newspaper placed under the vest. I found in this hotel a copy of the *Emporia Gazette*. I placed this where it would do the most good. It added greatly to my comfort or, perhaps better stated, it lessened my distress. No doubt this was due to the "hot" editorials which this nationally famous newspaper usually carried. At least the results of its use were unusually good.

It was necessary to catch a train at five in the morning. I had sustained an injury by a fall from a train which was moving faster than I had calculated (subgluteal bursitis to the doctor). As I limped toward the train the conductor, who knew me well, grasped my arm and exclaimed "Good God, Doc, where have you been?" My damp overcoat had attracted lint from the cheap bed clothing which caused my friend to opine I had slept with my clothes on.

The old coal-burning stove in the front of the car was a most welcome haven. As I sat there shivering beside the red hot stove I burst out laughing as I noticed that my shoes were clean though I had not had them off for two days.

At Emporia I got off the train to get some coffee. I quite forgot time and place and was startled when the conductor opened the door and said "Take your time, Doc. I'll hold the train." I have reserved this place to say that not in a single instance have I ever known a railroad man, from division superintendent to the most cantankerous brakeman, to refuse to render service to a sick person or a doctor. Railroads may be soulless corporations to some but not to us doctors.

Besides the mules and the hotel and my friend the conductor the account of this trip would not be complete without a mention of the chief actor, the patient. It was a case of intestinal obstruction due to adhesions of intestines to and impending necrosis of the gallbladder. I operated on this patient as she lay on the edge of the bed—sleeves rolled up, no operating gown, not even a face mask, operating under local anesthesia. The patient recovered. She recovered because I knew the principles of drainage. Principles learned, some will be horrified to learn, by operating on dogs. Of course I should have waited and learned these principles by operating on human beings.

This experience forms a fitting conclusion to this chapter because it embodies everything, arduous trip, the frosty hotel, an understanding railroad man, and the recovery of the patient after a desperately urgent operation under most unfavorable conditions. To make this record complete it is necessary to record that the memory of the experience is all that I did get out of it, but this remark is unprofessional. The patient recovered—that should be sufficient, but I cannot help but recall that the trip cost me thirteen dollars.

Because of the generally forbidding hotel accommodations if there was a depot and a night agent I preferred to repair there and share quarters with the telegrapher. Though it was forbidden to admit anyone into the inner sanctum of the depot I was never refused. Usually the message summoning the doctor was sent out from that office and the advent of the strange doctor was anticipated. The room was always warm, usually hot. I used the ticket table as a cot and using my instrument bag as a pillow was soon asleep. I have spent many, many an hour enjoying these accommodations.

The enduring thing is I saw many interesting cases, trivial, lifesaving and last stages, such as one does not see in office or hospital practice. I made many good friends, among both doctors and patients, who still bring a pleasant memory. But I am glad those days are gone forever, both for my sake and that of the young doctors who will follow after me. Hard, cruel experiences which, even in retrospect, give me now and then pangs of painful memory.

Yet after all it is quite possible that if the young doctor of today had to make great sacrifices to reach his patient, and then sit for hours watching the course of the disease, he might take a more understanding view of the sick human. At any rate, if so occupied the commercial side of medicine would not loom so large. Besides, few doctors of the bygone day died of heart disease as is the case now, be the cause what it may. The respectable way for the old-time doctor was to acquire pneumonia after an exposure and die on the fourth day while, in his delirium, he urged his team onward. Giddap Jack!

As I look back on those arduous days the impression I have retained was the universal brotherhood of man. A neighbor in distress received the voluntary assistance of his neighbors, each according to his capacities and talents. The doctor struggling to reach a patient received every aid. Nobody complained of hardships, certainly not the doctor. Though underprivileged to the nth degree as some of these people were, yet after all they knew the essentials of the more abundant life, the brotherhood of man.

CHAPTER

5 ⎯⎯⎯⎯⎯

IN THE PRECEDING CHAPTER I NOTED THE POPULAR PICTURE of the old country doctor driving along the country road in the daytime, hauled by a weary horse. The vicissitudes of the night are never considered.

Even so, the events of the road were an open book to the public compared to the scenes in the sick rooms. Each family of course had a vivid memory in so far as it concerned itself, but the country doctor's memory was a record of the griefs of the countryside as a whole. No old doctor would want to record his experiences even if he could. Sick scenes have been all but neglected by the painter, yet no subject in human experience offers a more fruitful opportunity to present intense human emotions. A notable exception is the famous painting "The Doctor" which graces the walls of many homes. This picture is typical in that it shows a fine old doctor sitting beside his little patient, lying with her arm flung out, mute evidence of a terminal stage of the disease. The father and mother are shown in the background paralyzed in their helplessness. The old doctor's face is perfectly calm. What thoughts are racing through his mind? Would he like to join the father and mother in their wail of helplessness? The old doctor too is helpless, but he sticks to his task, rendering his ultimate service to his little patient and to the parents. It was this silent faithfulness of the old doctor in the hour of grief that endeared him to the families that he served. The old country doctor was a man of few words because there were no words.

It is the purpose of this chapter to pull the curtains a little aside to show something of the events in the sick room. The memory of the more tragic scenes will paralyze any pen that attempts to record them, but a few things may be set down as a framework to which those who have experienced such scenes may attach the pictures of their memories.

Viewed from the vantage point of the achievements of medicine of the present day, the accomplishments of the old doctor seem pitiably insignificant. Yet the satisfaction one gets out of life is measured by the efforts one exerts in achieving a worthy end, not in the actual achievement. This philosophy touches the very heart of medical practice as it was then; in a measure it is even true of the experiences of today. The question of what the old doctor did is answered by reference to my old case records now covering more than forty-four years. It is amazing to what degree old scenes are brought back to memory by the reading of a few lines of a case history. It is at once fascinating and depressing, fascinating because it brings to mind the old sturdy pioneers, depressing because, in the light of our present knowledge, the therapeutic measures were so impotent.

From what has already been said it is clear that the country doctor's activities had less to do with the saving of life than with relieving a patient's pain and the mental suffering of the family. Whatever one may conclude in retrospect as to the importance of the doctor's ministrations, neither doctor nor patient then doubted the efficacy of the treatment employed. However, the picture must not be painted unduly drab. The patient's sufferings were relieved and in occasional cases the measures employed were unquestionably life-saving.

Let it be remarked that, exalted as are the achievements of

the present day, the younger man may well remember that possibly fifty years hence his achievements may seem as puerile as ours do now. Furthermore, what concerns the individual doctor is not so much what medical science can achieve as how much of this he can deliver to his patients. That is the personal element for which each doctor is responsible.

Regardless of what the old doctor was able to accomplish in a therapeutic way, the sense of security inspired by the doctor's arrival affected the patients favorably. The degree of this influence depended on faith, which again was based on personality and previous experiences. The most striking effect was on the family and it became obvious before one even approached the patient or started to render any service. If this be so how did we differ from the quack and the cultist of today? The answer is simple: We had measures capable of relieving suffering even though we could not curtail the disease. The quack and the cultist has only the influence of his presence which faith in him may bring. Beyond this he stands in his own barren pasture and reaches over the fence that separates him from regular medicine and surreptitiously garners the luscious clover of science. The cultist and the handsome quack may rival us in inspiring confidence in the malingerer or the hysteric. Let it be repeated that this type of treatment is effective only for imaginary ills which disappear on request or whenever the complainer tires of them.

The proof that the cultist recognizes the ineffectiveness of his treatment is found in the fact that when he himself is sick he wants a regular doctor. I want to say for him—that he makes a most agreeable and obedient patient.

Broadly speaking, the influence of personal contact in relieving the patient was in inverse proportion to the intelligence and the past experience of the patient. For instance I once examined an old lady's chest with my stethoscope, an instrument she had never seen and mistook for a means of treatment. After taking a few deep breaths she enthusiastically declared that she already felt greatly relieved. In appraising service rendered by the doctor at the bedside two things must be considered: the immediate relief of suffering by means of known remedies, and the cure of disease, or at least the staving-off of death. The doctor's most immediate function at the bedside was and is to make the patient as comfortable as possible by whatever means are available. Even today a convincingly careful examination with the assurance that the ailment is trivial or nonexistent relieves many patients permanently. The essential factor is that the patient have faith in the ability of the doctor.

This fact stands out with striking prominence as I review my old case histories. In ability to make the patient comfortable the old doctor could show cards and spades to his modern prototype. It was his chief function because in many cases he was unable to determine the nature of the disease. Morphine will relieve pain no matter if the doctor knows the cause of pain or not. These remarks apply to bedside medicine in acute cases. In chronic disease not attended by acute suffering the task at hand is to discover the organic lesion. This remark is, of course, irrelevant to the present discussion because in the old days there were no refinements of diagnosis as we, even we country doctors, know them today. In acute cases the relief of suffering and the diagnosis of the disease should go hand in hand. Young men should realize that the former need not be neglected in order to achieve the latter; that in fact it may be made a valuable ally—that is to say, while the doctor is relieving the suffering he may determine its degree. If an indifferent remedy relieves a "terrible pain," the pain simply was not so very bad.

The ability of the old type doctor was enhanced because he remained at the patient's bedside until his suffering was relieved, even though it required many hours to achieve that end. While so engaged the doctor learned much about the nature of the illness. If he was not impressed with its seriousness, perhaps

I ARRIVE AT THE PATIENT'S BEDSIDE

because of the prompt relief obtained from some minor treatment, he knew there was little likelihood of any serious organic lesion. Yet it must not be assumed that all serious acute diseases are accompanied by pain. This is particularly true in those afflictions associated with vascular accidents. But in the majority of these cases there isn't much the doctor can do. Happily they are most common in the aged in whom serious disease often comes rather as a benediction than as a disaster.

No reproach attaches to the practice of masterly inactivity, for in most cases the disease was self-limited and all that could be done was to make the patient comfortable until the disease ran its course. The modern doctor with his patient in a modern hospital does no more, though he does it more scientifically and in the doing adds the distress incident to examination to that caused by the disease. There may be justification for the legendary patient's complaint that "the disease was not so bad but the treatment was terrible." This obviously is true in all acute infectious diseases. Perhaps we did something to control incipient complications, though of course one cannot be sure. For instance, if the urine examination indicated kidney complications we busily combated it, but whether or not what we did served any useful purpose is questionable. Now we know that keeping the patient in bed for long periods is the essential thing.

I still possess my old case books which record nearly every call I have ever made and nearly all the medicines prescribed. In some cases I knew, even in the beginning, that my efforts would be futile in the matter of rendering service to anyone and fruitless in the matter of revenue for myself. Often I knew before I touched harness that the trips would be useless. These cases were chiefly those in which there had been nothing wrong in the first place, or in which the patient had recovered before the doctor got there. A child might have a fall that caused more apprehension to the mother than injury to the victim. A negative finding accomplished something by relieving the minds of the parents, even though it demanded no professional technic. In some instances a discomfort definite enough while it lasted had disappeared before the doctor arrived; nausea from the first round of tobacco had subsided, a kidney stone had passed or a cramp due to green apples had disappeared. Of course, one left some medicine in case of a recurrence of the trouble; this was largely the bunk, but someone had to pay for the axle grease and just plain advice never was productive of revenue unless fortified by a few pills. It was about as important as the deacon's "Amen" during the preacher's sermon—it did no harm and it was an evidence of good faith. Both just little byplays which fooled nobody and contributed to the amenities of human relationship or something like that.

Speaking in the concrete, I soon learned that as I looked on the illness might subside of its own accord after a remedy was applied. However, when or if a favorable result followed my ministrations I never had any doubt as to the causal connection, a happy faith shared by the patient and the family. I believed then that my services in many cases were responsible for favorable results, whereas I know now they were of little value. Even at this distance it is difficult to estimate the worth of the treatment adopted. One can in most cases find consolation in reflecting that the remedy expedited the spontaneous departure of the pain. Even in pneumonia I believed my treatment saved the patient's life. For instance, one winter I attended a large number of pneumonia patients. Very few died. As I battled the elements to reach my patients, I had the greatest personal satisfaction in my achievements. I did not know then as I do now that the epidemic was a mild one and that my efforts to control the disease were futile. But the experience did me good. I learned to endure hardships for the sake of my patients and I made good my boast that if a message could get through to me I would get through to the patient. Stubbornness grows on what it feeds on and this intensified tenacity of purpose stood me in good stead in later years when I had to combat a serious disease with only a remote chance of accomplishing anything. Perhaps when Pope wrote "For fools rush in where angels fear to tread" he had the young doctor in mind. This raises the question as to whether or not anyone with good sense ever accomplishes anything. Most achievements follow the efforts of those too dumb to quit. Life is that way.

The exanthemas of childhood are always tricky business for the young doctor, as I have had many opportunities to discover. The first symptoms are so insidious that in many cases even experts cannot be certain of the diagnosis. An instance in point occurs to me. I once had a case which stumped me because I was unable to determine whether it was German measles or scarlet fever. I had this consolation, however, that the very first patient I saw the distinguished von Leyden present was an exact prototype of my former patient; after lecturing for an hour and fifty minutes von Leyden had ended by saying: "We will observe this patient. If the skin of the palms of the hands and soles of the feet is cast off during convalescence it is scarlet fever; if not, it is German measles."

Grandmother was always a source of apprehension. She knew that patients just got well, for she had followed the course of many cases when no medical talent was available. She was disposed to scoff at the efforts of the young doctor and tolerated his presence merely "to watch for complications." Grandmother had small respect for the young doctor and she usually had some old doctor in mind who in her opinion should have been called. Whiskers indicated maturity and most young doctors attempted to emulate their elders in the matter of hirsute adornment, with the result that they made themselves ridiculous instead of venerable. But Grandmother was vulnerable; her faith in her own ability and a liberal coat of soft soap generally made her a friend of the young doctor. Her theory probably was that the young doctor must be smart to recognize her ability.

In the management of ordinary diseases Grandmother regarded herself as superior to the doctor, an opinion in which I soon learned to concur in many cases. She piled the incipient measles patient high with blankets in order to induce perspiration. After the eruption had completely developed the patient felt better, which was the case also without blankets. But I learned something from these experiences: to wit, keep busy and you are in line to receive credit for whatever salutary results ensue.

Grandmother had other abilities. Diagnosis of eruptive diseases is not always easy and I remember one patient whose eruption was atypical. I reserved judgment. The grandmother arrived. She gave a sniff or two as she untied her bonnet. "Measles," she remarked tersely. I concurred, though I did not know at the time that measles could be diagnosed by the smell. But Grandmother was not the only one who contributed to my education. There were the old prairie doctors who had never seen a medical school but had learned many things by experience. One of them taught me a lesson I still remember. I was called in consultation to determine the nature of an epidemic in a neighborhood in which many young adults had died. The eruption was like measles, but in the midst of some of the patches of eruptions were papules which looked exactly like smallpox. The old doctor said it was measles and events proved he was right. I had never heard of this complication of measles. My diagnosis was hemorrhagic smallpox. That came the nearest to anything like it I had ever seen. The lesions were hemorrhagic all right, but what I did not know was that they could occur in measles. However, it made little difference so far as the patient was concerned, for when hemorrhagic either disease will nearly always kill the patient. The important point was that my dignity received a terrible jolt. It has since received a lot of other jolts. In fact, it has been jolted until it has disappeared in the circumambient atmosphere. But it is no loss, for as one increases in experience dignity loses most of its value.

Leaving these abstractions, we proceed to the consideration of concrete cases as one met them in country practice. These included just about every disease the human being is heir to; one had to be prepared to meet anything, not only in the nature of disease but also meddlesome neighbors and friends and the dog when he made a country call. It was legal to shoot the dog.

Usually the call was brought by a horseman who dashed up the street on a foaming steed. The movies never produced anything quite so spectacular. The young doc usually answered the call in the same fashion: that is, at first—for he soon came to see how theatrical it was. During the trip he had plenty of time to reflect on the responsibility which awaited him when he reached the patient's bedside. To a young and untried doctor this anticipation was worse than the reality, for a case seldom turned out to be as serious as represented by the messenger. Almost anything from hysteria to postpartum hemorrhage might confront him. The hired man or a boy of the family usually brought the call before there were telephones. Generally, the messenger knew only that there was need for haste and nothing could be learned in advance as to the nature of the illness, though sometimes the hired man would announce that it was about time for an increase in the family. The vulgar might laugh at such a remark but it merely reflected an observant mind.

This lack of preparative information worked a double hardship. The doctor was neither able to take suitable supplies for the condition he was to meet nor to determine which of several calls received simultaneously was the most serious and should be answered first. I always followed this rule: children first, next women, then old men, and finally the adult males. Known cases of hysterics came last. The reason for giving priority to children was that they become violently ill suddenly and require early attention; hours counted. Then too, as it has sometimes been facetiously remarked, if haste was not exercised the child might recover before the doctor arrived. More seriously, the family might have one of those curious compilations, *What to Do until the Doctor Comes,* and might do it too. One hoped to get there before they did. We know now how important haste is in cases of acute abdominal disease, notably in beginning appendicitis and intestinal perforations. In those days the acute intestinal disease of childhood, more than any other disease, justified haste in applying treatment.

As an aside I may mention that once I was confronted by some ladies who requested that I relate to them instances where I had arrived just in time to save a patient's life or, *per contra,* had gotten there just too late. I replied that at the moment I could not think of such an instance but I could recall a number of instances when I arrived too soon—when, in fact, it would have been better for both doctor and patient if I had never arrived. This was perhaps an overstatement of fact in both directions. My idea was to combat the general notion that the hurry hither and yon of doctors is in most instances byplay. Even today the young doctor if nabbed by the police for speeding has as excuse an urgent call. If he doesn't hurry he may receive unjust criticism. A case in point. Once a hospital was criticized in a column-long, front-page article because an ambulance delayed half an hour in picking up a patient who had fallen. Yes, he had fallen several times and in several ways. In fact, he was just plain drunk. He had chosen his bed—to wit, the gutter—and he had a legal right to occupy it, I reckon. At least the public was misled, or at least that portion which was dumb as the reporter may have been misled.

The young doctor naturally took things more seriously than the seasoned old doctor, both because of the desire to establish himself in the community and because of the belief that his services always were of great importance. That is to say, his ignorance approached that of the patient. Then, too, the old doctor knew the people, both physically and financially, and if the patient's complaints were negative, he had urgent business elsewhere. One of my first calls will explain why. A boy came galloping to my house, the horse covered with foam, knees shaking and obviously at the point of dropping in his tracks. The boy, eyes bulging, shouted: "Come quick, Doc. Mother's terribly sick." I hastily hitched my horse and made the seven miles in considerably less than one hour—some driving! I rushed into the house only to find an assortment of women solemnly sitting about a stove doing nothing—except talking, of course. I asked, "Who's sick?" The lady of the house calmly answered: "Well, Doc, I reckon it's me. I ain't really sick, but I've been porely since Christmas and so Pa thought I better see a doctor. I didn't feel like ridin' to town so we sent for you because you are the new doctor." The significance of that last remark escaped me at the time, but I soon learned that they never paid any doctor anything and that established doctors turned a deaf ear to them. That is the way with deadheads. They make their call sound urgent in order to break down whatever sales resistance the doctor may have. Another thing this case taught me was that deadheads will call the doctor for minor ailments, whereas in similar circumstances those who expect to pay will go to his office. In this case the patient's family of ten or more children seemed to be the trouble. Any experienced doctor can tell from these remarks what was wrong with her.

This family was interesting in another respect. There were no beds for most of its members. All the boys were sewed into their clothes in the fall when cold weather approached. At bedtime blankets were thrown on the floor and the youngsters lay down on them, clothes and all of course, and were asleep at once. They woke up in the morning all dressed and ready for pancakes and 'lasses. In the spring the clothes were ripped off and the child saw himself, for the first time in a number of months. This was before we learned about the more abundant life. The interesting fact, anthropologically speaking, is that the people did not know they were suffering any hardships. It all depends on the point of view.

Even more trying than the false alarmist were those who invariably called the doctor about eleven at night. Such calls became more numerous after telephones came into use at about the turn of the century. Usually the background was something like this: an ailing child would keep the mother worried all day until Father came home. The hungry father took Mother's report lightly at first. But after a few hours, tiring of the child's lamentations, which interfered with his sleep, the father would send one of the boys after the doctor. One father I knew boasted that he never called a doctor before midnight and thus made him earn his money. Of course, this fellow never paid the doctor, so that phrase "earn his money" was merely a facetious hyperbole. I never after answered one of his calls. Tiring of this sort of thing one night, I phoned a chronic offender at eleven o'clock that I must see him at once about an important matter that concerned us both, a matter that would not bear discussing over the party phone. He demurred, saying he had been asleep in bed and that he was not feeling well. He had caused me this same feeling many times and I had known he would be in bed when I telephoned. I repeated my message in louder tones and hung up the receiver with a bang. In about an hour I heard a horse clattering, rapidly coming down the road. When he came to my door I feigned sleep but at his second knock I admitted him. Then I told him very calmly that I wanted him to bring me that load of hay he had promised. Being on a party line, one of the neighbors learned the facts and there was much kidding. The result was a greater respect for the doctor's hours of rest throughout that neighborhood. But in a measure he got even, for the hay he brought me was all weeds, wholly unfit for horse feed.

The doctor learned to know his families, and calls from such people as these were usually passed up for a while in the hope that in the meantime a legitimate call might come from the same neighborhood. One could then answer the call without feeling that the expenditure of time and effort was a total loss. Such patients as I have described called the doctor for the most trivial affections, because they never intended to pay him for his trouble. The country doctor cannot bluntly refuse a call just because the patient is a confirmed and joyous deadhead. People of this class do sometimes die, though I cannot at this time recall a case. If such a thing did occur the doctor was censured, even though everybody knew it was good riddance.

I never refused a call, no matter what the condition, or what the chances of remuneration. When I announced that I wished to study medicine my father asked me to promise never to refuse to attend a sick person, whether he could or would pay or not. My father, being a farmer, did not realize how exasperating patients can be or how useless some calls. I have kept the faith: that is, almost. I have always refused to attend a drunk with a headache. I figure that he might as well suffer from the present headache as from the one he will acquire as soon as he is relieved. This may sound complicated to some persons but it will be perfectly clear to others, I am sure.

Thereby hangs a tale. We had in our town a chronic inebriate. One day I saw him zigzagging down the sidewalk. Early that evening the wife called to say that her husband was very ill. I assured her I could substantiate her statement, for I had seen him a few hours before. I advised that she put him to bed, expressing my belief that he would bᴗ all right in a few days as had been the case many times before. A few hours later she called again, reporting that her husband was dying. I replied that in that case it was not a doctor she wanted but an undertaker. This gave me an idea. I called the undertaker and informed him that Mr. X was in need of his service. Would he attend? As is the wont with morticians even today, he expressed deep sorrow, but in a tone that indicated grief would not incapacitate him for business.

I thought there might be interesting doings, so I cut down the alley and across lots and hid in the shadows of the house. Soon the undertaker approached in his wagon, with his assistant. There were at that time no mortuaries and a body was "laid out" in the parlor or living room of the late lamented. This undertaker was up-to-date and carried a board and a pair of "horses" on which to place the board. On arrival he found the door slightly ajar, but no one visible. Gently pushing open the door, he entered and quietly arranged the board on the supports ready to receive the relict. Just then the wife came in from the kitchen and, recognizing the undertaker, let out a shriek. This partly aroused the patient and he fixed the undertaker with an uncertain gaze. Spying the board, prepared to receive his remains, he sat bolt upright. He took one good look, and then let out a howl that frightened children four blocks away. The bed stood in front of a screened window. The patient dived through the screen of the very window through which I was peeping, carrying the screen with him. He lit running and after two hours' search his friends found him crouched in the corner of a fence many blocks from home.

He stayed sober for the remainder of his sojourn in our town, some three years. I have always remembered with a devilish chuckle that this man's coworker was cured of his bibulous habit during a revival, but his cure lasted only nine months while my low-comedy one lasted at least three years. I took delight in reminding the local minister of the relative merits of the two treatments, because while the professional soul-saver, whom the local minister had called to his aid, was conducting the revival I treated him for a disease decent people do not get.

But to return to our mutton. What the doctor did when he reached the bedside can best be illustrated by citing actual events recorded in my casebooks. Naturally, the diagnostic problems varied greatly. In some cases the probable diagnosis was at once apparent; in many, careful study was needed, and, *voce dulci*, the patient just got well—or else. This was not so bad as it sounds, for as already related, diagnosis or no diagnosis, about all one could do in many cases was to relieve the symptoms, and to do this no pathologic diagnosis was needed. One of my colleagues diagnosed typhoid as malaria in all cases and he had the leading practice in this community: that is, for a while. Most doctors claimed to be able to break up a case of typhoid fever or "typhoid pneumonia"—"if called soon enough." I was too stubborn to follow this policy and boldly declared that if they had it they kept it until they recovered, that the breaking-up claim was all bunk. This cost me heavily, but only for a time. The fates are in the end kind to the stubborn.

The usual procedure for a doctor when he reached the patient's house was to greet the grandmother and aunts effusively and pat all the kids on the head before approaching the bedside. He greeted the patient with a grave look and a pleasant joke. He felt the pulse and inspected the tongue, and asked where it hurt. This done, he was ready to deliver an opinion and prescribe his pet remedy. More modern men had a thermometer and a stethoscope. The temperature was gravely measured, and the chest listened to—or at.

That ritual was followed by every experienced physician. I had ideas of my own. I passed the aged female relatives up, ignored the children and proceeded with the matter at hand. This was not based on bravery on my part, but ignorance. I had not yet learned that most of the things one needs to know in the practice of the art of healing never get into the books. But there were compensating factors. I at least examined my patients as well as I knew how. My puerile attempts at physical examination impressed my patients and annoyed my competitors, which, of course, I accepted as a two-time strike. Word went out that the young doctor "ain't very civil but he is thorough." Only yesterday one of my old patients recalled that when I came to see her young son I "stripped him all off and examined him all over." Members of that family have been my patients for the intervening forty years, so impressed were they. Incidentally, it may be mentioned that in this case I discovered a pleurisy with effusion which had not been apparent to my tongue-inspecting colleague.

The great majority of the country doctor's calls were for trivial and obvious conditions, such as sore throat with or without special involvement of the tonsils, recognizable at a glance. Grandmother might have a renewal of her attacks of bronchitis or asthma, or Father might have lumbago or rheumatiz. These conditions could sometimes be diagnosed while one was driving into the yard. Simple remedies sufficed and one came a day or two later to see how the patient was progressing.

If there was an injury involving the skin one sewed it up without ceremony. The patient was supposed to submit to this without a squawk. If the kids received the injury while up to devilment they stood it heroically, but if they received it in line of duty they did not fancy, there were likely to be loud lamentations. But the ordeal was brief. In case of fracture one went out in the barnyard and hunted himself a suitable board, a loose one if he could find it—otherwise he forcibly removed one from its moorings. From these he fashioned a splint, perhaps with the aid of a bed sheet, if there was such a thing in the house. X-rays were unknown but the results obtained by the country doctor of experience were surprisingly good. At least none died as now sometimes happens when fractures are operated on. Legs, it may be mentioned, in those days were regarded as things to be used, not to look at. Therefore, if a useful limb resulted, everybody was satisfied, even though the result was not a thing of beauty.

Though many of the calls involved trivial and ephemeral diseases, there were many serious and arduous problems to meet such as try the souls of even experienced men. At the top of these stood epidemics of typhoid fever. My introduction to this disease was an epidemic of sixteen cases scattered over a wide territory. This number required a great deal of time, since it was supposed that an attentive doctor would see each patient at least once a day—during the most serious period of the disease sometimes several times a day—and stay all night at the terminal stages.

Happily, no other disease, I can now say, demanded so much of the doctor as typhoid fever. This disease is so insidious and protean in its onset as to try the skill of the most learned. Obviously, it was a great scheme to diagnose any sort of obscure disease as typhoid fever, as my competitors did. For if the diagnosis proved wrong the doctor could say he had broken it up; if it proved correct he got credit for great diagnostic acumen. This worked a great hardship on me, but I stuck to my guns. Word finally went around, "That boy is honest."

The history generally gleaned on the first visit was something like this: headache and backache for a few days with complete loss of appetite. Usually there were general abdominal pains most marked in the appendicial region. Abdominal distention soon followed. Fortunately for our peace of mind, appendicitis was not operated on in those days, and the responsibility of a differentiation was not great. So one just waited to see which it would turn out to be. If there were other cases of typhoid fever in the family, or even in the neighborhood, this was sufficient to make the diagnosis of typhoid fever probable, even in the early stages. Examination showed a distended abdomen, some tenderness and gurgling in the region of the appendix. Later, in many cases, rose spots appeared on the abdomen and, to the practiced eye, clinched the diagnosis; but my eye then wasn't very practiced. The temperature varied usually with the duration of the disease, gradually ascending day by day until the maximum of 104° or 105° was reached. In the early days there were no laboratory tests to be made and observation of the course of the disease was the only means of arriving at a diagnosis.

As the fever increased, the tongue and lips became covered with a dirty brown crust and there was a low muttering delirium. As the end of the third week approached, the possibility of the dreaded hemorrhage and perforation kept both doctor and family in a high state of dread, and every change that might indicate the advent of these disasters was keenly watched for. If any untoward symptom appeared, a messenger was dispatched for the doctor, though there was nothing he could do when he got there. Irritating occurrences were common. Sometimes a new arrival, usually an ancient relative or the minister, observing the patient for the first time, would express the opinion that the patient did not look right and advise that the doctor be called. This, of course, was to impress the relatives with their great interest in the welfare of the patient. Such solicitude was noted particularly if the patient was a rich uncle. Fortunately ministers always visited the patient in midafternoon and one could answer the call before bedtime. I suggested to one young divine that in my opinion his great solicitude for the patient was inspired by the large number of young chickens in the barnyard.

Those weary trips were galling because one was fully convinced before starting that the call was wholly useless and was instigated by some fool interfering with what did not concern him. One cannot blame the doctor for educating the cleric not to butt in. One could not refuse the call because a complication might actually have developed and, if it had, the death of the patient would be attributed to the negligence of the doctor. There being no lawyers, there were no malpractice suits. Malpractice suits, it may be remarked in passing, are dependent on the presence of a lawyer in a state of malnutrition, and have no relation whatever to the acts of the doctor. The doctors of that day were tried at the quilting bees of the community, not in courts of law. This made it necessary for the doctor to make a display of great activity, a show staged for the benefit of the relatives. Those who feed on this sort of bunk now employ irregulars, who surpass regular doctors in the practice of legerdemain, though some of us were quite skilled in that line when occasion required.

Under certain conditions the doctor was able to be of some service. When the stage of high temperature and delirium was reached cold sponging was demanded, or at least that was the consensus of professional opinion at that time. There being no trained nurse, it fell to the doctor's lot to do the job. It usually required one to two hours of sponging to reduce the temperature to 103°. One was rewarded for his efforts by seeing the patient sleep peacefully, free from muttering, for several hours. I want to say to the young doctors of today that two hours spent bathing a delirious patient seems quite a long time. Occasionally a mother or a neighbor would undertake the task.

Typhoid fever, like most infectious diseases, had a way of affecting chiefly the most ignorant, and I might say the most impecunious also, so that all the doctor got for his pains was the satisfaction of doing his duty and the knowledge that perhaps he had saved another moron to join the great group of unemployables. The disease, of course, did not confine itself to this class, and distressingly often attacked those who were stricken while aiding an unfortunate neighbor. I know the graves of several such victims. I may say in passing that I figured up the per hour collections in an epidemic of typhoid extending over three months. It averaged a little less than twenty cents an hour, not counting the expense of the team.

Though a typical case of typhoid fever was usually easily enough diagnosed—that is, if one observed it for a week or two—many diagnostic problems presented themselves. An apparently typical pneumonia might end up as a typical typhoid fever. I made such an error which caused me great distress. Just at that time Osler reported three cases in which he made this same mistake. I felt better then. Sometimes a typhoid patient would begin with a sudden severe pain in the region of the appendix. Since, as noted, appendicitis cases were not operated on, a diagnosis was just a matter of professional pride. After appendicitis became an operable disease, many useless operations were performed. Ignorance sometimes saves the doctor from doing foolish things.

The disease sometimes runs a very peculiar course. One of my patients ran a temperature for nearly twenty weeks. Some ran the usual course, were temperature-free for a few days and then started all over again. Most perplexing were two husky young farmers who began their disease on almost the same day and progressed uniformly in a typical way. On about the tenth day one developed a severe headache and neck retraction. I stayed with him through the whole night. Nothing I could or dared to do relieved him. At daylight he died. Spinal punctures were then unknown. I hastened to visit the other patient and found him peacefully eating his breakfast, fever-free.

At the end of this grueling summer I emulated my patients and took typhoid fever myself.

During the summer season digestive-tract diseases were common, particularly among children, and when I was not sponging typhoid patients I was giving enemas to convulsed babies. Doing this, I have no doubt, saved the lives of many children. There was no ice, no sanitation, and there were few screens. Many children died in their second year, that dreaded "second summer."

When word came that a baby was in convulsions, I would drop everything else and hasten to attend. I would find a child in convulsions, with a temperature of 105°. A hasty dose of castor oil was administered, followed by an enema which was perhaps repeated. If the convulsions did not cease the child was placed in a tepid water-filled washtub. After the convulsions ceased it was given salol and bismuth. One of these children that I bathed for six hours one night is now in a penitentiary. At least he is not listed as unemployed, and that is something.

I ARRIVE AT THE PATIENT'S BEDSIDE

Nearly all my babies recovered, whereas those my colleagues treated with Dover's powders or other opiates died. This experience gave me my real start. The word went out, "That young doc stays with them until they get well or die."

In looking back over forty years I am glad to say no branch of medicine has made greater advances than that dealing with the feeding of babies. The young specialists in diseases of children, inheriting the modern knowledge from their teachers, know nothing of the trials of long ago. The art of feeding has now reached such a state of perfection that the acute convulsive diseases are now almost unknown.

If I were a great artist given to paint but one picture I should depict a young mother sitting before the crib of a convulsing baby, with the crushed father in the background. In cases of tragedy the mother nearly always stands up better than the father. No one who knows women as well as the family doctor ever calls them the weaker sex. That phrase was spawned in the parlor by some goof who did not realize that the "weakling" was pulling in the line.

Convulsions in adults, as seen in lockjaw, for example, are terrible to witness, but they are infinitely worse in a child with so-called summer complaint. The cherubic little body is contorted into the most impossible shapes: eyes half open, the balls rolled upward; face twitching and pale or bluish-white. After a few minutes of violent muscular contraction there is slight relaxation and one hopes that it is ended; but not for long, because the contractions soon reappear, perhaps even worse than before. With slight variations this may continue for hours, even days. Usually after a time a diarrhea begins and the child rapidly emaciates, becoming quickly only a skeleton, a mere shadow of its former self. The convulsions are generally absent now, but the temperature rises rapidly, trying the registering capacity of the clinical thermometer. The child lies panting, head buried in the pillow. The limbs grow cold. There is a slight quiver. The emaciated little limbs suddenly straighten, then relax. The child is dead.

I have done many desperate and, I hope, life-saving operations but nothing gives me so much pleasure as the memory of those battles with convulsed babies. To see the contracted limbs relax, the head lift itself from the depths of the pillow; to see the light return to the mother's eyes, and the smile to her lips— that is one of the greatest experiences in life. In that final day when Peter says, "You are one of those bloomin' docs. What did you do?" I shall say, "I did it to even the least of these."

I know of what I speak. I have sat and watched my own little daughter in convulsions for twelve hours, as utterly para- lyzed with terror as any layman. After a short sleep she awak- ened and asked, "Where is my doll?"—the sweetest words ever spoken. I have never attended a sick child since that day. That memory freezes the marrow of my bones after more than thirty years.

Of course, all sorts of cases were interpolated. My first stomach patients were a husband and wife with identical symptoms. I could not risk my whole practice on one line of treatment, so I gave one antacids, the other hydrochloric acid. Both promptly recovered. They thought it was wonderful that while they both seemed to be identically affected the young doctor discovered a difference that required a different treatment. I recently met the living member of this excellent couple, in good health and still grateful after more than forty years. Such an experience is what makes hard labor worth while. It also illustrates the value of fast thinking—and, incidentally, of keeping one's thoughts to him- self.

Similarly happy was my experience with my first case of prostatic irritation. Strumpel's *Practice* stated either salol or boric acid could be used. Instead of tossing a coin I combined them. He got immediate relief. I still use this combination.

Patients are grateful in proportion to the relief obtained, even though the condition does not threaten life. The hardest fight with snowdrifts I have ever made found at its end an ischiorectal abscess. The patient suffered intensely and a simple opening of the abscess, of course, brought instant relief. He thought I had saved his life. In such situations the diplomatic doctor does not dispute his patient's opinion. He just looks grave and modest and for this he need not apologize, since he is up against the law of averages. He is sometimes praised for doing nothing and often condemned for failures that are inevitable, despite the fact that his measures are both correct and timely. There is one consoling thought: it is generally the ignorant who condemn the doctor. Intelligent people give him credit for doing his best though it be futile, or even unwise or mistaken; having achieved something themselves in their own lives, they know that, contrary to the teaching of the Sunday schools, to do our best is often not enough.

Of different import was a case of empyema. To answer the call eight miles from town I battled mud for three hours. As I entered the sickroom I saw a boy fourteen years of age half sitting up in bed in deep cyanosis, with grayish-blue skin and heaving chest, his mouth open and his eyes bulging. It seemed that each gasp would be his last. I threw down my instrument roll, sat flat on the floor with my legs spread under the bed. Grabbing a scalpel I made an incision in his chest wall with one stab—he was too near death to require an anesthetic. As the knife penetrated his chest, a stream of pus the size of a finger spurted out, striking me under the chin and drenching me. After placing a drain in the opening, I wrapped a blanket about my pus-soaked body and spent another three hours reaching home. The patient promptly recovered and is now a useful citizen in his town and recently voted for Landon, but I have never recovered from the memory of that pus bath. Bah!

Just before I began the practice of medicine many women in this neighborhood died of puerperal fever, chiefly due to one doctor who divided his time between practicing medicine and raising hogs. It was his practice to administer a large dose of ergot in order to hasten labor so he could reach home in time to feed the hogs. He sometimes washed his hands after the completion of labor but never before. After making a digital examination, he used his pants—that is, trousers east of the Alleghanies, as a towel.

I was called to see one of his patients in the very first months of my practice. The following, printed elsewhere, is a better description than I could write now:

A woman in her eighth puerperium had been overcome on the third day after labor by a violent chill and high fever. When I saw her on the fifth day she lay motionless, eyes sunken, wide open, and fixed. Her respiration was labored and rapid and despite this labor her color presented a mixture of waxy pallor and cyanosis, as though some vulgar hand had soiled a marble statue of Distress, or Nature herself was seeking to soften the awful picture to spare the untried sensibilities of the embryo Aesculapian. The distended intestine found little resistance from the lax abdominal muscles and ballooned out to an astonishing degree. My first thought as I saw the patient lying in bed was that a canopy had been formed for her out of barrel hoops to prevent friction from the bed-clothes. My astonishment at finding that the whole mass was belly knew no bounds. My eyes at this sight, I am sure, rivaled the patient's in fixity and wideness and my respiration was equally labored. As I sought to feel her pulse the cold clammy skin made me shrink and as I sought the pulse I could find but a quivering string and because of the pounding of my own heart I never knew its rate. As I turned from this scene, standing about the room were the seven older children, the eldest a girl of twelve. These, too, were wild eyed and short of breath. Approaching the cradle I sought to calm myself by viewing the child. Much to my consternation here lay a replica of the mother herself. The infant vainly sought to emulate its mother in girth of abdomen but far exceeded her in rate of respiration. In one particular only was there essential difference. Instead of the waxy gray of the mother it presented a peculiar ochre yellow, the result of cord infection.

Noting my discomfiture, the old doctor with whom I was in

consultation said, "Never saw anything like it, did you, boy?" I had not, nor have I since.

I have the greatest pleasure in reporting that no case of puerperal fever has happened to me or any of my assistants. In fact, puerperal infection is rare, really almost unknown, among country doctors. The disease is not so rare, I read, in the hands of specialists in lying-in hospitals. I say this with pride in the country doctor, not in derision of the specialist under ideal surroundings.

There were many trials for the country doctor in attending labor cases. The following stands out. The patient was nearly forty years of age, small, chunky. A glance indicated that a difficult job was ahead. Only the husband was with her. The night was stormy. As soon as I arrived the husband, a half-wit, departed for a destination unknown and I was left alone with the patient. There was a little stove and a basket of corncobs. After a delay of many hours it became evident that instruments would be required. I had no anesthetic. The patient was in great distress. Her intelligence was just one jump ahead of her husband's. It was necessary to get on the bed and hold the patient's legs with my knees while I applied the forceps. I finally got a fine boy who, despite the none too high estate of his parents, grew up to be a fine young man. I felt that he was in a measure my boy, for I had earned him. He died in the war to save democracy, or to end wars, or whatever it was.

In most cases there was some woman about to care for the new arrival. Sometimes there was no one but the husband. A husband in a case of this sort is just one big cipher. In my first cases in such circumstances I attempted to wash the new arrival myself. Trying to wash a new baby is some sleight-of-hand job. Naturally I had no lap, so I would place the object of my efforts on the kitchen table, which was invariably covered with oil cloth. These youngsters are as slick as greased pigs. So, in order to prevent the baby falling to the floor, I was obliged to grasp one leg firmly with one hand, which left only one available for performing the ablutions. After a few such experiences I carried a bottle of sweet oil and just anointed it all over, rolled it in whatever was available and allowed it to await the ministrations of more experienced hands.

Even conducting a labor lone-handed was not the worst that could befall one. Some of the mothers or mothers-in-law were considerably worse than useless. My assistant and I had an experience that illustrates this. It was a case in which instruments would be needed and I worried about how to get rid of that mother. I had no need to worry. That resourceful assistant of mine was seldom at a loss in meeting any situation. He stared at the mother for a moment and asked if she was subject to heart disease. She stammered that she had been, though obviously it was a new thought to her. He stated very solicitously, after he had listened to her heart, that it would be safest for her to go out into the yard, as it might be necessary to give the patient an anesthetic. She not only went into the yard but across the barnyard into the pasture beyond. After everything was attended to she was recalled.

The most common pests were those who urged that something should be done to hasten labor, declaring that their doctor always gave them something to hasten the process. This type I set to boiling water, stating that it might be necessary to give the patient a Sitz bath. It takes quite a while to boil a tub of water in a teakettle. This kept them busy in the kitchen boiling water and out of the way until labor was terminated. Of course, one never intended to make use of the tub of water.

This same assistant furnished me many a laugh by the ingenuity which he displayed in coping with annoying situations. One instance comes to mind. We were attending a very sick man. A neighbor, a well-meaning but none too bright old bachelor, camped in the kitchen in order not to miss any food. One of the women asked if something could not be done to rid them of the pest. My assistant opined that something could. He went into the kitchen and acted surprised to find the neighbor there. Assuming a startled look, he beckoned the nuisance to come hither that he might have converse with him. They huddled in a corner of the kitchen and the doctor asked him if he was not aware that the disease was terribly catching, which of course it was not. The eyes of the old gent began to advance toward the end of his nose. With a frightened glance about the room he dashed for the door, nearly tearing it off its hinges. He did not stop even to get his cap and when last seen was traveling at high speed in a general southeasterly direction. Despite the seriousness of the situation, everybody had a hearty laugh.

Whether an incident is funny or tragic often depends on the viewpoint. Here is a case. I received a call from a doctor in a neighboring town. He had a patient, a young lady afflicted with a serious heart disease. Would I come? I would. It was a rainy day and the road was a sea of mud. I drove my horse until he became exhausted. Then I importuned a farmer to take me the rest of the way. His outfit was a farm wagon and a very sophisticated span of mules. When I arrived at the house the family doctor was awaiting me. The patient had been employed in a neighboring town. Previously always in the best of health, she had suddenly been taken seriously ill. The symptoms were very confusing to the doctor. Rapid respiration was all he could see and he concluded the trouble was a weak heart. I saw a fine plump girl with pink cheeks. She had been weeping. Her pulse was slower than mine and as regular. Knowing the disposition of the doctor, I asked him and the family to let me talk to the patient alone. It was a risk but necessary. I sat down on the edge of the bed and talked to her like a child, for she was only a child, though nineteen years old. "Now tell me," I began, "now tell me just what happened to him." She burst out weeping. "I don't know," she sobbed. "He just up and married another girl." I inquired in detail all about him, his appearance, his occupation and all that. No occupation, very handsome, with brown curly hair. I evaluated him in my own way. Handsome men, I volunteered, live off either the earnings of their wives or of their fathers-in-law. The commercial value of curly brown hair, figured in terms of buckwheat cakes, I opined, was not very high.

I talked to her at length on how fortunate she was that fate had intervened for her. Mere child, fine figure of a girl, beautiful face, young, she had no need to grieve. In calling a young girl beautiful one runs no risk of offending. One may take a cue from the newspapers. Every female that gets into devilment, if under seventy years of age, is referred to as "attractive." This, I presume, is following the usual newspaper habit of giving the people what they want: to wit, bunk. I explained to her that fate had much better things in store for her. I administered this sort of talk for a while and finally her face began to relax, just as that of a nine-month-old baby does when she is about to reach out her arms to you. I wrapped a blanket about her and said, "Let's go out and tell Mother you are all right." She tripped lightly out of the bedroom, through the living room and into the kitchen where the family doctor and the family were talking. The mother's look as she beheld her smiling daughter walking for the first time in weeks was something you do not see in books. "She will be all right," I assured the doctor. Then I sought the farmer and his mules and made the trip home; elapsed time, fourteen hours for the round trip. Now, is this tale funny or is it tragic?

In the same community, some years later, I received a call from that same doctor. A girl was in a terrible condition. She worked in a neighboring town and had come home sick, with a high fever and in terrible pain. That sounded suspicious but I could learn nothing further from the doctor. Mud as usual, and the team walked every foot of the way. Time, seven hours.

I ARRIVE AT THE PATIENT'S BEDSIDE

The doctor was awaiting me. He announced that since calling me the patient had become much better and was now quietly sleeping. She had an abscess where no lady ever has an abscess. The abscess had burst of its own accord and the patient was at once relieved. There was nothing to do professionally but I did make some remarks of a general nature. I had read during the trip out; I was too mad to read on the way back. I made uncomplimentary remarks, with special reference to professional incompetency and the general cussedness of humanity, all the way back. Twice seven hours. Of course, having done nothing I was entitled to no pay. But then that family never paid anyone anyway, so there was no occasion to make a concrete application of this remark. Five dollars for the team and fourteen hours on the road was all I was out. Personally I never could detect any humor in this incident.

Another case had a decidedly amusing feature. I was called to see an old Civil War veteran with a chestful of fluid which caused him much difficulty in breathing. That the family doctor had made the correct diagnosis was proved by examination. While I was preparing my apparatus to relieve the old man of his fluid he bawled out, "Say, Doc, you are the homeliest man I seen since I saw Old Abe." "Say, Pa, you better shet up," his wife called from the kitchen. "Old Abe saved your hide onst; maybe this young feller kin now." A death sentence for sleeping on guard when he was a boy in the army had been commuted by the martyred President. Fortunately, the old lady's prediction came true; he promptly recovered. "I oughtn't to have said what I did," he said to his family doctor, who relayed it to me, "I mighta knowed he must be good for something or somebuddy wooda shot him long ago." As an apology without loss of dignity this always has seemed to me a masterpiece. Low comedy such as this between patient and doctor was common in those days. Many of the older men were war veterans first and pioneers afterward—he-men all the while. Fearless and uncomplaining, they fought grasshoppers and drought uncomplainingly, voted their ticket straight and asked no return. We shall not see their like again.

The foregoing may be regarded as in general the business of the practice of medicine followed by all of us, modified by each doctor's idiosyncrasies and by the situations which arose.

The more intimate experiences do not permit telling and the more ridiculous would be out of place. Often, too, they are so intimately blended. The events recounted here are sufficient to give a general idea of the life we old fellows used to lead.

The human side varied much according to the doctor's bringing up and his general view of life. Despite what I have written and what I may write, I have always had close association with many ministers of the gospel and we often compared notes as to our personal points of view. The ministers of the old days were not learned in a book sense, but many were men of great earnestness and high purpose. These men in general had an idea that something notable should take place at the moment of dissolution and seemed to think I should provide pabulum for their discourses. I had to tell them that saints and sinners died alike and that at the time of death, whatever might have been the antecedents, there was no pain. I have seen only one man who looked on death with terror and he was a sanctimonious old sinner, the pillar of his church, at the sight of whom one just instinctively grasped one's pocketbook.

In most cases death is preceded by a dulling of the mental processes as the circulation to the brain lessens due to the failing heart. Those who die just go to sleep. Even in diseases in which consciousness is retained until the last, as in peritonitis, there is no fear. I have sat beside the bed of such cases and talked of things in general, such casual things as the prospect of quail hunting and the like, while the cooling hands denoted the approach of death. Anyone who ever became unconscious during the course of any disease has experienced the sensation of death.

I ARRIVE AT THE PATIENT'S BEDSIDE

Only favorable circumstances brought him back to consciousness again.

In the old day we remained with our patients during their last hours. We saw to it that they did not suffer. The interest in such a situation attached not to the dying but to the living. I can confirm that old saying that in the deepest sorrow there is no weeping. I have sat more than once on the side of a cradle with a mother while a baby died. Our eyes met as the last quiver passed over the little body. She recognized as well as I that life had become extinct. There was no weeping.

The saddest sight I have ever seen was at the deathbed of an old couple who had lived together many years. Both had pneumonia. I watched the passing of the aged wife and then went to see the husband. I made not a sound. "Mother's dead?" he queried. I did not need to answer. He closed his eyes, folded his hands over his chest and in a short time he also was dead. Don't ask me the meaning. The finest scenes I have witnessed have been the serene old age of such couples. As far as I can see, in order to arrive at the same place at the same time it is necessary to travel together. To so travel it seems that the burdens of life must be borne share and share alike. Whatever the more abundant life may be, this, I am sure, is the most abundant death.

Contrary to general belief, husbands are more nearly crushed than wives at the death of the mate. This is confirmed by the number of bereaved husbands who take their own lives on the graves of their departed wives. Such suicides are not unusual among men but are rare among women. I have said again and again, and I say it once more, that whoever it was that first called women the weaker sex certainly was not a country doctor.

Doctors nowadays do not stay with their patients during the last scene. What do they accomplish by remaining? Scientifically nothing; humanly much. I know of what I speak. In the saddest hour of my life, at the deathbed of my daughter, on one side was the magnificent and always faithful Carrie the nurse, on the other side the incomparable Dr. Campbell, calmly applying measures of resuscitation which he and I knew were utterly futile. Yet futile though it was, the battle of these professions inspires an indescribable measure of comfort. I know that my last conscious moments will picture that scene: nurse on one side of the bed, doctor on the other. Though scientifically futile, if my presence in a similar situation ever brought an equal amount of comfort to anyone I am sure it was more worth while than anything else I have ever done. Our mission in life is to lessen human suffering as much as we can.

On the whole those arduous experiences were happy days. When the roads were good and the trip not too long I took my black-eyed little daughter with me. Later on, she had a sister who was anything but black-eyed and another sister halfway between. No one ever achieves more than that, a reasonably assured living and happy children. No music of earth has greater worth than the prattle of a healthy child, it is said. I was established in practice, all school debts paid, eating three meals a day, with a prospect of earning enough to educate my children. Nobody expected anybody to break up typhoid fever or pneumonia and the diagnosis of typhoid fever was often a long and even uncertain procedure. Also there sometimes were diseases that just could not be diagnosed with certainty, and a confession of these facts implied not ignorance but courage and honesty. I had arrived. Beyond this fundamental fact no doctor ever achieves a higher estate.

Yet, despite this fact, I carefully counted my dollars for the time when I would be able to dive into the unknown, graduate study and a specialty. Ambition is a terrible affliction and followed to the supreme degree leads to but one end, disappointment. Anyone who reaches the heights of his ambition never had an ambition. The mirage becomes a pool when one reaches the end of his labors, be he cobbler or philosopher.

CHAPTER

6

THE OFFICE PATIENTS PRESENT THE EVERYDAY COMPLAINTS with which every family is familiar. They are, for the most part, trivial and tend to spontaneous recovery. There are more subtle disturbances not so well classified but recognized by all doctors in general; management of them is the same, but such patients are peculiarly the problem of the local doctor who knows the many imponderable influences to which the patient is subject. The local doctor knows the innumerable factors of home environment and heredity which are hidden from the consulting doctor but which play a great role in the prospective treatment. Many patients have their pet complaints which they retain for years without end. Many seem to acquire a sort of affection for them because they form a ready subject for conversation with friends and neighbors. Grandpa's "rheumatiz" becomes of neighborly interest because it makes it possible to predict rain—that is, in retrospect.

The doctor in his office has two problems constantly before him. The patient's seemingly minor complaint may presage a serious disease, and to overlook it may bring grave reflection on his skill and disaster to the patient. What seems to be a trivial complaint as far as danger to life is concerned may be cured by someone particularly skilled in that particular line. It is the business of the country doctor to bring these two together. In most cases when patients visit the physician there is some definite complaint, usually of a minor nature which they have some hope may be relieved. In general, it implies that only minor repairs are needed, as we say of automobiles: battery recharged, carbon removed or something like that. If major repairs, in automobile parlance, are supposed to be necessary; if valves are to be ground, or new rings put in; if the transmission has gone haywire, or something mysterious is wrong—the patient is a candidate for a specialist. When the doctor works alone he is a universal specialist, a wayside garageman. He is ready to make any minor repairs. In contradistinction, in the clinic a specialty is assigned to each doctor and each is supposed to be able to render maximum service in his line. The skin man takes the kinks out of your fenders, the eye man puts in new headlights, the stomach man adjusts the carburetor. Just where the surgeon comes in in this simile, I can't say; but some persons may suggest that he is the man in the office who makes the charge. Here is where the comparisons cease. For in the auto business, if the united efforts of the various mechanics avail nothing, one can trade in his car on a new one, but man has no trade-in value; he just is carried out and a brand-new model takes his place. Here comes another similarity and a difference: some people buy the new car on the installment plan, but we can't get a mortgage on a baby.

The great advantage of office practice is that the patient can receive in a few minutes adequate treatment for minor ailments. The patient may have his ailment anytime he sees fit without waiting for office hours. The family physician is on call from year's end to year's end. The clinic, on the other hand, begins and closes at a certain hour, and one must have an ailment that is durable or severe enough so that a distinct memory of it survives until the time of the clinic's opening.

The general practitioner's office has changed completely in the last fifty years, so it is of interest to take a look at the typical office of the old-time country doctor. It consisted usually of two rooms: a waiting room in which the patient waited for the doctor and another in which the doctor waited for the patient. Such was my first office. And as my first year's practice netted me two hundred and sixteen dollars, it is obvious that my waiting room was seldom cluttered up with patients. My other room was euphoniously designated the consulting room. The reading matter available in the patient's waiting room has long been a subject of jokes and jibes. One could usually guess the age of the doctor by the date of the literary appurtenances of his office table. The jokes about the hoary age of the literature offered to the waiting patient is still revived now and then by the local press. That old joke, if it is one, was not on the doctor, for he kept current periodicals in his room to while away the weary hours he spent waiting for patients. If offices were ever subjected to a cleaning in that old day no one has recorded the fact. Mine was kept clean—that is, as seen through a male eye—for I attended to that job myself until I could afford an office boy to do it.

The typical doctor's room contained a desk littered with advertising except one corner reserved for the doctor's feet. Since he wore no spurs it had to be free from litter, otherwise his feet would slip off. A chair that had been fairly comfortable in the long ago before the seat broke out was placed before the desk. A few chairs for the patients, a ten-dollar-examination table, for which he paid seventy-six dollars. I made my own tables at a cost of four dollars and eighty cents for the lumber. Then there was the instrument table, which was a kitchen table purchasable unpainted for a dollar.

The doctor was the entire staff and it was up to him to help the lady undress, counting the petticoats the while, and to help her reassemble them after the examination was complete. If one ever witnessed this process, or procedure, whichever it may be, one can readily understand why the doctor was tempted to content himself with feeling the pulse and inspecting the tongue. In the beginning of my practice six petticoats formed the customary number. This may seem incredible but it is the literal truth. I counted them many a time. Furthermore, many of the patients had achieved such a degree of plumpness that even when one divested them of their clothing one was not much nearer the seat of complaint than before. Hunting for a needle in a haystack is practically child's play compared with locating a pain in three-hundred-odd pounds of gross weight. The general topography of his patients made it safe for the doctor to examine them without being chaperoned by an attendant; that should be fairly obvious. There was that consolation: a patient with six petticoats had no sinister designs and, it may be added, presented no temptations.

That is history. The modern country doctor's office is as carefully kept as the city doctor's. Nowadays no doctor would think of examining a woman patient without a woman attendant being present. In many cases the woman attendant also takes care of the office and keeps accounts. Before the advent of the income-tax collector, if the doctor wished to determine his assets he compared the unpaid bills on his table with the money in his pocket and by the simple process of subtracting the lesser sum from the larger sum determined his assets or liabilities as the case might be. Nowadays one pays taxes on his hopes as well as his assets, and deadhead patients thus contribute to the wealth of the nation, using the hapless doctor as intermediary.

Though usually the office patient does not present great responsibility it must not be imagined that the seriously sick patients did not sometimes visit the office. A patient who visits the office one day may be sick in bed at home the next. For instance, a patient with walking typhoid fever visited my office one day, and was sent home to bed and died of hemorrhage the next day. Another patient, one with a perforated appendix, had a general peritonitis and his chilling hands indicated death was already on him when he visited the office. A slight complaint may terminate as an inoperable cancer. It is such cases that keep the country doctor in a state of more or less apprehension.

The chief convenience of the house visit was that the patient was definitely anchored and one could at once gain a reasonable proximity by simply clawing off the comforter or feather bed. Just a word of caution. The feathers had a way of assembling along either side of the patient and if the turning back was carelessly done the whole would fall to the floor. In my day there were usually a few sophisticated old aunties in attendance who enjoyed any happening that obfuscated the young doctor. Without going into detail, I may say that the scenery revealed by a mishap with a feather bed may be considerable.

Since office practice usually has to do with chronic diseases, the doctor could make his examination, if any, as superficial or complete as he wished. Such typical diseases as typified by the itch or the asthma demand but little examination. He cures or he palliates, or he does no good at all. In most cases, fortunately, the patient just gets well as a matter of course. If nothing at all happens and either or both doctor and patient tire of the treatment the patient is sent to a clinic, or to a specialist if either doctor or patient can determine the likely organ at fault.

This was not the manifestation of carelessness. The country doctor himself had to do everything that was necessary in order to reach a diagnosis. He took the patient's history, made a physical examination, did what laboratory work there was to be done and finally put up the medicine. He was, in other words, a universal specialist and a druggist besides. I recall very distinctly that on my twenty-seventh birthday I "examined" forty patients in the office and drove a total of sixty miles on country roads and was just an even twenty-four hours doing the job.

Though most office cases presented minor ailments the doctor had to be constantly on the alert for serious diseases of insidious onset. He was supposed to diagnose the disease at the very beginning while the symptoms were as yet indefinite or inconclusive. For instance, behind the cough might be a beginning tuberculosis; behind the digestive disturbance, a beginning cancer of the stomach.

Quite commonly a fever presaged the advent of an acute disease. If there was an epidemic in the community he played probabilities and diagnosed that disease. But not infrequently something entirely different was in the offing. The embarrassing thing to the country doctor was, and is, that he was supposed to diagnose a disease in its beginning—say, like a rattle in a car. If he fails to do so, after a time the patient consults a specialist. Usually by this time the disease has developed sufficiently so that anyone can determine its nature—say, like when the rear axle has come off a car. Naturally the specialist gets credit for extraordinary acumen, though in the beginning, while the symptoms were indefinite, his opinion also would have been indefinite, because often in the beginning of a disease a diagnosis is impossible. The joke on the office doctor rates par when the specialist collects all the patient's visible assets and the doctor gets nothing.

Office practice has one great advantage over visits to the patient's bedside. If the young doctor does not know what is wrong with the patient he can adopt the lawyer's tactics and stall. He can give the patient something to take and ask him to return, and in the interval read up on the various possibilities. However, the doctor must read fast, for it is not his habit to charge a retaining fee and there is a possibility that in the meantime the patient may stray off to another doctor. Lawyers are smarter that way. If the patient paid a retainer fee to his doctor as he does to a lawyer he would be much more likely to return. I could never understand why our customers are called patients and a lawyer's are called clients. For it certainly takes a lot more patience to deal with a lawyer than with a doctor.

THE PATIENT COMES TO THE OFFICE

A doctor cannot stand customers off until next term of court. The doctor's judge just doesn't tolerate delay.

Therefore, the doctor just naturally has to know right now, at least do something without delay. For no other profession is so much discriminated against. We are subject to suits for malpractice, always by disgruntled patients who never pay their bills. All it takes to make a malpractice suit is a hungry lawyer or two and an envious doctor. The treatment and the results have nothing to do with the matter. A lawyer's patients may go to the pen but they do not sue the lawyer for malpractice. Perhaps it is because the statute of limitations runs out, or whatever it is a statute of limitations does, so that by the time the lawyer's patient is released suit is no longer possible. Ministers also are fortunate. They accuse us of burying our mistakes. Suppose the Reverend Mr. Brown says to his client, Mr. Smith, "Now, if you will stand for my sermons and pay your church dues and don't get caught at any of your cussedness, I will assure you of a seat with the elect." And suppose that in spite of faultless preaching the plan slipped up and Mr. Smith returned from a less comfortable sector of the hereafter than that promised and sued the Reverend Mr. Brown for malpractice. A few such experiences would teach preachers to wrap their promises in Latin phrases as we doctors do.

Lawyers and clergymen sometimes form a coalition. If the lawyer makes an awful botch of it, and his patient is consigned to the hot seat the lawyer turns him over to a member of the cloth who prepares him for a seat with the just. That is what is vulgarly called passing the buck. At any rate, everybody seems to be well satisfied with the results. The executed person was saved, the clergy vindicated and the sheriff has done his duty; nobody comes back to complain.

We doctors never derive any comfort from either of the other learned professions. They both keep us on the griddle throughout our lifetime. Though I have always lived an honest life I invariably get the jitters when I receive a letter with a lawyer's name on the corner of the envelope. Of course, there is one place safe from lawyers—in heaven. It is reported there are no lawyers there. Unfortunately, there is no haven when confronted by a malpractice suit. But I have it figured out for myself that if one stays broke the lawyers will not bother him and if one plays golf or goes fishing on Sundays the dire warnings of the clergy will not excite any apprehension. Anyway, perdition sounds as if it might be restful to one who has practiced medicine for a lifetime.

The country doctor is not altogether helpless, however. If the patient's disease refuses solution, or if he has no disease at all, the doctor can refer him to a city specialist. It may be said that one of the most important problems of the family doctor is to determine when or if the patient should consult a specialist and select a reliable one for him. It is something more than a facetious remark to say that the doctor's function is to protect his patient from the specialist. Certainly he renders distinct service if he keeps the patient from falling into the hands of the pseudo specialist.

The best example of the pseudo specialist is the surgeon too desirous to cut. The most diabolical were those who treated young girls with minor disorders by radical operative measures. Many a girl with mild menstrual pains had her "chronic appendix" removed, and worse still, an ovary or two tinkered with. Fortunately, it is now generally recognized that there is no such disease as chronic appendicitis and it has come to occupy the same place in pathology as the dodo bird does in ornithology. Hemorrhage in a girl was another such condition. Fortunately the surgeon has learned that these patients are not to be treated by operation, but they are now threatened by the radiologist. Life certainly is just one thing after another for the girl who does not know what is the matter with her. Her friend is the family doctor. He knows that she will recover from her ailments if he can protect her from the surgeon. He knows those pains are not found pushing a perambulator so he stalls for time to bring the remedy.

The complaints of women make up a large part of office practice. These are vaguely termed female complaints. At least, these complaints are the exclusive right of women. I have a distinct aversion to referring to women as females, but one cannot entirely avoid the use of conventional terms after listening to the complaints of some of them. Some of the species admit of no other designation for the reason that the term is all-comprehensive.

By female complaints are generally understood disturbances of organs peculiar to women, but they do not include all diseases that women complain of. Those doctors who specialize in the former are called gynecologists. I like the older designation better, "specialists in the diseases of women." It makes it easier to distinguish between diseases of women and female complaints that have nothing to do with diseases. I once had occasion to teach this subject and I gave the boys a definition which the passing years have caused me to feel rather well satisfied with, though the boys thought it was a joke. It is as follows: "A gynecologist is an unfortunate individual whose mission in life it is to aid the human female to correlate her biologic instincts with the dictates of Christian ethics."

The diseases of the organs peculiar to women are easily recognized by any experienced doctor. The measures required for their correction is common knowledge. The doctor has merely to recognize complicating factors, which may require all the astuteness that long experience alone can bring. Organic ailments are easily diagnosed and may require operative correction. The biologic complaints are more complicated, not so much as to their nature as to the problem of their management.

Female complaints are capable of rough classification. There is the middle-aged woman who is suffering from many complaints chiefly because she is middle-aged. The approaching menopause so disturbs her that she is likely to fall a prey to pseudo specialists and some that are not pseudo. The old family doctor who has known his patient a long time knows that she will settle down after a few years, despite certain minor displacements or lacerations which would excite the specialist to action. All he needs to do is to reassure her and prescribe medicines to relieve the minor discomforts.

The complaints women suffer from, as distinguished from diseases, as indicated above, are of a wide variety. The most perplexing for the family doctor to manage is the nervousness incident to the fear of conception. Few tell the doctor the basis of their complaint. One must guess it from general appearance. The patient may have some organic ailment which in the absence of the fear would warrant operation but in the face of the fundamental cause of the complaint one hesitates to recommend operation, knowing the cure will not be complete. Nothing in medicine requires so much judgment as does the handling of these patients. What is disease and what worry tries the skill of the most astute.

A perplexing problem is the adolescent girl. Christian lady and plain animal sometimes wage a terrible subconscious battle. Sick or well she is a problem. The commonest complaint is monthly pains—a symptom more often than a disease. We doctors sometimes forget, as well as learn, about the young dysmenorrheaic. The trouble used to be perfectly amenable to treatment by us country doctors when we got hold of her first. The treatment was well described in such recent books as Hartshorne's *Practice of Medicine.* My edition is about eighty-five years old. We now know polyglandular disturbances are responsible. Dr. Hartshorne does not say anything about that. We just added it. It doesn't mean that we know any more than he did. And, while advancing in theory, we have forgotten his treatment. He gave potassium iodide. These patients have small goiters, and when these disappear the dysmenorrhea does likewise.

The old doctors all knew potassium iodide would relieve dysmenorrhea in young girls. That is true yet. It will cure all cases except those complicated by other things, particularly malformations of the pelvic organs which naturally are not amenable to treatment. The use of potassium iodide for dysmenorrhea is one of the most valuable contributions ever written in a medical book. Yet it has been forgotten except by a few old papas.

When I began practice with a horse and road cart, women never complained unless they really had something wrong with them. They had eight or twelve children—just imagine a woman with twelve kids having hysteria or malingering. All, the children and mother, were part of the domestic machinery. These mothers produced something besides children, too—things ranging all the way from soft soap and rag carpets to mince pies. Everyone, including the children, was engaged in the gentle art of trying to make a living. When any of those people complained, they were physically sick, even including the daughters. We old doctors have had the advantage of growing up, so to say, with the complaints. We have seen the number of petticoats diminish—well, literally to the vanishing point. We have observed the development of complaints from the beginning. It is just like the experience gained by having driven all the different stages of automobile development. That is to say, a complaint may be crude in the beginning but when it is passed on from mother to daughter it gains a finesse that is confusing to the inexperienced doctor, old stuff to the old doctor.

Office practice is not made up wholly of tongue inspecting and pulse counting. There are many complicated problems which confront the doctor. They are medical but only in small part concerned with organic changes. To be prepared for these states the doctor should have a thorough knowledge of the laws of biology and also a fundamental knowledge of the history of religions, if anyone knows what I mean, which I hope they do not. I most emphatically state that it is not an expression of cynicism. If ministers would just forget the hell hereafter and concentrate on the hell on this earth, and if lawyers would forget the law and concentrate on justice, they would become our powerful allies in alleviating human suffering from the face of the earth, instead of, as now, our chief deterrents—more, our chief obstructionists. The moral sense of doctors of medicine is as highly developed as that of any other profession.

To return to the female complaints. One may divide them into two general classes: the female complaints and the male complaints. The former include those due to maladjustments between the biologic and the ethical. Male complaints, on the other hand, are those in which man is the aggravating factor or, maybe, the regressive factor. These are subtle things which only doctors can hope to understand. If written they would need to be sent by express or freight. They involve some real or fancied dereliction on the part of some man; usually, of course, Papa is the alleged offender. The bodily complaints are secondary and are invented to corroborate the dereliction mentioned. This really is a complicated matter of the widest range. These cases should, in fact, be divided into two groups: those due to traits inherent in the male species, ranging from cigar ashes to fist fights and beating Wifie; the other group is more serious, both to patient and to the doctor, has a more primitive biologic basis, and includes the imaginary, ranging from overlooking the wedding anniversary date, to suspecting the blonde stenographer. Any surgeon who cannot evaluate these different types of complaints will find himself doing many useless operations.

It is said that truth is wholly foreign to the divorce court, and one may say almost as much for such cases when they reach the doctor's office. Even the wisdom of Solomon would be unequal to the solution of them and he had ninety wives, or was it nine hundred? Even if one suspects the cause of the complaints one never knows whether or not the patient's answers represent the truth. Here is where the woman doctor has a distinct place. Women are less hesitant to tell one of their own sex the real cause of their complaint. Moreover, the women doctors are less likely to be misled by the statements of patients of their own sex or any sex for that matter. However, our big handicap is that we men doctors lack the nerve to quiz these patients regarding intimate details. As a result, we follow the clergy and shut our eyes to the troubles of these women despite the fact that both professions will have to face the problem sometime. In the meantime they are compelled to flounder the best they can in their ignorance. Fortunately, their ignorance is not so abysmal as we try to make ourselves believe. This reminds me of the mother who remarked to her mate that she had just had a talk with Daughter. Papa asked, "Well, what new did you find out?"

Herein lies the starting point of a large proportion of divorces. The blonde stenographer is the accessory after the fact, as the lawyers say. We fail in our opportunity because of our own timidity and because of ecclesiastic and legal restrictions.

One patient presented her problem without equivocation. She came to my office with a flock of children and flopped exhausted in a chair. Her opening remark was, "I am twenty-nine years old and have eight children and am completely worn out. What would you do?" That she had eight children was a fact; I counted them. Also, she was completely exhausted; and the children lacked proper food and clothing.

There are borderline cases which suffer from both female and male complaints. These include matrons of all shapes and sizes. One of the most striking types is the young woman of, say, twenty-one who has had two or three children. She married just as soon as she discovered her legs. As far as I can see, those patients just simply suffer from overadvertising. They run around with their little legs bare, and marry at fifteen and proceed to follow the biblical injunction until they have exhausted all their strength. Then they expect the doctor to remedy their trouble. Greasing a car will not remedy a burned-out bearing.

Then there is the socially satiated husband, aged twenty-one. He has seen all there is in life. I wonder sometimes if Edmund Burke could have written that wonderfully classical tribute to the French dauphiness if he had not seen her legs? These patients are beyond the pale of adequate treatment. Usually they are the victims of malnutrition, because they come from families larger than could be cared for. This explains their disposition to marry long before their majority or maturity, or even the legal age. Their parents give their consent, though generally these people are incapable of forming an intelligent judgment. Lawyers and clergymen graciously hand this problem over to the doctor, but with the warning that if he solves it, to the pen he goes.

Now, there is another type of patient even more troublesome. They come to the office alone. No hubby is to be seen anywhere in the background. He has made his getaway, a deserter or just a plain refugee. You have to figure out which. If he has deserted, you can do her some good with sedatives. If he is a refugee, the thing to do is to send her to a neurologist as a temporary port on the voyage to the lawyer's office. These patients are taciturn. Sometimes the trouble is the same as that which sent Sam Houston to Texas. There is some maladjustment, biologically speaking, which the doctor is not told about but knows just the same.

Another type suffers from too much Mamma. Friend Husband is not along but Mamma is. This is one of the most prolific sources of female complaint. Mamma has had all the symptoms and Daughter unconsciously imitates her. Hence you must diagnose the mother. In cases where there is a strong nervous element, and even if there is pathology, the operation must be avoided if possible, because the result will be a disappointment to all concerned. One can sometimes get a lead as to the nature of the trouble by noting her given name. If it is a silly one, there is a queer psychological quirk in the family, not necessarily on the mother's side. It merely indicates a family trait which may manifest itself in unusual acumen or in nervous complaints. Therefore, one must not place too much emphasis on such leads, for while usually of significance, they may lead one astray. On the other hand, if a child is named Edith and blossoms out as Edythe or if Anna becomes Annette you know there is a neurotic quirk in the case even though a family relationship cannot be identified. In the former case you are dealing with a possibility; in the latter, with a fact. These are social and not medical problems, unless some hapless surgeon begins to operate. From then on it is, in fact, a medical problem. Unhappily one cannot put back what has been removed. The difficulty is that sometimes such patients are afflicted with an organic disease which demands operation. This may cure the organic disease but the patient's nervous disorder, or her pure meanness, as the case may be, still flourishes. This is the type of person who goes in for malpractice suits, hence the wise surgeon refuses an operation even when the patient really needs surgical treatment.

There is a type of female complainer of greater obscurity. She comes alone, unattended either by husband or woman companion. She announces that she wants a physical examination. Her general attitude puts the doctor on the alert. You can see icicles hanging down from her chin, that is how friendly she is. Now the diagnosis is plain enough. She thinks Hubby has been out visiting the blonde and has brought something home. The chances are he hasn't. If he is a real rounder, his wife will swear by him. If he is faithful she swears at him. This is a funny situation only for those who don't have to live in it. The jealous woman nearly always has a faithful husband.

Such a woman is difficult to handle. You examine her carefully—Wassermann and all—just as if you are falling for the whole story. Then you tell her everything is negative, and ask, "Why did you think there was something wrong?" The chances are that she will say she knows better. Your diagnosis is wrong. She is going to believe what she wants to believe and no doctor's opinion is going to stop her. Probably she hasn't any idea who the blonde is, but she is certain there must be one. It must be a blonde. Possibly Hubby has given in too easily for her last new dress or a new radio. If you do not kick on what your wife wants, she is bound to be suspicious. She thinks there is something to cover up or else you would howl at the proposal to spend money.

The foregoing account may seem cynical, but the fact is that these are very real and very important problems both to patient and to the doctor. No one suffers more than the jealous woman. It is distressing to the doctor because it is an incurable state. Once the cause of the complaint is known his course is clear, but if he searches for some organic lesion his labor will be lost. The precursor of jealousy is usually self-pity; and this usually comes into evidence if searched for, because no one is more loquacious than the woman who pities herself. The difficulty from the doctor's point of view is that listening to details is time-consuming. Worse still, the patient may find the doctor is the only one who understands her, if he be too sympathetic. Many a doctor has lost his happy home trying to unravel such cases.

These are only in part medical problems. The complainers for the most part have too little to do. We have, or had in the past, the woman who is burdened with both childbearing and work, the other with too little of both. This is one of the things, like cancer, we can diagnose but seldom cure. In both cases much more could be done if the condition were anticipated and prophylactic measures instituted. Unhappily, the doctor cannot deal with such problems. The problem is ecclesiastical and legal. In the abstract the doctor should render a decision and then forget about it. Unfortunately, he must deal with such patients one at a time and perhaps through years and decades at that. Why do they not tell the clergy and the legal profession their troubles?

These women come with complaints suggesting some disturbance peculiar to their sex. This is by way of introduction, say like the young swain who introduces the evening's conversation by remarking how beautiful the moon is. Others mention other organs as the seat of their trouble. The stomach is the organ most commonly mentioned in office practice. There is much overlapping. Many women patients tell of some distress in the stomach, just to make the history complete. For instance, one patient in her history to an assistant described her stomach as the cause of a considerable part of her complaints. I asked her how long her stomach had troubled her. "Oh, just since this morning," was her reply.

In the study of stomach complaints one must estimate the intelligence of his patient. The stomach in certain strata of society means the front of the body. Better-educated persons means the upper part of the abdomen below the ribs with an indefinite lower border line. Others, when they say "stomach," mean stomach.

By stomach complainers is here meant those patients who blame their stomachs, though there is no direct relation to stomach disease. It can be said in a general way that when the stomach is really sick it does not complain. Therefore, those who come presenting stomach complaints are likely to have some other disturbances—in fact, anything but disease of the stomach.

One need have no compunctions in calling certain types of patients "female complainers," for that is just what they are. If they weren't females there would be no complaint. It is convenient for office practice mentally to catalogue them. They are a numerous group.

The most perplexing of them are the alimony hunters. They can be diagnosed at a glance by an experienced practitioner, even though they mention only their stomachs as the source of their trouble. They have faces that would congeal boiling oil in August. Their faces have as much expression as a Chinaman's. When one is confronted by a five-hundred-dollar necklace encircling a forty-cent face he may know that he is up against a real problem. They are not voluble but they are very emphatic and indefinite. They complain of gas, of some burning and discomfort after eating, all aggravated during the night. Some are wise enough to give a clear-cut history of ulcer. They give one the glassy eye. I am reminded of days on the farm. I learned then that whenever a cow kept her eye on me while I was placing my stool in position I was not going to get much milk but I might be kicked out of the barn any minute. I have often wondered why this type of patient comes to the doctor at all. Nobody can tell them anything and they know it.

Unfortunately, such a patient usually has a spouse who if kept as a work horse will pay bigger dividends than any alimony would amount to. But occasionally it is necessary to fake some sort of illness in order to squeeze out of him a fur coat or a trip to Florida. These cases belong to the neurologist and the wise doctor will suggest a specialist at the first meeting.

Some are crafty prenuptial gold diggers. No long sour faces for them. They are a cheerful lot, illy concealing the glee of a Nimrod who has just snagged big game. Theirs is not the exuberance of the amateur landing a first fish, because they are old campaigners. Theirs is the satisfaction of the experienced angler who knows exactly where to go and what kind of bait to use. This type, it is apparent, belongs in a lawyer's office, and it is best to tell them so. If for any reason it seems necessary to unharness such patients, a trivial procedure, the doctor should take the precaution to have present not only a nurse but two nurses and a stenographer.

Social mismates may be more difficult to figure out. They may have some of the attributes of those just described but the motif is different. In their own minds they have been unfortunate, unappreciated, mismated. In a word, Heloïse, the waitress, has married Clarence, the head bookkeeper. The patient is attended by a retinue of sympathetic female friends. No one can weep well without the stimulation of an understanding audience. The neglect is a sad one. George Ade depicted this type. Heloïse can sing and Clarence can write, but neither can convince the other of the talent—nor anyone else for that matter. The doctor knows the real trouble is that Heloïse, deprived of the exercise incident to her late calling, has too much idle time which she devotes to taking on too much weight. Clarence, on the other hand, comes to miss the graceful lines that deftly handed him his ham-and in just the right way just over his shoulder, and he loses interest in authorship. Here one must take care lest he overlook a real stomach disorder. The delectable dishes Heloïse was wont to place before his noncritical eyes were the product of the chef's skill. Mistaking the transportation line for the factory, Clarence may develop a real stomach disorder, attended by loss of weight, maybe an ulcer.

In such case the family doctor has the advantage over the specialist. He has known both *dramatis personae* since they were children and could, if called on, write the history of the case that started when Clarence began to take his nourishment at the Greasy Spoon, the well-known emporium specializing in home cooking, even though it were not so bad as all that.

The question is sometimes asked by the sociological wise guys, Should a girl continue to work after marriage? If you ask the family doctor he will enthusiastically advise, "Keep Heloïse pushing hash until she has a baby, twins preferred."

Obviously, in such cases one has to deal with emotional states chiefly. If there is a physical basis it plays a minor role. I have learned much about the management of such patients by recalling and studying the technic of the old revivals. The preachers of long ago had never heard of psychology or of social science, yet they were powerful persuaders. That they changed the course of many lives there can be no doubt. The drunkards ceased their drinking, at least for a couple of weeks; and there were many other evidences of improved conduct, until next pay day. Of course, some sinners changed only on the surface, but it helps some when people hide their cussedness. Hypocrites were often the by-product of these revivals, as well as the instigators of them.

The old revival is a thing of the past. The old type of preacher is gone; the terrible ravages of infectious disease are gone. A diphtheria epidemic was the best possible "build up" for a successful revival, and the old preachers were quick to sense it. Fear was usually a dominating factor and diphtheria antitoxin has done much to allay it. Oddly enough, no one seems to have thought of accusing us doctors of making the world irreligious, though we are obviously guilty. We do get a break now and then.

In cases where emotions play a part the astute doctor will consider them. Idleness is the thing that feeds the emotions. And here the cults serve a purpose. It is a mistake to condemn categorically things that attract human beings. Take a look and see what makes the world go round.

Sometime when I get time I shall establish two new cults. The one: "Every day I shall chew [the rag] faster and faster." This should attract maiden ladies of mature years. The other:

THE PATIENT COMES TO THE OFFICE

"Every day I get wetter and wetter." This should attract young mothers. I figure that these will prevent many people from drifting into a mental state that demands the sacrifice of some perfectly normal organ they imagine is the offending member.

The most irritating of stomach complainers are those who tell about vomiting. It is absolutely impossible for her to keep anything on her stomach. Perhaps she requests a "blood examination." I have already explained the conclusions we draw from this request. One starts out without one positive fact; the stomach is not at fault.

First of all you inquire her weight prior to the alleged onset of the stomach illness. Then you put her on the scales but keep her guessing as to her present weight. The weight is unchanged and it is no job at all to decide how much credence her statement regarding vomiting is entitled to. Many of these patients are actually sick; and it is difficult to say where self-pity ends and disease begins. A physical examination may reveal some anatomic anomaly: a goiter, a heart lesion, some pelvic disease. Anatomic evidences of disease are recorded but ignored for the present. They may have organic disease but that is not what ails them. And right here is where the specialist falls down. He treats the organic disease but does not cure the cause of the complaint. Blondophobia is an absolute contraindication for any but a lifesaving operation. For the time being, one must concentrate on the cure of the stomach lesion which does not exist. Does the doctor tell her she has no trouble with her stomach? Not if he is smart.

The patient must be individualized, the treatment depending on the type of patient. The younger women usually supply the greater number of complainers. You explain that the stomach trouble is due to nervousness. If there is any excuse for assigning the trouble to overwork, seize on that. The laziest person on earth is complimented if you suggest he is overworked. The mixing of genders in this description is deliberate and I would be insulting the intelligence of the reader to explain the reason for doing so. Suggesting overwork as a cause of complaint is always a safe lead. If her face lightens up at this suggestion one can give her full doses of bromides and ask for a later interview. If you cannot relax her face by this talk, and vomiting continues to be the dominant complaint, it is necessary to take her into the hospital. Explain to the nurse, out of sight of the patient but within her hearing, that the patient must have very small quantities of broth for a day and then be put on full diet. "If she vomits," you conclude, "get the stomach tube ready at once, for gastric lavage will be necessary." An empty gnawing stomach with threats of the stomach tube causes most of them to eat everything that comes within reach. Some of them actually must have their stomachs washed out: that is, if they have never before had the experience. It leaves very few of them with any heart for their act. Blondophobia, as stated, is incurable, but some of these cases are due to a negligent or a fugitive sweetie. These patients are curable because of the natural self-limitation of goo-goo eye disease and the perennial hope that a new sweetie will appear on the scene.

One of the most common type is the middle-aged woman approaching midlife. One can help her by helping her to understand herself. Explain that the stomach disturbance is a reflex just like the vomiting of pregnancy. In many of these cases the psychological apple cart is upset by the sundering of family ties. The children establish homes of their own and Mother is left alone again. With this her labors are lessened and she tends to take on weight from inactivity. Such a patient does well with sedatives and, after a few years, heads into a serene old age, particularly if she inherits a bunch of grandchildren to care for while their mother works in a restaurant. These women are well off if they have outside activities, such as memberships in the club for the study of the heathen Chinese.

Deserted women and widows are a different proposition. Instead of parading their troubles, they hide them. The grief is real and permanent, as are the physical complaints. They do not apply for aid but struggle along through weary years. I often wish the foreign-missionary-society ladies could find these women who live in the next block.

Another group includes women who are overfed and under-exercised. These cases are most commonly seen in those past middle life. Usually the children have grown up and established homes of their own and Mother has lost incentive to all exercise except that attending the consumption of food. These patients usually have ruled the home and its inmates so long that any suggestions looking to a change in their routine is welcomed only with a glassy stare. One explains that it would be well for them to limit intake by gymnastic exercises, the same consisting in pushing themselves away from the table when they think they are still ravenously hungry.

These patients complain of distention of the stomach. It is because they eat too much. They have difficulty in breathing, also because they eat too much. Quite commonly they complain of high blood pressure; and some do actually have it, because they eat too much. Some of them even suffer from it. If the doctor is in need of attentive clients he can increase his revenue by telling the patient that she has high blood pressure. He need not be more specific. The patient knows no more than we doctors about high blood pressure, but it is something that one can fix on. In rare cases in which management is necessary, it can be done without picturing the dire results of these conditions. That only makes matters worse. One can tell them that high blood pressure, in the absence of organic disease, is just one of those things and need occasion no alarm. The doctor then has done his duty without inconveniencing the patient in the least. Thereupon he anoints himself with his own self-approval and a pleasant time has been had all around.

The saddest class of all are those patients underdeveloped from birth. They are usually the product of heredity and not of malnutrition in childhood. Usually they come complaining of "dropped stomach" or an equivalent expression. They have had a "complete examination" elsewhere and the stomach lies in the pelvis and they seek relief. They are dysmenorrheaic and usually have had a "chronic appendix" removed; often they have had an ovary resected, and possibly the gall bladder drained, and, even yet, sometimes a kidney anchored. The stomach may be accused of anything under the sun. They are not sure if the pain is in the stomach or in the back—and topographically there is little difference. These patients are born to mourn.

It is not important what one does for them so long as he does nothing to them. Suggested: mild sedatives and a sympathetic explanation that the position of the stomach depends on the shape of the individual and has nothing to do with the complaints. Remind her that much of the work of the world has been done by frail persons. This is a safe line and one can produce historical evidence to prove it. Of course, there is something else needed besides being just physically under par, but no one ever catches one up on that. We all fool ourselves and there can be no harm in fooling others occasionally when it is for their good. As a matter of fact, if we all became suddenly truthful we would most likely wreck society. We must not think on those things. They are pleased to find someone who understands and appreciates their troubles and they will take your little pills years without end uncomplainingly. What the pills contain is less important than that they should be big and pink. By this means you keep them out of the hands of cults and too eager operators and so render them a real service.

This type may combine a degree of cussedness along with congenital frailty. She pities herself and demands everything for herself. This includes the resources and the man power of the entire household. From this class are recruited many of the most selfish persons in the world. They furnish tragedies too deep for stage or screen, which cannot be represented running their course in any given time, for they are matters of a lifetime and, so far as I know, they never die.

Some of these patients have a real malady. From these most of our migraines and neuralgics are recruited, so it is difficult to distinguish suffering from selfishness. Usually the husband is all devotion, drawing heavily on his own resources, both physical and financial, in order to administer to the patient.

Speaking as a male, it is cheering to note that many of these women never marry. If they do the result is sometimes tragic for the poor man who talked too much, or at least asked too many questions. I have known several victims who found relief in narcotics and many more who resorted to alcohol. One is disposed to excuse them because of their desperation. A case in point. The husband of a woman of this type had become a narcotic user because of the eternal nagging of his wife. One day the husband calmly told his spouse that he had his fill, that he was going away for good, but if at any time she should conclude to behave herself to send him a note. At the end of two weeks she sent a letter begging him to return, which he did. He died soon after, likely of shock.

Many of these cases could be cured and many more prevented if the husband had the understanding and courage to demand his rights. This is not easy, because the sweet young things get him going long before he wakes up. The easiest thing is to drift along. The wife goes to Florida for her health, and the husband takes the stenographer out to dinner for his health. Someone writes the wife and the fireworks start. It is a social and not a moral problem, certainly not medical.

The best cure for a neurotic woman is to marry a profligate and drunken husband. I have seen many cured either on the first or some subsequent gamble. I would not advocate kicking the nervous ladies around because it requires a finished technic to accomplish results. Just cussing them gets nowhere; physical measures are necessary. Friend husband must both get drunk and beat her up. The drunken state is required as an excuse in Wifie's mind for the beating. After Hubby becomes reasonably sober he says he is sorry and everything is lovely until the gong sounds for round two.

In most cases the husband suffers in silence. If one sees a patient half reclining while the husband diligently fans her with a toothpick or a postcard as she looks appealingly up to him, one has the diagnosis, and also, one may say, the prognosis. To do anything for these patients one must have an understanding husband. If anyone essays to write a drama on this subject it is necessary to have the husband die in his devotion to her. She mourns for him ever after. The facial expression of these women reminds me of a pup that has lost his bone.

In rare cases the husband has understanding as well as sympathy. With such a combination he can assist the doctor by taking presentiments of impending death from starvation with composure. I have known the suggestion of a steak at the Harvey House to stop instantly a persistent vomiting fit.

I feel that I must apologize for treating these things in an apparently cynical manner. The truth cannot be told and by treating the subject in this manner I leave space between the lines for those who understand. I am pleased to be able to state that the great, great majority of women will not understand what I am driving at. For this they should be profoundly thankful.

The psychology of these chronic complainers is a matter of general interest. The fundamental factor in many of these complaints is introspection, the next step is self-pity. They have the more abundant life thrust upon them by the simple process of matrimony. The more abundant life means a more affluent state than the recipient has known heretofore. The essential factor is that it be unearned. This more abundant life grows by what it feeds on. The more abundant life today becomes neglect tomorrow. To remain a more abundant life it must be increased.

The lack of it engenders a sense of neglect, self-pity, introspection. Starting from these simple fundamental problems it is possible to trace the progress of many of the complainers above enumerated in the abstract.

This state is not a matter for levity. These patients suffer and they suffer intensely. They are not malingerers. They are the victims of circumstances. Because these states are incurable prevention is important. It is only by emphasizing moral responsibility that the end may be achieved. The more abundant life can be achieved by honest effort to achieve something worth while.

My father chose as the text for his funeral sermon: "We sow in tears that we may reap in joy." That was his idea of how to achieve the more abundant life. It can be achieved only with palms down, as he viewed it. To hope to achieve it palms up leads to a moral breakdown.

Though women furnish the vast majority of these cases, their brothers are sometimes likewise affected. Of all the animals that inhabit the earth the neurasthenic male is the most pestiferous. His stomach complaints are notable but indefinite. His expression is that of a defeated candidate the day after election. We recently have had these, even in Kansas. In days gone by, when mustaches were standard equipment, one could spot these boys a block away. The mustaches dropped down, contra-Kaiserwise. The history is difficult to obtain. If one inquires whether or not the stomach pain radiates, "It certainly does," he says. And then enters into extended explanations of the various radiations, especially those to the occiput or the groin. He holds forth with enthusiasm. This question breaks the ice and the regular history of the sexual neurasthenic is showered on you. Once started on this line, the stomach complaint is forgotten. He uses his stomach merely as a respectable object of complaint, knowing full well that the real trouble is elsewhere. All lying is not done in divorce courts by any means.

I once asked a very wise doctor what he did with this class

of patients. He replied, "Send them to some man I dislike, preferably in another town."

The worried businessman often presents himself as a stomach complainer. He represents a large class of patients with stomach complaints without an organic basis. Quite commonly there is loss of weight in addition to epigastric pain, distention, and acid eructation. There is history of night pain. Kind of food makes no difference. There may be food and alkali ease. There is generally disturbance of sleep and quite frequently nervousness during the day. The apprehensive look, the epigastric pulsation, the general solidarity of the individual is sufficient to characterize these cases.

One can sense the business condition of the country by these cases. Immediately after the war it was the cattlemen. They were big-fisted men from the plains with stomachs that had laughed at sowbelly and beans from childhood—until the depression came. Then came the bankers with wobby notecases representing frozen assets reflected by their faces. Then came the millers. Speak understandingly to these men of business conditions and they will tell you that they have been under a great nervous strain synchronizing with their stomach complaint. A wily stomach specialist told me of a patient of his whose stomach condition could be foretold by watching the cotton market. If there was a big drop the patient would most assuredly appear for treatment. These patients respond to nerve sedatives and understanding.

This extended discussion of the experiences and vicissitudes of patients has been entered into for the purpose of showing that there are many complaints which are fundamentally not medical. Furthermore, if associated with some organic disease the correction of that affection will not relieve the patient of the chief source of his complaint. The patient goes to the surgeon, is operated on, recovers from the operation. To the surgeon it is a cure and he so records it. But to the family doctor it is a failure, because the patient returns to him again and again with the same complaint as before. These cases give the laity the idea that the operation was unnecessary. Perhaps so; we all know that such things happen to the best of surgeons, but usually the operation was justifiable though inadvisable at the time. Therefore, the family doctor advises against an operation because he knows the associated conditions which will not be removed by an operation, the facts that the patient will not reveal in the history. And if the surgeon should divine the true state of affairs it is by intuition, as it were, rather than by scientific investigation. This is what we mean by the art of medicine. It explains why working at the profession is called the practice of medicine. The doctor learns by practice what patients not to operate on.

These are things of plain everyday experience. There is a more intimate side to the exercise of the family doctor's field of usefulness which will be discussed in a separate chapter. The foregoing appear to me to be his most useful activities. He treats his patients as well as he is able, to alleviate their complaints as much as he can, and prevents them, in so far as he is able, from rushing into operations the results of which they cannot foresee nor comprehend.

I have always courted close contact with my patients. Such instances as the following delighted me. A woman, leading her small male offspring, rushed into the office and burst out with: "Say, Doc, Willie just fell off of the piano and hurt his arm. See if it's broken." A cursory examination showed nothing wrong. "It's all right. No charge," I said. Time about one minute.

Sometimes a joke will relieve fears at once. Two women, both chatting loudly, leading a small boy between them, rushed into the office of one of my assistants, an irrepressible wag. He was sitting with both feet on his desk and did not remove them when the cavalcade entered. The chattering women and the wailing boy made known that the lad had swallowed a penny. "Cut out the chatter," drawled the assistant, slowly removing one foot from the desk. "You'll get your money back. He's only hiding it from the income-tax collector." In a moment everybody was laughing at the joke and the patient was forgotten, and, so far as I know, the penny.

Sometimes one's jokes go awry. One day a lady led in a gangling male offspring of seventeen years, obviously an only child. He was long and very thin, a replica of his mother, a fact which she had not noticed. He did not click with the weight chart in the high-school athletic director's office and that worthy sent a note to the mother that Percy was underweight. She wanted to know the cause. A careful examination disclosed two reasons for his apparent malnutrition—his name was Percy and he inherited his mother's constitution. So far so good. She anxiously inquired whether it would be attended by any undesirable effects if Percy should practice on the saxophone. I essayed to relieve the tenseness of the situation by casually remarking that I could not answer with certainty because I did not know the neighbors, but if they were long-suffering they might not shoot him. Viewed from all angles I still believe that was a very witty byplay, but the mother had other ideas. She was very angry, in fact she was mad; and despite my explanations, retractions and hastily improvised compliments, allegedly complimentary to Percy, she remained so.

One meets situations that are nonmedical perplexities. One of my assistants was consulted by a refined, apparently intelligent woman. The diagnosis made, he proceeded to write out the prescription. She extended a detaining hand. "I not want your treatment," she said. "All I want is the diagnosis. God will cure me." "Remember the address," my assistant replied, "and if you are not cured by the Powers, come back and we will fix you up." One is at a loss to know how to deal with such cases. Of course, this woman thought the doctor sacrilegious. But from the doctor's point of view no organic lesion is ever removed by a mental treatment. The attempt to do so has allowed many curable lesions to reach an incurable stage. When only the patient is concerned one may argue that it is his right to do with his life as he pleases. This exemplifies the inconsistencies of both ecclesiastic and the civil law. Both countenance willful refusal of agencies that would rescue from death. But if the citizen uses a gun to attempt suicide, he is damned by the cloth and is promptly arrested by civil authorities. Those things are too deep for us doctors.

The following incident illustrates the difficulties we often find ourselves in. I was once confronted by a patient with an abdominal tumor which it was necessary to remove by operation. My audience consisted of the patient's daughter and a lady of generous proportions designated as a friend of the patient. During the course of the operation she kept chattering to the daughter: "Now you think you see something, but there is nothing there; you just think there is." This was Fletcherized unceasingly. Now when a surgeon is battling with a serious problem in operative technic he works at a high tension and may actually become irritable. This incessant chatter grew decidedly irritating. An unbidden thought entered my head that it was time to enter a counterargument. I slammed the tumor, a mass weighing about ten pounds, on the feet of my tormentor. As may be anticipated, the lady jumped. Also, she shrieked as she viewed her bloodstained stockings and shoes. I addressed the daughter with the refrain I had been listening to for a quarter of an hour. "Don't mind; there is nothing there. She thinks she sees something but she doesn't. She just thinks so." There followed then a profound silence.

These are attitudes we constantly meet in office practice, unhappily often associated with hopeless states. I try to view these things in an impersonal light. As long as it concerns the individual, I repeat, I can view any state of neglect with equanimity but when children are involved I cannot be so generous. The last death I saw from diphtheria came as a result of a denial that the child was sick.

The human being is a perverse creature. If those ladies troubled with the thought of interloping blondes would just say, "There is no blonde; I just think there is," and repeat this a thousand times a day it would at least keep them occupied. That is, after all, the real requirement. Here is one time they would be right in almost every instance and a prayer might relieve their pains. We hard-headed doctors can only conclude that the female instinct not only transcends their faith in Hubby but also their faith in prayer.

These situations and conditions are described here in order to show that many patients are better off in the hands of an understanding family doctor, though he may be somewhat shy on the latest laboratory examinations and the newest untried therapeutic measures. Many patients, for instance, are permanently injured by a false positive Wassermann reaction.

Whether these patients above referred to have had adequate medical treatment depends on the point of view. The fact should not be overlooked that such borderline cases may be actually harmed by extended examination, for this may fix the patient's mind on other symptoms of which they had previously been unaware and, in general, give them the impression that they are worse off than is actually the case. It will be a sad day for many not sick of body, but with a mental background, when or if the family doctor is replaced by the political clinic. No clinic can displace him in cases in which a human understanding is necessary preliminary to therapeutic efforts.

No one understands so well as the family doctor that a great part of human suffering is not due to organic disease. Really, the sufferings caused by disease are for the most part of short duration; many are not attended by any pain at all. The suffering of grief, whether it be due to circumstances beyond the individual's control, or if it be superimposed, endures throughout the years. It may be voluble or silent, but it is real. In the passing of the old family doctor these patients have lost their best friend, and their chief protector.

CHAPTER

7 —————

UNDERGRADUATE COURSES ARE VERY NECESSARY IN MEDICINE, as in any other branch of knowledge. We make large talk about the basic sciences, but after the student has submitted himself to them we do not tell him what he should do next. He is allowed to graduate in medicine without sufficiently realizing that the receipt of the diploma is but evidence that he is ready to commence the practice of his profession. He is not adequately impressed with the fact that his scientific years are but the barest introduction to the basic sciences which he must pursue after graduation if his preliminary work is to be of any real use to him. As a natural result, only a few young doctors do anything about the basic sciences except promptly forget what little they learned in the preclinical years.

After teaching pathology for thirty-five years more or less intensively I have yet to find a graduate sufficiently versed in this science to apply it to a clinical problem. He may emit simple pathologic platitudes, but while so doing his eye envisages nothing. The clinical years of the student's course are designed to teach him to use the tools he was supposed to have acquired in his preclinical years. He hears but little about the basic sciences, for the simple reason that the clinical teacher is unable to apply basic knowledge to clinical problems. It is the study of the art of medicine that occupies him from the beginning of the junior year until old age overtakes him. We hear much of the science of medicine but see only a little of it.

In order to acquire more basic work the young doctor must resort to graduate study. By graduate education, schools mean the studies one pursues in residence after the completion of the primary undergraduate course, a continuation of the same thing as it were. That is the university's notion of what graduate education consists of. It implies that you go back to school and get a little more of what you already have or have had. It implies study in residence under the guidance of instructors in an accredited school. That it may or may not lead to a degree is of no importance. Many schools now offer graduate courses in basic sciences either as such or as a preliminary to advanced study of clinical subjects. If the end sought is clinical, the preclinical subjects are all studied with the idea of forming a more extended basis for clinical study than is furnished by the undergraduate courses. If the student has a scientific career in mind, usually that of teaching, as a rule only one of the basic sciences is elected.

To the recent medical graduate the internships and the residencies are but a continuation of their clinical years in school. They learn to apply what they have already learned; their science becomes an art. Such studies, unless preceded or accompanied by study of the basic sciences, do not fulfill the requirements for graduate study.

Universities do not recognize graduate work unless it is done in residence. The reason for this is that but few students, unless under definite guidance, pursue a subject with sufficient definiteness and persistence to master any subject of a fundamental nature. But it can be done, though it entails greater effort than when done under competent guidance.

Even after the definitely planned graduate courses of three years or more now offered, the student, unless he gains momentum along a certain line and secures a vision of his own, will remain at just that point where this added course has brought him: that is to say, unless his studies have brought vision, the ability to do advanced work on his own lead, his graduate studies have been a failure even though done in residence. It is a mistake categorically to regard such work as research. To do research work one must have an idea of his own, a thing that comes to but few. As a matter of fact, when the graduate course is pursued to a sufficient degree to be rewarded with the doctor's degree in philosophy some such study is required. Theoretically, the candidate must contribute to the advancement of knowledge. The addition to knowledge, of course, need not be true but it must be original. The thesis required for such degrees, allegedly containing a new idea, is supposed to indicate that he will be able to continue in independent work after he leaves the university. This sometimes actually happens.

In contradistinction to graduate study as above outlined, postgraduate study, as the medical man regards it, is what he gives himself according to his own plan after he has taken up his life's task. He seeks no academic recognition and seldom troubles himself about new ideas. He converts his knowledge into understanding and his understanding into art and these find expression for his own personality and capacity. He may go far in his profession and never have an original idea in his life. He need not even acquire any new knowledge. Most of us know far more facts than we can intelligently use. This point is illustrated by a statement the great German clinician, Traube, was wont to make when the autopsy showed that a wrong diagnosis had been made: "The facts were there but we did not think right." To think logically from the evidence at hand is the ultimate aim in the education of the vast majority of medical practitioners.

This ideal preparation for a doctor as above outlined I carried from school. It was the product largely of two teachers, Jaggard and Fenger. I had in mind to do graduate work for a few years and then continue the same line of work as I built up my practice. This must needs consist of a thorough course in the fundamental branches of my chosen specialty. This plan had to be interrupted, for economic reasons, by several years of strenuous general practice as already recorded.

I realized that the details of the postgraduate course must depend on the material available. I figured that if the Fates were kind I would have forty years of graduate and postgraduate study. Most young men, according to my observation, are in too great a hurry to emulate the position, professionally and economically, of their older colleagues. Strong trees grow slowly.

That this is no recent idea on my part I possess documentary evidence. Many years ago I read a paper advocating the granting of degrees for graduate work in medicine. This paper antedated by some years the offering of such courses by any university. My idea was to encourage the study of the fundamental branches by men in actual practice. It has been my privilege to conduct a few picked students to a higher degree. More would do so if there was a little more spoon feeding on the part of established men.

While yet in medical school, due to the fact that one of my teachers talked much of the opportunities for study in Germany, I resolved that I would spend two years in that country before I was thirty years of age. My preliminary education having been devoted chiefly to the study of mathematics and classics, according to the old plan, to the utter exclusion of the biological sciences, it appeared to me that in order to prepare myself for needed graduate study a knowledge of biology would be necessary. I sought to remedy this defect on my own account and by correspondence course after I had begun practice. At that time a number of colleges offered correspondence courses in a variety of subjects. A number of universities of first rank still offer help to those who cannot study in residence, though this does not lead to a degree.

In my correspondence course I selected biology as a major and psychology as a minor. The work required was designed to be triple that required when done in residence; the idea was, I presume, that the influence of his teachers was twice as valuable as the work the student did on his own account.

In biology it was necessary to secure a certain number of butterflies. In order to save time I rigged myself a net with a ferrule on it which fitted on the end of an umbrella. The net I carried tucked beneath my vest. When I spied a specimen I needed I tied my horse to a fence post, hooked the net on the end of the umbrella and gave chase. The insect secured, it was placed in a cyanide bottle; the net replaced under my vest, I resumed my rounds of visiting patients, presumably with unperturbed dignity. A moving picture of those pursuits after butterflies would be a very interesting exhibition. Bugs were more easily secured but one had to be on the lookout; I accumulated a respectable collection of both, about two hundred of each—a ridiculously small number, of course, but enough to give me a fundamental knowledge as a basis for the study of the vertebrates. I felt much grieved when I discovered that mice had eaten the whole collection while I was entertaining myself with a case of typhoid fever. Each specimen had for me a personality.

These studies were carried on between my professional calls and between days for a period of four years. I kept my work hidden from the view of my patients as well as possible. I feared they might think I was wasting my time in trivial things if they knew how I spent it. One day, however, I inadvertently left a bug sticking on the usual long pin. An old farmer came in; spying the bug, he said, "Ah, Doryphora decemlineata," thus making the diagnosis for me. In other words, I had found a potato bug.

I soon found that the people, instead of looking askance at my studies, were amused; some even became interested in what I was doing. To illustrate, I was working on an absorbable bone button for the anastomoses of intestines. I dressed my dogs, after operation, in a plaster cast extending from the front to the hind legs. One of them escaped from the dog "hospital" and came downtown on an inspecting tour. I was horrified that the people should discover that I was operating on dogs. The cast I mentioned somewhat interfered with the usual dog amenities, but instead of my being censored for my activities the people got a tremendous laugh, very much to my relief. Sometime later I was called on to repair a gunshot wound of the intestine for a boy who had had a difference of opinion with a pal. The patient recovered promptly from the operation. The city marshal, who had supplied me with dogs, was very proud of this achievement since he had supplied the material for my studies. He was indeed entitled to a great measure of credit, for without his cooperation my studies would not have been possible.

An amusing incident occurred during this time. On a trip to the western part of the state, where I went to recuperate from a privately conducted case of typhoid fever, I found a well-preserved buffalo skull. I packed this in a box and on the way home placed the package on a seat in the depot. A sneak thief seized it and fled. One can imagine his chagrin when he inspected his loot. But I needed this specimen, for I had an excellent collection of bones as I was then studying Flower's *Osteology of the Mammalia.*

As noted above, I also studied psychology. Why I do not know, except that it was available as a minor to go along with my biologic course. I had the obsession as a child that I had a philosophic mind, but time has proved that it was a lamentably bad guess. I have studied books on psychology and philosophy at intervals during my entire life but without ever grasping a single fundamental idea. Of late years I have abandoned these efforts and have taken to the reading of detective stories in my leisure moments.

My struggles with things psychologic began early in life. When I was twelve years old a phrenologist came to our town and gave lectures and demonstrations. For a dollar he would feel your head and predict that you would sometime become a Congressman or a Senator. In those remote days this was supposed to be a complimentary prediction. My head did not get felt but my brother's did. He was supposed to become a governor but escaped by going into the lumber business. I did get hold of a book on the subject and found out that Webster's head differed in size and shape from that of idiots. This was supposed to be proof of the correctness of the phrenologic hypothesis. About the same time I acquired a copy of McGregor's *Psychology*. It had no back and twenty-five cents was the price asked, but as I had only a dime this was accepted in full payment. I pored long and hard over this book and learned just what one would expect a thirteen-year-old boy to accomplish.

So I welcomed a chance, in my correspondence course, to study psychology under guidance. Ladd, Wundt and Calderwood were the texts assigned. Ladd's *Physiological Psychology* was the principal book studied. The others were just to be read. I got along fairly well except with the chapter on the Presentation of Sense. That was a mystery. It did not seem to have any sense. I literally committed that chapter to memory but no light responded in my brain, or wherever it is psychology is supposed to register. One dark night, in making a call on a patient, I inadvertently fell into a considerable ditch. As my head struck the opposite bank, the meaning of that chapter came to me like a flash, revealed by the stars I saw from the impact. This experience confirmed my previous opinion that in order to understand psychology it is necessary to have suffered some serious head injury.

About that time I discovered that I must pass an examination in logic. When I had secured a copy of Jevon's *Logic* I had just ten days to prepare for the examination. I stayed with that book day and night, scarcely leaving it except when actually confronted by a patient. Most of the study was done in my buggy. The examiner was good enough to say that my paper was the best he had ever read. I mention this because it is an excellent example of intensive study of one subject. The general opinion is that such "cramming" has no value. That is not true. I liked that book and read it at least once a year for many succeeding years and this led to the study of more pretentious books on the subject, including John Stuart Mill. In reading medical papers I am still able to detect the fallacy when the author gets his conclusions out of line with the minor premise, as most of them do.

As a further preparation for my contemplated foreign study I gained what I thought then was a reading knowledge of French wholly by study in my buggy. I am sure my old horse learned the irregular verbs as I repeated them to him. In fact, it seemed to bore him. I pause here to note that what I acquired was a translating knowledge of the language, not a reading knowledge. There is a vast difference. German was the first language I learned as a child and I was ever after able to understand conversations—and sermons on those occasions when I listened. Feeling that I should have a knowledge of medical German, I subscribed for a medical weekly and translated a German book on the anatomy of the nervous system into English. It was a difficult task and the results were not brilliant. I discovered later that this book presented a most difficult and involved presentation of the language. I could scarcely have selected a more unsuitable book. I also learned a little Italian and Spanish. This was fortunate, for the first day I spent in Professor Virchow's laboratory he gave me a page-and-a-half article in Italian, which he requested me to read as a preliminary. It took a whole evening to translate it and the Professor gave a look of surprise when I presented him the translation. He was just trying me out.

When I began practice I was deeply in debt but I borrowed two hundred dollars with which to buy a microscope and microtome. I made diverse histological studies of available material. I recall making a section of a cat's spleen. The slide showed round collections of cells which looked to me like tubercles in the books. That shows better than anything else I can say how utterly inadequate was our course in histology and pathology. I knew that the cat had not been sick, and it became evident that I must find some source of pathologic material. So I wrote Dr. Zeit, then assistant to Professor Klebs, of Klebs-Loeffler-bacillus fame. He wrote me at great length, clearly setting forth the absurdity of trying to study pathology by correspondence. In a postscript he added that since I was so enthusiastic he was willing to try to teach me for a few months for twenty dollars a month. He sent blocks of tissue labeled by number each week. I made sections of these tissues, sent him slides together with my diagnoses. He must have learned a lot from the original diagnoses I made. The study of material so sent, though pitiably inadequate, proved of great help to me, for later when I applied for a laboratory space in Berlin I was asked if I was able to make sections. I replied, "*Yah wohl.*" This statement required a charitable interpretation which happily was accorded it. I have always felt the greatest sense of gratitude to Dr. Zeit for helping me through a very dark period. More than that, we established a friendship which lasted as long as he lived. He gave me much help in later years when I came to teach pathology. He was a sharp but always helpful critic.

While I was a junior student in the medical school I chanced across a reprint of an article written by Hektoen describing the appearance of a section of gut anastomosis as made by Dr. Murphy with his button. This excited my curiosity and I sought to make some sections too. I saw some very interesting bands, which later became the foundation for my theory of the formation of connective tissue. I made sections of the material obtained in my experimental surgery. Thus I had a problem before I had a degree, a problem that has been constantly in mind all these years and will be for a long time.

It was necessary to earn sufficient money to pay for a resident graduate study. After four years enough was saved and preparation for the start made. The amount was inadequate, but it seemed to be now or never. I realized that the preparation I had been able to make was pitiably deficient—but experience has taught me that such a feeling is inescapable. No matter what is done, the end is a feeling of disappointment. If one achieves his visions he never had a vision.

Though a period of study in Berlin was constantly in my mind, friends advised me to find out what was offered in my own country. So I wrote to my alma mater about research work on the peritoneum and in wound healing. My letter was referred to the department of zoology. The head of that department wrote me that he was not able to offer me work such as I desired, and suggested that I do an *Arbeit* on the embryology of the eye of the cricket instead. The relation of the structure of the eye of the cricket to practical medicine seemed remote to me. I wrote to the head of the department of anatomy of a large Eastern university. He expressed the opinion that the problem of wound healing could be approached only by the avenue of embryology.

While I was planning my European trip it was suggested that I prepare myself for teaching anatomy in my alma mater when I returned. Therefore, anatomy should receive special attention during my studies abroad. I may say in passing that when I returned from my trip abroad the views of the university changed and they desired a full-time teacher of anatomy. I had seen too much of practical medicine to care to take a full-time job. Hence I escaped.

On arriving in Berlin, with my family, I proceeded to the university and registered for the courses I wished to take. As was the custom, one took his registration cards to the various halls where the courses were to be held and the *Diener* assigned seats in the order of appearance. This seemed unnecessarily strenuous to my partner and me, so the next semester we went to the functionary who held the reservations and by paying a few marks were allowed to select seats and then present our cards and claim our seats at leisure.

The act of registering, as far as my academic work was concerned, was easy; but registering my children took several days. I may explain that when you register you give up your passport and receive a student's card. This student's card made the student immune from arrest for almost anything except major crimes. If a student got drunk and mixed up the steins and waiters' heads, a police officer would get the number of your card and report to the university that Hans Americus did in Karlstrasse 20 at 4 A.M. break a stein on Karl's headpiece. Then Hans was called before the university authorities. Likely the fine would be one mark, eighty pfennigs, to replace the stein. (This incident is fictitious in detail but true to life though based entirely on hearsay.)

After securing my student's card, I proceeded to the nearest precinct and registered my family. They refused to accept my student's card and demanded that I produce my passport. I went down to the university and related my predicament to the functionary. The secretary got red in the face and roared. He remarked something about thick-headed police officials who, he suggested, *"können den Teufel aufsuchen."* Then a faint smile lighted his face and he said, "How you say in America, you can take yourself to the devil?" So I returned to the police station and delivered the secretary's message in two languages. The police officer was very apologetic for having caused me all this trouble. He just wanted to be sure I had a passport.

Nor was that all. Returning from the university, I found an official document half the size of a billiard table—it looked like that—commanding me forthwith to come to the police station. The document stated also that the charge for the document was thirty pfennigs and the constable fees fifteen pfennigs, respectively 8 and 4 cents. I learned that the offense was that I had given the name of my baby daughter as Helen. Now, he argued that there was no such name. "Well," I said, "that was her name in Kansas but I am not sure even what my name is by now." There was a deadlock. An older officer was called. He explained to my contestant that Americans are a funny lot and when they try to say Helena they say Helen, because they are all tongue-tied. So the seance ended amicably.

After getting myself registered, I again sought opportunity to study the peritoneum. With considerable trepidation I approached Dr. Hans Virchow. His reply to my question as to whether I might do an *Arbeit* on the peritoneum was that no one knew anything about the structure of the peritoneum, but since I was interested he would be glad to offer me what direction he could. "What is needed," he concluded, "is someone who will live in the abdomen for twenty years and then write of what he saw." And so I was registered as a graduate student with Professor Virchow, doing a research on the peritoneum. Though a foreigner, I was given anything I needed in the way of material. I continued to work under his direction for two years, and since to date on my own account.

I still marvel at the kindness shown me throughout that period. He seemed to have my welfare constantly in mind. At lunch he would come to my desk armed with a rat-shaped zwieback in one hand and a cup of tea in the other and then proceed to discuss my work or, as was often the case, twit me about my ignorance of the English language and things American in general. When he discussed things scientific he invariably spoke German, but when he was in a facetious mood he spoke perfect English. He was fond of quoting poetry and then laughing when I did not recognize it. I once told him the only poem I knew was "Twinkle, twinkle, little star." He insisted that I recite it, so incredulous was he. He laughed uproariously when I could not get beyond the first verse.

He had the capacity of criticizing my work severely but he

always left encouragement. When I offered a new point he would counter, "Well, yes, it looks that way but what counter-argument can the other fellow make?" I discovered, for instance, that the so-called stomata, universally believed to exist as normal structures of the peritoneum, were artifacts. I could make them or not make them at will. Still he was playfully skeptical. Then I learned to make them out of egg albumen and silver nitrate on a clean glass slide. That, he admitted, would answer any argument. The so-called stomata have gone out of the literature.

I got a shock while studying this subject. Certain reactions were said to produce silver albuminate. I spent a whole day in the royal library and could not even find the word. I confided my difficulty to a fellow American who was doing a research with Professor Fischer, one of the greatest chemists of his time. He suggested I go with him to see his chief. I did so. When I stated my problem the huge professor chuckled and said, "There is no such substance; there cannot be." There, you see, was a word indicating a substance that was nonexistent yet had been in the literature for years. Pure assumption. Professor Virchow had a tremendous laugh when I told him. It confirmed so well his constant caution, "Don't believe all you read."

He was constantly bringing reprints or literary citations to my desk and expressing his interest in innumerable ways. He had no children and I am sure that for the time being I was his son. He remarked to a friend of mine near the end of my residence that he had never seen anyone so capable of intense and continued toil as I. I was always proud of my endurance; there didn't seem to be anything else to be proud of. I regret that I did not publish my *Arbeit* in German. I did not realize how much he desired it. It would have been a small compensation for the many favors he showed me. His constant caution—"Is it true?"—remains with me still.

After I returned home I continued the study of the peritoneum. I did much experimental work during my full-time teaching days. When my clinical work increased I was able to study the pathology of the peritoneum in the living. After some twenty-odd years I followed the advice of my old teacher and my two-volume work on *The Peritoneum* was the result. Though it did not meet the optimistic prediction of the Professor I had a thoroughly thrilling time doing it.

This research was conducted with the idea of offering it as a thesis for the doctorate in philosophy. Professor Virchow strenuously opposed the seeking of such a degree, because he said it implied that there was something higher than the degree of doctor of medicine. This degree, he strenuously maintained, represented the highest scholastic honor.

An interesting occurrence took place while I was studying the embryology of the peritoneum. I needed embryos. My co-worker volunteered to see what he could find. He went to the Women's Clinic and by the payment of a certain sum obtained from the *Diener* all the material on hand. The lot contained one hundred and seventy-six embryos, ranging from the smallest I have ever seen to one of five months. This material formed the basis of the study that appeared in my book.

With intensive work in anatomy in mind, I heard Waldeyer's lectures and demonstrations two hours a day for two years. Descriptive anatomy was covered in the fall semester and surgical anatomy in the spring semester. I attended clinics during the remainder of the day. All my spare time I spent in the dissecting room during those two years abroad. I had a key to the Anatomic Institute and could work whenever I wished. I spent several hours in the morning before the regular university work began, and the numerous holidays and the long vacations also I spent in the dissecting room or making slides of the peritoneum or of pathologic tissues. During vacations I sometimes devoted as many as ten hours a day to sitting beside a cadaver.

In my regular work in the dissecting room I came across a

ligament in the hip joint which was not described in the books. The Professor became interested and directed the custodian to give me all the hips I could dissect. He had preserved a number of simians which he placed at my disposal. After I had worked out the problem thoroughly and had come to the conclusion that the structure was necessary due to the fact that the genus homo had for a long time walked more or less like a man I discovered an excellent description in Latin written in a pre-Darwinian day. The Professor chuckled when I showed him my literary discovery. "Too much curiosity," he commented in a taunting way.

As an example of the thoughtfulness which he exercised for my needs the following will illustrate. One morning while I was going to my room in the Anatomic Institute at break of day, as I passed through a large room I was horrified to see a large lion lying on the floor. I retreated. What I mean to say is that I removed myself in great haste. On careful inspection from a distance I concluded the beast was dead. So I cautiously stepped past the huge animal to my room. When the Professor came he explained that the lion was killed in a fire at the zoo and he thought I might like to dissect his hip, there being no record of the structure of the ligament of the hip joint of a lion. I later published a paper on the ligaments of the hip joint.

Professor Waldeyer had the reputation of being the best teacher of anatomy since Henle. He drew pictures of the structures on the board and demonstrated them on the cadaver as he discussed them in his lectures. We were supposed to emulate him in the dissecting room. The need, he insisted, was for the student to develop a third-dimensional anatomy, to be able to actually see in the mind's eye the structural relations of the various parts to each other without effort of memory and without troubling to think of the names of the various parts. He contended that unless a surgeon knows his anatomy with this degree of thoroughness he is obliged to hunt around at each operation to see what comes next. That certainly is true; this needlessly slows the operation and is a fruitful invitation to infection. I once saw a good surgeon spend fifteen minutes dislocating a caecum. I have often wondered what he thought was lateral to it—probably a branch of the aorta.

Generally speaking, prolonged operating, as one so often sees it, is due to lack of anatomical knowledge, making the operator fearful to do long arm strokes and sharp dissection so indispensable to clean and rapid operating. The poky operators sometimes excuse themselves on the grounds of thoroughness. A couple of years spent in the dissecting room will save time in later years by increasing operating speed. Also—it is better for the patient. After all, it is just the structure the surgeon is afraid of injuring that he is most likely to injure. Pure native awkwardness, another cause of slow operating, can be largely eliminated by constant work at dissection.

The central idea in the teaching of anatomy in Berlin was to stress the practical phases of the subject. Things one would not see in practical medicine were ignored. For instance, I made a very careful dissection of the nerves of the arm, following each nerve to its finest detail. It was a good job and I awaited Professor Waldeyer's inspection with confidence. With a wave of his arm he roared, *"In allen Himmeln, weg damit,"* which was all the comment I elicited. He then explained that the demonstration of branches too fine to be of value to a practicing surgeon was worse than useless, since it obscured the presentation of the important structures. Just the same, a dissection I made of the sympathetic nervous system still reposes, I am told, in the museum along with the dissections of such anatomists as Schlemm.

This plan of teaching is quite a contrast to that presented by the biologists who teach anatomy in this country, very much, I am sure, to the detriment of those students who afterward become surgeons.

Though I taught nothing but dissecting-room anatomy after

my return I have always been thankful that the possibility of a teaching job led me to a more thorough knowledge of the subject than is acquired by most surgeons. I have never had to fondle a structure to determine what I had in hand nor to speculate on what lay beneath. Though I spent many hours in the dissecting room I feel that I have more than saved this time by the more speedy operating it has made possible.

While I was making these studies with Virchow I worked with Frederick Kopsch on histological technic, particularly as it pertained to the structure of the individual cells. This led to the use of many different kinds of dyes. The purpose was to see how the different cells reacted to the different stains. This is called tinctorial chemistry. I may say in passing that during this time I examined a number of goiters and noted that the colloid of the various glands I had at my disposal stained differently. I have continued these studies during the passing years and it resulted, after more than thirty-five years, in the publication of my theory of thyroid degeneration. Of course, no one understands this except me, but one must be patient. It took twenty years before I could get my fibrous-tissue theory published; in fact, not until the work was confirmed by a professor in an Eastern university. No one, it seems, trusts the veracity of a Kansan, unless it is about tornadoes and dust storms.

Aside from my studies in the fundamental branches, I saw many clinics while in Berlin. This included all branches of medicine except diseases of the eye. From the very beginning I made it a point to learn everything I could pertaining to medicine, including, I may add, a really extensive study of the history of religions. For instance, when I was doing general practice I learned to fit glasses. A knowledge of this branch apparently unrelated to surgery sometimes helps. If one finds a nice lady who is wearing almost plain glass with assertedly great benefit one thinks that maybe she does not need an operation. Also, while I was doing general practice I did what I could in the study of the nose and throat. In fact, I did every operation performed at that time involving this region.

Speaking of the nose and throat, an instance occurs to me. My pal and I registered for a special course on the nose and throat with the distinguished Professor Janzen, just because we both had the idea that a surgeon should know the entire operative field. There were forty-six students registered, all specialists except my pal and me. The students operated in turn. Janzen had a special technic and in turn the specialists failed. We got a bright idea. We got a set of Janzen's instruments and bribed our way into the deadhouse and did tonsillectomies on the late deceased. We became expert after doing several hundred operations on the cadaver. When it came our turn to operate on the living, we went through the procedure without a hitch, using either hand *à la* Janzen. After watching us perform, the Professor did a flipflop and yelled, "Natural throat specialists!" and pled with us to abandon thoughts of general surgery and become laryngologists. Of course, we never told anyone how we had become experts. Silence was, in fact, a part of the agreement with the custodian of the deadhouse.

We did another like trick. Operative courses on the mastoid were done on temporal bones which were removed during routine autopsies. By deft persuasion on the part of my pal, we acquired eighty-eight of these, just forty-four apiece. By practicing on these we became so expert that we could expose the ridge that houses the facial nerve as it passes out, in three minutes, without ever exposing the nerve. We sprang this on Janzen too. He had another fit and at once urged us to accept assistantships with him. Of course, we were very modest about the whole thing.

My old pal has passed the Great Divide and I must hasten to say in his defense that he secured these materials in a perfectly honorable way: that is, by plain and fancy bribery. That was his part of the job. I accepted my share of the loot with sanctimonious complacency, because being more fluent with the

Kaiser's language it was my part of the job to work the professors. A line from Professor Virchow gained ready entrance to anything in town except the Kaiser's icebox, and we never thought of that.

I worked regularly eleven hours a day at the university. Usually four of these were devoted to attending surgical clinics chiefly with von Bergmann and Lexer. With von Bergmann I had a chance to make the slides of the material from the clinic. This was most valuable, because the Professor was a past master in surgical pathology and besides teaching me much he renewed the inspiration previously germinated by Fenger. He was a hard taskmaster and I can still hear his roaring at me: "If you had half an eye you could see it." He was, of course, right. With a single lightning glance at a slide he would turn to his audience and describe it in detail. I learned from him the fundamental difference between surgical pathology and the pathology of surgical tissues. Few specimens went from his operating room undiagnosed.

I spent two or more hours a day for more than a year on diseases of the chest with one of the best diagnosticians in Berlin. It seemed to me that a study of these organs was very necessary, no matter what one's future work might be. I learned to determine lung affections accurately. This experience served me well in after-years when I came to diagnosing and draining lung abscesses. I have never learned to determine heart murmurs; but, after all, if one can estimate what the heart is doing, or is capable of doing, he gets along very well in ordinary clinical work. At least, that is the ointment I used for salving my ignorance.

This course with Brandenburg illustrates how one might go about getting wanted instruction. One could start with the premise that just what he wanted was to be had. One must needs find where it was, this to be followed by getting it. Many of the younger teachers were open for private courses. The usual price was fifty marks a month each, for classes of ten students. We concluded after investigation that this was the man we wanted because he was Gerhardt's right-hand man and because he had available the great number of patients the Charité afforded. I approached him. Yes, he would take a class for an indefinite period at the rate above mentioned. At the appointed time my pal and I appeared and I handed him five hundred marks. "Where are the other eight students?" he inquired. "We are all ten," I replied. He was delighted. Pay for ten and only two to bother with appealed to him. It worked out as we figured it would. Being just the two of us, we would be given the run of the wards. We appeared at four o'clock and examined the patients admitted during the day. We were not allowed to ask the patients any questions. It was to be purely a matter of physical findings. We marked our findings on the patients' skin, my pal using one system, I another. This enabled our instructor to see at a glance the findings of each of us. The instructor came at six o'clock and examined the patients, as was his regular job, in order to pick out suitable patients for the Chief's university clinic. These examinations usually lasted until seven o'clock. The most interesting cases would be shown in the clinic the next morning. We could, if we wished, attend these clinics and learn what one of the greatest internists of his time, Gerhardt, had to say. If this did not satisfy us, in most cases we had but to wait a certain, or uncertain time, and then attend the autopsy by Jurgens. That was the ideal way of studying diseases of the chest. We kept this up for a year.

Following our usual plan of learning about everything, we studied dermatology. It chanced that Lassar's clinic on diseases of the skin was located near the Anatomic Institute and it was possible to attend these clinics at the noon hour by abbreviating or canceling our lunch. I continued this during my entire stay. The result was when I returned home I was able to diagnose almost any skin disease. In fact, I was more of a skin specialist than anything else, and I knew enough big words to start practice in that specialty but it had no attraction for me. It seemed to me that the practice of the specialty of skin diseases involved only observation and conversation. In fact, I had the idea, untrue of course, that one could practice dermatology very successfully if he could attach his optic nerves directly on his medulla, thus dispensing with what lies above. Of course, dermatology was a much more simple specialty at that remote date. Learning this branch consisted almost entirely at that time in looking and remembering.

My seatmate in Virchow's laboratory was Erich Hoffmann of Schaudinn-Hoffmann fame, discoverers of the *Spirochaeta pallida,* the cause of syphilis. He was the first assistant to Lessar, head of the syphilis hospital of two hundred beds. I had the chance to see a great many cases of this disease in that clinic. Osler has said that if one knows syphilis he knows medicine, or words to that effect. Be this as it may, one thoroughly schooled in clinical syphilis has small patience with those who are satisfied with the routine Wassermann test and are guided by the result.

The close relationship between professor and pupil as manifest in Berlin—namely, the chiefs bore affection to their assistants and, of course, the reverse was equally true—was a surprise to me. Two illustrations will suffice. The summer before I arrived in Berlin an event happened in the Alps that rivals the storybooks. Dr. Nasse, von Bergmann's first assistant, was climbing the mountains with a guide. Somehow both slipped and fell into a deep cavern, both hanging onto ropes. There was extreme peril. The guide said to Dr. Nasse, "We cannot both get out; your life is worth more than mine." With this he cut his own rope and fell to the bottom of the cavern. Nasse was dead when the searching party found him—but strangely enough the guide was hauled out alive. This is beside the point. Ever after when Professor von Bergmann had occasion in lectures to refer to some work his late assistant had done, he would say, "My recently deceased Nasse" in the most sentimental tones. Some years later I purchased a set of yearbooks in surgery. I was surprised and delighted to find on the flyleaf, "Dr. Nasse."

The other concerned Waldeyer. He came into the lecture room one morning, palely glanced about the room at the assembled students and began: "Gentlemen, I have to perform the saddest task that comes to a teacher, reporting the death of a beloved student. Word has come of the death of Dr. Steinbach." As tears rolled down his face he continued, "He gave up his life in Africa for the glory of German medicine." With this he turned his face to the blackboard and began to draw furiously.

I got a touch of the kind consideration these famous men had for their students. After I had attended Waldeyer's lectures for a year he called me into his office to tell me that he noted that my eyesight was defective. Therefore, he had reserved seat number one in the pit, seats usually reserved for the army officers, the best seat in the house—within a yard of where the Professor stood while lecturing. When the lectures began I was in seat one in plenty of time. Soon half a dozen army surgeons in full uniform came in, swords clanking. They formed a circle around me and looked fierce. I noticed nothing, because I had a card for seat one in my pocket. They were still standing about me when the Professor came in. He said a kindly good morning to me but did not notice the officers. Their feathers subsided at once and they took to their seats. But during the whole semester they spent their spare time glaring at me.

No American teacher ever showed me the many favors that many of these German professors did, me a poor scared foreign kid. To them there was no nationality, just somebody who seemed anxious to learn. That was enough. And at that the total cost in the laboratory was just sixty marks, about fifteen dollars a year. Everything furnished except the absolute alcohol used in making slides. At the end Waldeyer offered me an assistantship in anatomy and Virchow urged me to abandon the idea of becoming a surgeon and to stick to my researches. "A man with ideas should not waste his time treating the sick. At best, sometime the patient will die. Truth is eternal," was his admonition.

All in all, it was a glorious experience. In twenty-four months I missed working in the university six Sundays, just gadding around; and one weekday I was sick. The climate was ideal for working, always cool, though usually cloudy.

In thinking over my experiences in Berlin, I have the memory of having heard some of the greatest men of all time. What they talked of was in the books, but there was the stimulus of personality. Most of them were between sixty and seventy years of age. They were all working full blast. Waldeyer was studying anatomy more intensely than anyone in the Institute. Litten still hoped to determine how blood corpuscles were formed. Virchow, though eighty years old, still reached his laboratory in the early morning and still labeled all the specimens with his own hands. The memory of the intensity of their labors in their maturer years is a good stimulus now. They all worked until they died. That after all is the final test of the degree of interest in one's work. Professor Hans Virchow once said to me while I was laboring with an exasperating lymph-vessel injection: "He who has never shed tears over his work does not know what it is to try."

The material of all kinds was abundant, the library facilities adequate.

One thing impressed me—that what one got out of study depended on his own efforts. Material and books were not the whole thing. This is as true of the *Geheimrath* as of the country doctor. Labor incessantly from now on.

Then the journey home. The Statue of Liberty was the most fascinating sight I have ever seen. I can say with the returning soldier: "If the old gal ever sees me again she will have to turn round." One incident irritates me. A friend returning from Europe before I did was charged duty of a considerable amount on each slide. I had accumulated a large number of slides of things anatomic and pathologic. I could readily figure that if I were charged the same amount I could never get them home. So I selected a few slides of surgical pathology and abandoned the rest, many thousands of them. When I reached the inspector's office I learned that there was no duty on slides one made himself. Also my microscope and some five hundred books were duty-free, being all in foreign languages.

Having thus exposed myself to two years of graduate study, I returned home with a lot of added knowledge but with little that could be called my own. It all had to be made over again.

After ten years of medical study—four of undergraduate, four in general practice and two in Berlin—my school days were ended and I was nothing more than what could be charitably called a "promising young man." A career in surgery was a vision, a hope, nothing more. Undergraduate days, graduate days were over and from then on it was to be postgraduate study of my own designing. Nobody to feed me knowledge: no specimens, no patients, no books and considerably less than no money. All these I would have to find when, where or if I could.

CHAPTER

8 _____

IN CONTRADISTINCTION TO GRADUATE STUDY AS WE DOCTORS regard it, wherein one is guided by some institution, postgraduate study may be defined as that which one does on his own initiative. The term is most commonly applied to short courses of a month or so spent at a school designated as Postgraduate. Newspapers are prone to use the term "research." For instance a friend of mine spent three weeks in the Maine woods and stopped on the return journey in New York a week "to do research" according to the local sheet. In a broader sense postgraduate study includes all study, whether done at an institution or on his home grounds. It begins when he leaves school and lasts from then on.

We may pause here to inquire what is the present attitude of the medical profession toward the manner in which the aspiring surgeon should go about preparing himself for his specialty. It has been a process of evolution and the tracing of its development may be of interest.

Certain associations of literary colleges require that in a member college a certain proportion of its teachers must have doctor of philosophy degrees. That is, the college must ape the university even though the functions of the two are quite different. A good teacher cannot be measured by his degrees, for ability cannot be standardized, hence something else must be selected that is capable of measurement. Medical schools are imbued by much the same idea, standardization.

There are three essentials for the physician's postgraduate study: material, books and the will to do. Material, his patients, will come in far greater numbers than he can possibly utilize. Books are now available to everyone no matter how far removed he may be from medical centers. They are of importance in inverse proportion to his experience. The last named, the will to do, is by far the most important essential because it automatically brings the other two. But it is a gift of the gods.

There is no standing still in medicine. The young doctor soon finds out that much of what he learned in school turns out to be premature, that it does not stand the test of time, or that it has no place in the field of practical medicine. His stock of knowledge turns out to be largely counterfeit. Time eliminates the nonessentials. Many things which were useful in the beginning of the young doctor's career, such as an understanding of drugs or technical procedures, are in time superseded by new knowledge. Only an exceedingly small part of this can be supplied by schools and teachers. The great bulk must come from his own study of the patients that pass him day by day. If knowledge so obtained is properly assembled, intelligently classified and if logical conclusions are deduced therefrom it may have a real graduate importance far exceeding the usual university course.

Never has the progress in medical knowledge been so swift as during the period of my activities. The advance has been so rapid that no one has been able to keep up with more than a small part. The old measures have been superseded by something different, if not better, that, as I figure it, by the time I have ended my period of activity I shall come out about even. It is as if some legislature repealed all the established laws which a lawyer had studied and followed in his practice.

I EDUCATE MYSELF

History shows that as knowledge has increased some men have collected the new facts along a certain line and have become specialists. It is often argued that as the old specialists had a background of general medicine all specialists should begin in general practice. But the reason the old timers did not begin as specialists was because there was no special knowledge. That was developed as the men extended their knowledge and it was the development of this knowledge that made specialization necessary. To argue therefore that the specialist now should begin with general practice is as reasonable as to say that because I began with horse and buggy, instead of an automobile, others should begin with horse and buggy and work up through the Model T to a Packard.

It is argued that experience in general practice was valuable to the specialists because it offset any tendency to an unduly narrow viewpoint. Thus a backache indicates to an orthopedist something which requires a cast or brace. A gynecologist will suspect it indicates need for a pelvic operation. But one with a general experience will first think of lumbago. There is a measure of truth in this, but it applies only to those who make their diagnosis by exclusion. A specialist who recognizes the positive lesion before him is not likely to fall into this error. A specialist who sees in every complaint something that belongs to his specialty is simply not a good specialist. A good one is able to say that he does not know what the trouble is but that it does not belong to his specialty. This is the best type of specialist. He makes his diagnosis from positive findings and not by exclusion.

Most commendable efforts have been made to classify the specialties. Specialists inspect prospective specialists and brand with their approval those that qualify. That is a standardization that has some sense in it. In other words, instead of a man waking up some fine morning and declaring that he is a specialist, as has been the method in the past, he goes to a group of specialists and has himself inspected in order to see if he is a specialist. If he qualifies the public may be assured that he is really pretty good and worthy of confidence. The violin maestro recognizes a promising violinist, and separates him from the fiddlers. That is quite in a contrast to the policy of hospital standardizers. They would look at his fiddle and ask the price and base their approval on that. What else could they do, not knowing how to play themselves?

Even after a modern medical course, including an interneship of a year or two, the making of a doctor has just begun—at least no more than begun, maybe not even begun. Not all eggs hatch. One of the most learned men I have ever known was a total failure in practice. He lacked the ability to see or feel, and he took his own life after seven years of disheartening failure. He should have been a professor. Then no one would have noticed these defects.

What the student has acquired, even at best, is merely knowledge, and a long process is required to convert it into understanding. Knowledge gained in school is largely abstract and its application is not always concrete. He learns much of percentages of cases in school but he deals with them one at a time once he gets into practice. Our professors are too prone to regard only the abstract as scientific. Yet the study of one case at a time may be as scientific as basic abstraction. It may be said in passing, however, that the knowledge of percentages has its value. As Billings used to point out, given a case which resembles several diseases the wise doctor tentatively diagnoses the more common. It is generally recognized that the beginner is likely to diagnose rare conditions, living testimony that such have been overemphasized by his teacher.

The greatest defect in our educational system, however, is the failure to bridge the gap between the scientific and the clinical years. After the examinations are passed, the subjects of these years: chemistry, anatomy and physiology are relegated to oblivion by the student because he notes that a clinician whom he strives to emulate seems not to have any use for them. The chemistry of the bedside is delegated to laboratory technicians. Pathology, if referred to at all by teachers of the practical branches, is mentioned in a vague way suggesting a lack of living familiarity. Since the clinical teacher is obviously not conversant with these branches the student is not likely to be much impressed by their importance. He sends his pathologic material to the laboratory, just as his teacher does, and he sees it no more. As a result the student soon forgets the little he learned in the preclinical years and it becomes merely a "cultural" subject, no more a part of his clinical thinking than the irregular Greek verbs of his academic days.

We speak much of scientific medicine. Just how scientific is scientific medicine? In days gone by the young doctor entered practice immediately after graduation. He saw the various diseases and learned a little. He saw more cases and learned more. He advanced in proportion to his natural capacity for observation and to his stock of horse sense. Anatomy and pathology, so far as he was concerned, were nonexistent; they never had been. Only in this did he differ from the graduate of today. The young graduate now acquires practical knowledge in exactly the same way. The fundamental branches have nothing to do with his subsequent advance in practical knowledge. He did not learn enough in the first place and he long ago has forgotten what little he did learn. This is in a measure a confession. After teaching pathology for more than thirty years I know of not one of my students who has ever used his knowledge of pathology in the practical branches in his later clinical thinking. The reason is obvious. They never learned enough pathology to make it possible for them to use it. Don't blame the teacher. The time is too short to make it possible to acquire anything worth while. What little the student knew was largely memorized to pass the examination. This achieved, everybody was happy. I nearly got kicked out of my job once. The students had had so little chance to learn anything that instead of going through the farce of determining the density of the vacuum by means of an examination I took the whole class to a ball game. The Chancellor heard of it.

In a word, a doctor learns medicine just as an Indian learns to track, that is by tracking. If the Indian were scientifically educated he would start by learning the anatomy of the feet of the various animals and the physiology of mammals in the act of walking. He would learn the geology of soils in order to estimate the degree of imprint an animal's foot would make, and the botany of trees in order to learn their friability on contact. By the end of such a study he would have so injured his eyes that he could not see any tracks. But he would have the dubious satisfaction of knowing he was a scientifically educated tracker even though he could not track an elephant.

That most first-class practitioners attain skill by studying cases and ignoring the scientific branches is exemplified in every section of the land. One might be embarrassed if required to show wherein these men are less capable in a practical way than those who do occupy themselves with the fundamental science. I for one could ill afford to essay such proof. Most of our able surgeons do not use the fundamental sciences in their clinical work. Perhaps such knowledge is of no use. It would seem so. However, I have heard surgeons say many times that could they live their lives over again they would study surgical pathology. Bridge and golf do not mix with the study of surgical pathology. One must give up something. Be this as it may, by neglecting the fundamental branches they miss most of the fun in the practice of medicine.

Certainly he who wishes to acquire class as a specialist must first acquire knowledge, the fundamental knowledge, of his field, the anatomy, the physiology and the pathology. The special field is not so large but that this is possible, but those engaged in general practice cannot hope to acquire basic knowledge in all branches.

It is said that imitation is the sincerest flattery. So many men pretend to know pathology who do not know it, that there must be a subconscious conviction that it is of value. I once knew an eminent surgeon who emitted platitudes of pathology, and had in some circles of the profession a reputation as a pathologist, but as soon as he opened his mouth, which he did most handsomely, it was at once evident that he had not the slightest first-hand knowledge of the subject. During operations he never once referred to the subject with tissue in hand and once it left the operating room he saw it no more.

If one must summon his will in order to study his material it is an impossible task, but if one thinks it is fun it has an irresistible appeal. Some surgeons have a queer notion as to how a knowledge of pathology is acquired. The general notion is that they will vicariously become surgical pathologists if the hospital where they do their work has a good pathologist. The standardizers think so too. Still more ridiculous is the man who thinks he can borrow a few mounted slides and thus acquire a science. One young man came to me with the statement that he had come to realize the importance of surgical pathology to the surgeon; he asked me to lend him a lot of slides, say twenty-five, so that he could study them and thus become a pathologist. He still thinks he is a surgeon.

But the new scheme has its drawbacks. Those who attach themselves to an experienced practitioner or to a clinic are influenced by the abilities and deficiencies of their chief. The young surgeon learns the technic practiced by his chief, usually in a routine way, it being a process of memory rather than one of reason. It is amazing how long a young man can watch one certain operation without knowing what it is about, meanwhile wholly ignoring the anatomy of the region and the pathology of the tissues involved. The chief knowing nothing about pathology obviously the student hears nothing about it. Thus he will at best become nothing more than a mechanic like his chief.

Postgraduate work is essentially personal effort, regardless of environment. Unless the student puts forth effort on his own initiative his advancement ceases with the acquisition of technic. It is not recorded that anyone ever became a great botanist by simply sleeping in a greenhouse, but it is supposed to be possible for a prospective surgeon to become a great surgeon by sleeping in the operating room. Somehow the hard and fast rules set down by those brain trusters just do not make sense.

I know one surgeon who will not consider a candidate for assistant who has not had special training in anatomy and pathology for two years. This is a gesture which seems to satisfy the said surgeon. Does one with such a viewpoint insist that his subordinate continue to increase his knowledge of these subjects beyond the two years? Unless the chief is actually and continually engaged in such studies and is thus able to lead the way, he merely fools himself and his assistant; his precept is useless. As this surgeon's plan worked out, a candidate who desired to become his assistant spent two years in a pathological laboratory in order to qualify for the job. And there everything stopped. No one ever learned any pathology in two years.

Some specialists of the highest order devote part of each day to such study. I knew one nose and throat specialist who spent two hours each day, for more than twenty years, studying the anatomy and pathology of his field and at the time I was his student he was still hard at it. As a matter of fact after a man has followed this plan for a score of years there is no way to stop him. He has discovered what real fun is.

This brings us up to date. The prescribed plan now for those who wish to specialize in surgery is to enter a clinic, or at least to attach themselves to a busy surgeon, for three or five years. Near the end of this service they are supposed to do operations under the immediate supervision of their chief. This does very well in free clinics but has its difficulties for surgeons who devote themselves to private practice. This is the simplest plan and likely the ideal plan. Not all students who desire to become surgeons can follow this plan. Perhaps it is a good thing. Perhaps us old fellows who of necessity followed a less ideal plan serve as horrible examples for the brain trusters in the argument for their scheme.

No matter, effort and merit will soon become a liability. Hospital attendants will be selected according to approved political methods and surgeons will become glorified shovel cleaners.

We now proceed to the examination of my own experiences in graduate study. After spending two years in Berlin, where I was fairly swamped with material and opportunity, I returned to Kansas where there was nothing at all to work with. My ears became worthless appendages: there was nothing to hear. This was quite a shock after having had distilled wisdom poured into them for two years.

At this time the devil sought me out. I was offered the chair of Professor of Anatomy in one of our large universities. After long consideration it became obvious to me that where I belonged was in the wide-open spaces from whence I came. I was smart enough to know that the odor of saddle leather would never leave me. So I wisely resolved to fight it out alone.

My study abroad had provided me with a nice bunch of intellectual tools. I had learned laboratory technic in all its branches, particularly that used in the making of microscopic sections. Some of my slides still are on exhibit in the Berlin museum. I had also learned about books and their uses. I was now confronted with the necessity of getting something to study with and about and then planning a course of procedure.

Postgraduate study in surgery was a much more perplexing problem. For the study of surgery, patients are needed. For the acquisition of a surgical practice, a very necessary element is patience. There is nothing more necessary while one is waiting for patients. One must learn to "labor and to wait." In order to study surgical pathology some patient must give up something, ante or post mortem, that one can section. So this phase of my study had to wait. My studies on wound healing and the peritoneum were unfinished business and I at once proceeded to continue them. I had brought much undigested material home with me, slides and books, and I began again an intensive experimental study of the processes of wound healing which had occupied me at intervals for a number of years. Kansas may run short of almost anything but never of rabbits and cats. I repeated my studies on the formation of fibrous tissue once a year for ten years before I sought to publish the results of my work. As noted in the last chapter, no journal would publish them until years later.

Fortunately I soon had a large general practice and was favored with gradually increasing consulting practice. I had an able assistant who did much of the country work, so that my team and buggy days were largely over. Train travel took its place. Because of this traveling hither and yon I saw some very interesting and unusual cases and now and then I found a patient docile enough to allow himself to be operated on by me, particularly if he had no money to command a more experienced surgeon. Money or no money, if I got a specimen I felt repaid. Hereon hangs a joke which I still hear from the old-timers. The story has it that I had operated on a patient who yielded an interesting tumor. This was placed in my instrument bag and left in the lobby of the hotel. When I returned from the dining room the bag was gone. The bag contained instruments to the value of more than four hundred dollars. It is alleged that in consternation I exclaimed that my specimen was stolen, the joke supposedly being that I thought of the tumor and not of the instruments, which, of course, was no joke at all— just a different sense of values. I could buy more instruments but the specimen was priceless. I recovered both. A traveling man had taken my bag by mistake and he was glad to return it when he found therein a ten-pound hemorrhagic myoma.

Located as I was in a town of a thousand population, it was obvious that there was little prospect of obtaining surgical material with which to continue my postgraduate studies. While I was pondering possibilities fortune came my way—the offer of a position as teacher of histology and pathology in the University Medical College of Kansas City. The job actually was offered me: I would not have had courage to apply for it. Dr. Cordier knew I had been abroad and presumably had acquired some knowledge. He probably figured that anything the school could get would be better than what they had: to wit, nothing. Therefore, as I knew the predicament the school was in I was not unduly puffed up. This acceptance of an untried kid to head a department shows how pitiably inadequate was the teaching of the fundamental branches in the proprietary medical schools as late as 1901.

I was to give full time, five or six days each week, to teaching. The salary was to be fifty dollars a month, which happened to be just what the school janitor received. In fact, the faculty regarded me as just a little above the janitor in scholastic standing: that is, they did at first. I was the first full-time professor in this part of the country. That is something for the grandchildren. I sometimes had Saturdays and Sundays for myself in which to earn what I could to add to that measly fifty dollars. I spent these two days at my country practice and in starting my "hospital," the pitiable tale of which is related elsewhere.

Even though it was insignificant I was delighted to get the job, because the hospital connected with the school would provide specimens for study. It provided not only surgical specimens but also a surprising number of autopsies according to bed space. This gave me a splendid opportunity to see what surgical patients die of and as a direct result I learned much about what things not to do, the crown piece of the surgeon's education.

My laboratory was next door to the dissecting room to which I had ready access. Too, I hoped the lecturing to students might relieve a congenital case of tongue-tie. Possibly it helped a little.

Here I taught in turn, or simultaneously, histology, bacteriology, pathology, experimental surgery, gynecology and ran the dissecting room for two years. I taught or prepared material ten hours a day. I had to prepare the sections of the students as well as to demonstrate them to the class. I divided the class into two sections in order to facilitate personal instruction. In order to accomplish this more easily I wrote manuals on bacteriology and histology which proved to be a great help. In writing these booklets I got the smell of galley proofs from which I have never recovered. While dissecting was in process, two hours were added to my day.

If one wants to know how it feels to be slow of speech all he has to do is to try to teach a bunch of howling medical students. Lecturing was impossible for me, so I assigned lessons in the students' textbooks and quizzed from these. I knew what was in the books but to talk it off in the then approved style was beyond me. I was too smart to be dishonest and I made no attempt to pretend to know what I did not. Therefore, my students and I became in fact, much more than they realized, just fellow students. Despite their inadequate teaching, most of them have become able practitioners. I still prize their loyal friendship gained because I was honest with them; certainly I had no other asset.

In this new position I had an abundance of all sorts of surgical material obtained at operations and at autopsies at the college hospital, as well as material from surgical operations performed in other hospitals and from autopsies performed for the coroner and private practitioners. I learned that the position one occupies is not a matter of knowledge one himself possesses but of comparison with others: that is to say, a relative thing. An involuntarily silent tongue also is a great asset when one has nothing to say.

I continued my full-time teaching job in this institution for seven years. Though I received only fifty dollars a month for my long hours of labor it was a very valuable experience. I had material to work with; that is, I was conducting my own graduate school. Of course, I was ill prepared in the beginning for teaching the branches mentioned above; but each year I was farther and farther ahead of my classes and could face them with less fear.

The students were of all ages and previous conditions of servitude—butchers, barbers, bricklayers, reformed schoolteachers and clergymen. Living with them in the laboratory much of the day, I learned to know them well. The fine regard these boys have favored me with down through the years is still a constant source of pleasure and a magnificent reward for doing my best for them. Though there is no evidence that any of them remembered any of the pathology I tried to teach them, they seem to have remembered all the jokes. My stories at least must have been good.

In the dissecting room it was another matter. Here I had a thorough preparation and I did my best to follow Waldeyer's methods of teaching. The usual period in the dissecting room was two hours a day. I asked for four hours. The dean was very skeptical. If the student could not be pacified for two hours, as had been the experience, four seemed hopeless. Nevertheless, my argument won and soon the janitor had to complain that he had difficulty in getting some of the students out of the room at nine o'clock. My teaching was practical. I made them see that they were doing the first steps in practical surgery and they liked it. I knew every student thoroughly and paired the good students together. Those who did not wish to learn I ignored and concentrated my efforts on those who were anxious to learn. They rewarded my efforts by making some of the finest dissections I have ever seen.

Along with my teaching I continued my experimental work, notably in the study of the rate of absorption from the peritoneal cavity. Being myself at the time a victim of pulmonary tuberculosis, I made extensive studies of this disease. I induced it in the peritoneum of guinea pigs and then studied the effect of various agents on the progress of the disease, notably the effect of air and bile. Nothing came of it.

My teaching position brought me some autopsies and as a consequence demands to testify in court. I learned that the game is to cause you to swear that you will tell "the truth, the whole truth and nothing but the truth," and then the lawyers battled to see to it that you did not do any of the three things you were under oath to do. But it was a lot of fun. Unfortunately for the lawyers I was not so dumb and timid as I looked. I soon learned that if I played the smart game they played with me it was all right with the judge. One thing one could count on in the beginning of cross-questioning: I never used any money I received as an expert witness for my own use. I gave all the fees to Mercy Hospital because I wanted to make sure I would never testify for money. It was a common practice with lawyers to make the jury feel that the medical expert was to receive a large fee: therefore, the testimony must of necessity be prejudiced. I would parry with the attorney as long as I could draw him out. Then I would offer to make a pact with him to give the hospital above mentioned the whole fee each of us received, adding quickly that it was my practice invariably to do so. Of course, an assistant lawyer would move "strike out, incompetent, irrelevant and immaterial." But the jury got a laugh and somehow no lawyer seems to like to have a jury laugh at him. Lawyers have a small sense of humor.

One instance may be mentioned. I was testifying in a notorious case. The opposing lawyer was a very able man, large of physique and positive of language. When he came to cross-question me he walked near the witness stand and fairly bellowed his question. I looked at him calmly a moment and then placed my hand behind my ear and meekly said, "A little louder, please." Everybody bellowed with joy. The lawyer was so mad he sank in his chair and his assistant had to follow up the cross-questioning. The morning paper had a headline: "Prominent attorney did not scare the modest young doctor."

Another prominent attorney once became peeved at me for insisting that the nursery yarn of the cow jumped over the moon violated no rule of logic and was as plausible as the point he wished to establish: to wit, that a plump lady could produce a displacement of the uterus by sitting down in the vestibule of a streetcar. The judge allowed us to wrangle quite a while and then said to the lawyer: "You asked the question and I would suggest you allow the doctor to answer it, as he seems determined to. And then we can all go home to supper." My idea was that inasmuch as I was not permitted by any lawyer to tell any part of the truth I retaliated the best I could by keeping him from establishing something that certainly was not true.

As I became busier I came to avoid court service as being too time-consuming and the labor of avoiding the traps of clever lawyers too exhausting. Besides, it is not particularly edifying to have the average jury ponder on the correctness of the conclusions of a medical witness. At the same time one cannot blame them, for there seem to be doctors available for testifying to anything a lawyer may wish them to do.

About this time, without any provocation on my part, a prominent publishing house invited me to write a treatise on tumors. Naturally, I was flattered at the suggestion and started to work with enthusiasm. In fact, enthusiasm was all I had. There were no books available; nobody had a library. No one had heard of borrowing books from the Surgeon-General's library as I later learned to do. Books I had to have.

At this time the first automobiles came into use. Many of my colleagues bought machines. I reasoned that in due time these contraptions would collapse and all they would have would be a headache. So it proved in about a year. Instead of following their example, I concluded to buy myself a library. So one evening I ordered from a foreign catalogue many thousand dollars' worth of books, mostly complete journal files. I had not the remotest idea where the money would come from with which to pay for them and in due time the firm that sold the books to me began to wonder even more distressingly than I. But I did pay for them ultimately. Thus recklessly I acquired the second requirement for graduate education—books.

In the writing of the tumor book, pictures were the real problem. Slides I had a plenty from my Berlin days and from material I had collected in my teaching, but gross specimens and pictures of patients were almost totally lacking. Fortunately, the late John W. Perkins had many photographs of patients and he placed his entire collection at my disposal, a most generous act. For gross pictures of tumors I had to depend on drawing. Here I made a most happy contact with Tom Jones, the prince of medical artists, resulting in a friendship which has continued, I am pleased to say, to this day. I lugged the gross specimens to St. Louis and after the pictures were made I carried them back again. Two nights on the road riding in the smoker. I had no money for Pullman fare and, besides, my bags of specimens emitted odors despite the greatest pains in packing. A number of times, as I waited in the depot, policemen attracted by the odor made inquiries. One threatened to throw me out if I did not leave. I suggested to him mildly that I was on railroad property and had a ticket for the midnight train and, if he intended to fulfill his threat, that he summon several fellow officers, just in case. He glared at me a while and then went away. Lugging these specimens was indeed a grueling task.

The experience of writing this book was of the greatest

value. It compelled me to start the accumulation of a library and forced me to examine gross specimens more closely than I had ever done. It gave me practice in writing. The chief value, however, lay in that, after the book was published, it brought me much consultation practice in tumors, with the result that after a period of years I had accumulated enough material so that it would have been possible to write a real book.

Incidentally, I learned here the professional as well as the intellectual value of authorship. For some strange reason the general opinion among doctors is that if one writes a book he must have superior knowledge of the subject. Since no one troubles to read the book the delusion is not discovered. Of course, the only one benefited by the writing of books is the one who writes them, and conversely he is the one for whom he writes the books. I suspect this is true of all books but the financial compensation in medical writing is a negligible quantity.

It may be added here that after the first large order of books I continued to add to my library. I obtained many of the classics that have to do with surgical pathology. The building of a library requires something besides money. I obtained many complete files of journals, forty-four of them in fact, and this is no easy task. It was great fun. At one time I had a library of eight thousand bound volumes and ten thousand pamphlets. I donated these to several institutions, the last just recently. I am trying to break myself of the habit of writing.

Each year my private practice continued to increase and brought me more material from my own patients. This was fortunate, because the only material really satisfactory for the study of surgical pathology comes from operations which one has himself performed on patients he has studied beforehand. Besides, many of my friends were good enough to send me interesting specimens, obtained at their own operations, for examination. I rendered a report for the privilege of examining the tissue and, of course, kept the specimen as all good pathologists do.

The experience of writing the tumor book made clear to me the value of photographs as a permanent record. As soon as I was able to provide myself with suitable cameras I engaged a boy who gradually has, by his own efforts, become second to none in this class of photography. He has been with me twenty-five years and is technically known as "Jim." It has been a standing order for many years in my clinic that everything which can be seen must be photographed. Photographs, aside from their value if one plans to write, make the very best possible adjunct to the record.

Fortunately, I early recognized the value of case records. I have a record, inadequate though it may be, of nearly every patient I or any of my assistants have examined since my first, a case of acute appendicitis, May 1, 1894. In my early practice these records were very meager, but even so it is a satisfaction to discover that they are sufficient to recall to mind patients one saw forty years ago. Naturally, all hospitals now keep records of all patients.

Owing to the impressive teaching of Professor Fenger, I have sectioned every specimen I have ever removed at operation. I have kept the gross specimen, if not too large, and of the large ones a characteristic part of the tumor. I am able to secure within a few minutes, with the aid of assistants, the gross specimens and microscopic slides as well as the hospital charts of all my work throughout my whole operative experiences. The photograph of the patient before operation, if any lesion is visible, the case history, the record of the operative findings, the gross specimen and a photograph of it, and finally the microscopic slides make the ideal material for the study of surgical pathology. Such records, however, are a temptation to write: mine resulted in a ten-volume work on surgical pathology.

It is evident from the foregoing that the postgraduate course a surgeon gives himself is made up of several factors. These may be discussed more in detail.

What it takes to make a surgeon has occupied my time for many years and my summary must be only tentative. To make a surgeon we may begin with a young man who is thoroughly rounded in the fundamental sciences, notably anatomy and pathology. These are to the surgeon what the musical instrument is to a musician. The instrument may be high-class, the student thoroughly versed in the theory of music but the sounds emitted by the instrument are more agreeable if the musician has tried it a few times. Surgeons are born just as musicians are born. A born surgeon may not become a surgeon because of the failure to exercise diligence in developing his talent. The fundamental factor in success in surgery is the ability to give absolutely everything that is in him to his task—from now on.

Waldeyer was wont to say in his course in surgical anatomy that the born surgeon is marked by the ability to see answers. "Now," he would say, "we folks when we want to add up a column of figures begin by noting that six and four make ten and three are thirteen and so on down the line. Now a mathematician sees the answer without seemingly noting the individual figures. So the surgeon," he continued, "must see his problem and the answer." It must come as a picture when he picks up his knife, without the slow process of reasoning. He must see the anatomy of the part as though the patient were made of glass, a third-dimensional anatomy. He must see the pathology just as it will ultimately reveal itself after careful study in the laboratory. He must see the process of wound healing from the time he has placed his last suture until the patient leaves his charge cured. Just as one approaches this ideal is he a good surgeon.

This ideal is never fully reached. There are degrees of achievement. One player may play his violin and make no mistakes but it does not do things to your insides as, say, Zimbalist does.

These things cannot be explained. The best one can do is to say that it is the product of native talent and eternal practice.

As I have intimated, the first requisite in the study of surgery is to get yourself a patient. To get the first one there is no general rule. It is a sort of accident. Having got one, the thing to do is to keep him. Keep him above the ground first of all, and keep him as a friend. To achieve the first requires some technical skill. The latter is accomplished by convincing the patient that you are honest. The surest way of achieving this is to actually be honest. Only a fool will be otherwise.

Having acquired a patient, the first thing to do is obtain a history of his ailment. The securing of an adequate one is a work of art. It requires a knowledge of disease and of human nature. It is hard work and is time-consuming but it is necessary, because in many cases it is the most important factor in the whole procedure. A good history may even anticipate what the microscopic slide will show.

The taking of the patient's history, a task usually assigned to a junior resident, really is a most difficult task; nothing requires more experience. The old adage, "Tell the truth to your doctor and lawyer," is good advice. Even though the patients try to do it, there are many difficulties. It may be difficult for the patient to interpret his own feelings. This is obvious when one attempts to diagnose ailments of one's fellow doctors. The location of a pain and its intensity, particularly in the abdomen or head, may be most difficult to express even by a doctor in evaluating his own ailments. In fact, doctors furnish the most difficult problems when one attempts to obtain a history of their complaints.

I once had an internist, the late-lamented Watson Campbell, who was a past master in obtaining an adequate history. An internist of first rank, he questioned the patient carefully; but this was not enough for him. He would question a patient again and again. As he thought over the case, points would occur to him that he had not thought of at the first session, or about which the patient's answers had been vague. Sometimes the patient, too, had thought about his answers and recalled events he had overlooked at previous examinations. Facts of greatest value were often obtained in this way. Data so carefully obtained is as worthy of scientific consideration as any other class of investigative research.

Patients sometimes use superlatives in describing pains, and personal observation must verify the choice of the adjectives. The "terrible pain" the patient reports is modified in the doctor's mind if he finds the patient smoking or reading the funnies while in the throes of alleged agony, or if the patient has been engaged in a careful make-up. Rouged lips sometimes tell the doctor more than the sounds that come out of them. A patient who cannot sleep all night or who hasn't eaten a thing for three weeks and has lost no weight is just overstating his suffering. It is obvious, therefore, that even the best efforts at the elicitation of facts may result, if one accepts them as such, in giving the examiner a wholly wrong impression. Willful lies are much more easily detected than wrongful interpretation of symptoms.

Obviously the validity of the conclusions in such cases is dependent on the investigator's capacity to reason logically and to judge comparative values. Scientific thinking of the highest order can find play here.

The taking of the history of the disease as above indicated is more or less alike in all branches of medical practice. The various branches of medical science require different talents.

Having obtained the patient's history, the physical examination is in order. This may at once clinch a diagnosis suggested by the history. It may involve, in addition, laboratory examinations, including X-ray and chemical examinations. In most instances a correct working knowledge is obtainable. In some instances this must be supplemented by knowledge that can be gained only as the operation is in progress.

The examination completed, the plan of operation is considered. Before the surgeon operates on the patient he does his operation in his own mind. From what the patient tells him and what he can see and feel he determines the problem. He must also see the individual characteristics of the patient—old, young, fat or thin, the state of nutrition and the mental attitude of the patient both toward the operation and toward him as a surgeon. Then comes the real fundamental problem. What is the risk of the operation and what will become of the patient if no operation is done must be carefully considered. In general, there are two classes of patients; the one must be operated on to save life—as, say, for a perforated ulcer; the other must have an annoying lesion removed—say, a wart on the end of the nose or a big fatty tumor on the shoulder. In many, the problem is not so simple. The disease at the time may be but an inconvenience—as, say, a simple goiter or gallstones, conditions in which the surgeon must envisage the future. Simple today, but in the future—there's the rub. What is the basis of the decision? He just turns the table. He imagines himself on the patient's side of the table. Would he want the operation done on himself if he were the patient? That is the real test. This was once referred to as the Golden Rule.

The chief thing that concerns the surgeon is, naturally, the risk to life. Aside from other considerations his reputation depends on it; on his reputation, his practice, his position. The operation in itself may entail no risk; at least, it should not. One can estimate what the risk should be but there are factors which cannot be foreseen. Infections have been all but eliminated as factors of risk. But there are elements that cannot be foretold, complicating lesions that cannot be detected. There is the dreaded embolism, in which a blood clot escapes from the site of the operation and goes on its destructive mission to the lungs. In this the surgeon is in the hands of the gods. It is a possibility that constantly haunts the surgeon. Many a person dies of heart disease, drops dead without a moment's warning. What if some accident should happen while he is in the hands of the surgeon? Not so long ago during an operation on a goiter patient her husband, who was an observer, dropped dead from heart disease. What if the patient had had the heart attack? Such things cannot always be foreseen nor prevented, yet the responsibility is the surgeon's just the same. Such things do happen and the thought of it makes the surgeons old—old in mind, if not in body. Surgeons of long experience, as I have known them, consciously or subconsciously long for the day when they shall do their last operation. The reason is that the disasters remain firmly implanted in the surgeon's memory. His successes, though vastly predominant, come to be taken as a matter of course and do not counterbalance the unfortunate occurrences. Then there are the cases in which there are no disasters but the results are not satisfactory. Would a different plan of procedure have secured better results? Such questions may remain unanswered or are answered only by added experience. There is no consolation. Does the surgeon say, when disaster occurs, "These are the things no one could have foreseen, therefore I am not responsible"? He does not. If the patient dies while he is under his care he chalks it down against himself. This is as it should be. By so feeling there is the greater urge to prevent it. There may be no measures known today that enable us to do so. Perhaps, if we all worry about it, some time some measures will be found that will make it possible to prevent or lessen such disasters. On such fundamental urges progress depends.

The fourth factor is the gross examination of the tissue. The nature of the lesion, as it is exposed at operation, can be more accurately determined than through the intact skin. In the vast majority of cases a diagnosis can be made on the evidence here available. Cancer hardness is one of the most characteristic signs in all medicine. Never any doubt there. Sarcomas present a more difficult situation because of their resemblance to one another and to infections, granulomas and inflammation. Always uncertain ground here. The surgeon must rely in large part on the past history of the disease.

During the operation there is time only for a cursory examination of the lesion's surface. Once they are removed, the surgeon can study the tissues at leisure. He gets the feel and the look of the surface, he makes cuts across it, finds new areas to feel and look at. He learns the microscopic appearance later in the laboratory. The next time he encounters a similar lesion at the operating table he immediately recalls how the tissues looked on cross section in his previous examinations and how it felt and what the laboratory revealed. By this means only, can the surgeon hope to add to his fundamental knowledge.

The fifth factor is the microscopic study in the laboratory of the material removed. Sections are taken from the specimens for the preparation of slides. Most surgeons have this done for them by a technician. Young surgeons should make their own slides in order that they may know the meaning of the variation in staining reaction of tissues. The detailed microscopic examination represents the final link in the surgical examination. Here the surgeon must bow to the pathologist, with whose aid he must test the accuracy of the operating-table diagnosis.

The sixth factor—it was stated above that the pathologist must pass on the surgeon's diagnosis. However, the patient may need to be appealed to before the question can be finally decided. I once in my youth received a shock. I was visiting my friend Dr. Zeit, then an assistant to Professor Klebs, one of the greatest pathologists of all time—he of diphtheria-bacillus fame. Dr. Zeit had a slide made from a tumor sent in by a doctor, from Kansas in fact, and took it to Professor Klebs for comment. "It is not malignant," was the Professor's diagnosis. Later, calling to Dr. Zeit, "Tell the doctor to write me if the patient has a recurrence." Was it possible that he might feel uncertain? Thus, in many cases, only by following the patient in the years after the operation is the diagnosis confirmed or disproved. The facts revealed by the aftercourse may take one of two general directions. If the pathologist regards the lesion as benign and the patient dies of a recurrence of the tumor, obviously the diagnosis was wrong.

The aftercourse may be needed to check the diagnosis in lesions other than tumors. If the surgeon believes a pain is due to lesion of an organ and removes that organ, if the pain persists the pain was not due to an affection of that organ. The most common example is the removal of the appendix for an ovarian pain as has been so often done. The net result is that the surgeon has the appendix and the patient still has her pain.

Surgeons vary in their range of study. Some depend on the family physician or on internal medicine specialists to make the diagnosis as to the nature of the complaint. The surgeon must make his own examinations and arrive at his own diagnosis no matter how able the medical consultant. Unless he knows all that can be known about the life history of the disease he may be seriously handicapped during the progress of the operation.

Very few surgeons make any intensive study of the material removed or of autopsy material in case of a disastrous result. It is the nature and intensity of such studies that ultimately determine the place he shall occupy in the field of scientific surgery. Not his reputation by any means; this does not depend altogether on his actual achievements. His reputation is what the public thinks of him. His reputation may depend on his shape and social graces but in general real achievement as a surgeon ultimately breaks down any personal handicaps and gives him his rightful place both in attainment and reputation. The capacity of a surgeon cannot be gauged by inspection. Some surgeons are fiddlers; others, violinists. It all depends. The final answer must come from a study of the results. This requires the study of the subsequent history of the patient. Some patients do not die but they are not well. Why? The lesion operated on may have been only a part of the cause of the patient's complaint. If the patient is mad at Papa the most skillfully performed operation will not cure her complaints: that is to say, the lamentations will not cease. The surgeon is held responsible, as he should be. He should have learned before he operated on his patient what the end result would be.

Surgeons, therefore, habitually study the after-effects of treatment more than do physicians. The latter has the satisfaction of knowing that if his treatment does no good it will at least do no harm. The surgeon, on the other hand, when he takes his scalpel in hand is on the road which will make for better or worse. Consequently, he is more acutely alive to determine what happens to the patient after the treatment has been concluded.

Happily, not all the patients require operative treatment. When the surgeon gives medicines he becomes for the moment a physician. If only medicines are required there is chance for the play of the personal equation. When a new drug appears, a large number of doctors using it probably will believe that it acts beneficially. After a period of years its usefulness is found to be limited or nil. I remember very well when quassia was believed to cure cancer of the stomach. Nothing, in fact, requires so much careful observation over so long a period of time as accurately appraising the value of the drugs as modifiers of the course of a disease. New drugs are introduced that are said to be more effective than the old ones, and the doctor must personally test this claim by observation. This recalls the old joke about the doctor who tells the patient that if the medicine he is prescribing does not bring effective relief, "Come back and I'll give you something that will." The patient replies that he would like to take the second medicine first. The fact is that the doctor was trying to secure results with milder remedies, reserving more potent drugs in case the milder ones should fail. That doctor just talked too much. He should have contented himself with telling the patient to return after taking the medicine.

Operative treatment is the spectacular part of the doctor's life. Mere technic may require considerable skill, obtained only by experience, but on the whole it is the function requiring the least mental effort. In fact, I believe a man could become a good operator with nothing above the medulla, and I have seen many who seemed to be in precisely that predicament. It is much easier to acquire technical skill than to learn the indications for doing so. This is attested by the fact that many surgeons never advance beyond this manual dexterity. The master surgeon declares his class, not only by his operative expertness but by his understanding of the entire situation. Professor Koenig once said it took him ten years to learn when to operate, and forty when not to.

In the experience of many surgeons some phase of their practice takes on especial prominence either because of special skill or because of especial interest, usually both. This has led to many specialties within specialties. For instance, neural surgery has become a very highly developed specialty. Even more commonly, the surgeon retains his specialty intact but does develop certain operations beyond the average. This may become profitable if it succeeds in bringing additional practice, which need not be primarily commercial. Some surgeons like to fish, just why is a problem obviously not commercial. Just a hobby perhaps. A specially developed operation may attain the same prominence in the surgeon's eye and it is a lot less work.

My experience with local anesthesia may be interpolated here. Many years ago I read a paper on the use of local anesthesia. The official stenographer representing a surgical journal was present in an official capacity. He suggested that I write a series of articles on this subject for his journal. I did so. It was suggested then that it would be a good idea to extend them and print them in book form. Of course, this pleased me. The sixth edition of this book recently came from the press.

The distinctive feature of this book is that it represented my own ideas of how it should be done. Most books on this subject reflected the German technic. Mine was a much more gentle one, better fitted in my opinion to the more high-strung American patient.

This experience with local anesthesia illustrates the origin and effect of a hobby. I began the use of local anesthesia during the very beginning of my practice. By its aid I could do many lesser operations in the home, or in the office, anything in the nose and throat. People figured that if the operation could be done under local anesthesia it could not be much of an operation and it would be all right to let the kid do it. By degrees I came to do anything in the whole field of surgery without the use of a general anesthetic. It is harder for the surgeon but saves the patient certain inconveniences in many cases. The advent of spinal anesthesia largely wrecked my doll house that I had so carefully built up throughout many years. This is a part of any doctor's life. By the time he has made himself a comfortable place, the procession moves around the corner and he must scramble on.

The indication for operation expresses the personal equation and often reflects the age and experience of the surgeon. The young surgeon is more ready to operate than his more experienced colleague, both because he is likely to place too much importance on his findings and because he is not sure of his findings. For instance, if one is not sure whether or not there is rigidity of the abdominal wall he is more likely to operate than an experienced hand who says there is no rigidity. There is nothing so futile as to attempt to remove an imaginary pain, or a nonexistent lesion like the so-called chronic appendix, by a surgical operation. The patient retains the pain and glorifies it and

Papa who pays the bill gets a headache. The surgeon loses a patient, though she lives.

Then, too, indications for operation are often relative. Some discomfort may exist due to conditions which may right themselves in time, or which may continue producing only minor discomforts throughout life. The old surgeon may feel that the patient had better endure an inconvenience he now has rather than undergo an operation with the inevitable risks he knows not of. He realizes that complications may arise which may make the last condition worse than the first, a caution born of experience. The young surgeon reads that such and such an operation has a mortality of, say, two per cent. He feels that the patient had better take this risk than suffer the annoyance of a disease which in itself does not endanger life. The old doctor may feel that the patient in hand may be one of the two per cent risk. He knows that the mortality published as two per cent, at best, is such only in the hands of the most experienced operators, and finally most likely the statistics are wrong. He probably has a feeling that when anyone publishes statistics he is going to paint a situation as favorable as possible, else he would not be publishing them. When anyone essays to publish statistics it impresses me in the same way as when someone starts to relate a fishing experience. One must admit that the truth is theoretically possible.

Here arises a difference of opinion as to whether to operate or not, often resulting in a disagreement between doctors which so delights the layman. Just why people are so delighted when doctors disagree it is difficult to say, most likely it is because they are usually in agreement. People do like novelty. Why laugh at us? If lawyers agreed it would be as big a novelty as when doctors disagree. Even ministers disagree as to the best or only road to the pearly gates. The clergy in times past even made bonfires of one another. So far as a layman can say, the clergy have not yet determined whether or not the Civil War is over—a conflict which, incidentally, they had a large part in starting. Therefore, the division of the public at the squabbles of the doctors is really an unconscious compliment. As a matter of fact, what appears to be a difference of opinion may be but a difference in the point of view, as in estimating the comparative beauty of the so-called bathing beauties. It is really a very complicated problem, why people disagree.

Yet even the collection of data as above outlined is not enough. The patients must be restudied by a rereading of the history, a reexamination of the gross specimen, a restudy of the slide. Restudy of patients of years past expands a surgeon's knowledge. It is better than seeing a new patient, because the passing years have brought added wisdom.

The plan of study so briefly outlined here is my interpretation of what postgraduate study for the surgeon should entail. Each surgeon must make his own outline.

Just what one should do with data he has obtained is a matter of election. Having been invited to write a book on tumors, it was but natural that I should find this experience repeated. Besides the tumor book and the book on the peritoneum already mentioned, a book on the diseases of the thyroid gland, a book on minor surgery and a two-volume work on clinical surgery followed—the last two but hackwork done at the request of a publisher. These were time wasted. They dealt with superficialities in no wise calculated to extend my own knowledge. There is a slight satisfaction in the fact that the first named may have been of some value, since it has seen three editions.

A collective study of my surgical material has found expression in a work on surgical pathology in ten volumes. These are but an expression of what the patients taught me—at least, what I thought they taught me. Of course, one's independent observations in such a work will crop out. These may or may not be true. At any rate, the facts are there; but, in the language of Traube, possibly I have not always thought aright. But that is secondary. The restudy of this vast material has been valuable to me. A friend once found De Condoyle the great anthropologist hard at work late at night. This friend remarked that he must love his science to be working so late—the professor was then eighty years of age. "No," replied the old scientist; "it is not love of science that drives me. It is to drown my grief."

Such extensive authorship, it might appear, calls for explanation or apology. I have neither. I write only to please myself and in that I have succeeded.

Such an outline is my conception of a postgraduate work in surgery, so far as I have gone. There is yet much to do. Pleasing to state, there is now no lack of material.

CHAPTER

9

YOUNG DOCTORS NOWADAYS THINK THAT WITHOUT A HOSPITAL operations are not possible. Doctors who do not operate sometimes excuse themselves by telling the patient that they cannot operate because there are no hospital facilities. This is a subconscious salving of their own incapacity. Whole communities are sometimes so impressed by this idea that they build hospitals in order that their local doctors may be able to operate. But they discover after the hospital is built that there was a miscalculation somewhere. If one gets a nice new gun for Christmas, that does not make one an expert marksman. Something more than a hospital and equipment is necessary.

The story of kitchen surgery should not be lost, because it presents many lessons which would be of value today if they were heeded. The one fundamental fact that surgeons must get results is incontrovertible. How they get them is of little importance, from the patient's point of view.

Kitchen surgery emphasized that two things, and two things only are necessary for the performance of an excellent operation: to wit, a surgeon and a patient. In comparison with these everything else pales into insignificance. Persons are prone to denounce what they know not of. Surgeons trained in hospitals scoff at the possibility of doing expert surgery under unfavorable situations. Let me pick the surgeon and I will guarantee a good job whether it be performed in our modern palaces or in a fence corner. I have been privileged to work for many years under the most favorable conditions in hospital appointments and capable assistants, but some of my best work has been done in kitchens under the most unfavorable conditions, as we view these things now.

The kitchen surgeon had to be content with only the very essentials. These are amazingly few as I shall set forth. The important point is that he learned what the essentials were and how to use them. That is more than the modern surgeon knows.

Visitors to my hospital are often shocked, sometimes only surprised, to see our "sloppy" technic. True enough, I have never fully cast off the experiences gained in the kitchen. They wonder about infections. They may save themselves this needless worry. We will match the healing of the wounds of our patients with any hospital on earth. We know exactly what we are doing; our critics do not. I have developed a system; they have inherited a ritual. Clean, rapid operating will do more to minimize infections than all the face masks ever inflicted on a docile profession. Surgeons bedeck their faces with raiment and fine linen until the operating rooms look like the pictures of an oriental harem. The sight gives me a pain. This uncomfortable garb tends to slow operating and bungle technic, which are the parents of infected wounds.

Kitchen surgery made it necessary to learn the essentials of technic. The surgeon found that only the wound matters. What goes on round about is of very little importance. During the time I was doing surgery under these conditions I was also teaching bacteriology. I studied extensively two problems, the sterilization of the hands and the influence of respiration on infection. In the sterilization of hands I followed the methods then in use—prolonged washing and dipping the hand in some sort of chemical after the scrubbing was completed. I failed to demonstrate that the elaborate scrubbing had any great influence on sterilization of the skin of the hands. I once saw a meticulous surgeon scrub his hands for just exactly forty minutes and he got a wound infection in a hernia. He required two hours for its performance. I learned that the cleaning of the nails at the time of scrubbing is more likely to do harm than good. The time to clean the nails is at the morning ablutions and then leave them alone at the time the hands are scrubbed in the operating room. The use of chemicals after scrubbing, was, of course, ridiculous, if one considered the length of time it took the solutions used to kill microbes under the most favorable conditions. Happily, the use of them in the operating room has been discontinued, not that the uselessness of the process was recognized but because it was inconvenient. The advent of rubber gloves, of course, did much to lessen the ardor of hand sterilization.

The wearing of masks has for its purpose the prevention of wound infection from the exhaled breath. I did many experiments to determine the likelihood of infection from this course. I exposed two sets of gelatin plates to the air. One set of plates I placed before me so that they were exposed to my expired breath, as I was occupied in making slides, in as close contact as the wound does during an operation. The other set of plates were placed at the other end of the work table of the laboratory. There was no difference in the number of colonies in the two sets of plates. I repeated this experiment many times. Of course, if one is going to talk into the wound, or even spit into it, the mouth should be covered. I prefer to keep my mouth shut while operating. This makes the use of masks unnecessary.

The placing of sterile cloths about the site of operation is aesthetic. If one is careful to keep his instruments away from the area of skin not washed, no sterile linens are needed. If one places his instruments back into the dishpan after he has used them they do not become contaminated. No one touched them except the surgeon. Under the conditions of kitchen surgery, of course, the number of instruments in use were a very small fraction of the number one now sees on the instrument table of the modern operating room. The placing of sterile linen about the site of operation makes it unnecessary for the surgeon to exercise eternal vigilance as to what and where he touches; this is a convenience, but when layer on layer of sterile linen is placed about the site of operation the situation becomes ridiculous. I recently saw no less than five layers of sheets placed about the site of a goiter operation. These served but to handicap the operator. Five layers are no more sterile than one.

The important factor in the prevention of the infection of wounds is to keep the hands out of infectious material all through the twenty-four hours. The importance of this is often overlooked. A friend of mine once did an operation for necrosis of a jaw. His subsequent five laparotomies became infected. So shocked was he at this disaster that he precipitously went on a vacation. I opened up the wounds, with gloves on, and afterward for four successive days scrubbed my hands for thirty minutes, treating them also with a chemical solution as was the custom in those days. On the fifth day I operated on a patient of my own in another hospital and got a severe infection with the same bacteria that had infected my friend's case and which were demonstrated in the jaw infection.

The biggest factor in aseptic operating is the prompt performance of the operation. This implies the minimum trauma of tissues. Tissues long exposed to the air form a much more favorable culture medium for the growth of bacteria than do recently severed tissues. When incisions are left open too long the fibrin of the wound coagulates and when the wound is finally closed the tissues are no longer in the best state for prompt healing.

During my early years I had a very illuminating experience. We had a surgeon who was an expert anatomist and had had vast clinical experience. He tried to learn aseptic technic late in life and he did not learn it well. He made many ludicrous violations of technic as we young fellows viewed it. Yet he had fewer infections than did we younger fellows, despite his imperfect technic. He completed operations in fifteen minutes that took the rest of us several hours to perform. We were so occupied with the aseptic technic that we forgot to do the operation promptly. He was doing kitchen surgery in an operating room.

All that is necessary in the performance of an aseptic operation is a reasonably clean skin—for no matter how elaborate the preparation, it is not really clean, only reasonably clean—a few clean tools and, of course, an operator who knows what it is all about.

The chief disadvantage of the kitchen surgery of days gone by were two. There was the need for the operator to journey, often long distances, in order to reach the patient. This invoked all the difficulties incident to travel described in a previous chapter. A fatiguing journey is not a good preliminary to a trying operation, but we were a tough lot and could and did good work when we were dead on our feet. Then there was the labor of preparing the patient and the environment with our own hands.

The major subsidiary annoyance was the anesthetist when a general anesthetic was needed. Nothing is so distressing as trying to do a difficult operation with the patient only half asleep. Yet I hasten to say the country-doctor anesthetists have not tried my soul so much as some professional anesthetists found in the city hospitals. The country anesthetist will give some heed to the pleadings of the surgeon; the professional anesthetist is contemptuous of such lamentations. Sometimes one had pleasant surprises. I once went into a remote backwoods hamlet. My patient was a huge woman, the removal of the gall bladder was in prospect. The local doctor was to give the anesthetic. I felt sick. But this doctor went about his job in an expert fashion and the result was a perfect anesthesia. To my astonished inquiry, he replied that he had been assistant and house surgeon in a large St. Louis hospital for four years and there had given many anesthetics. He is the only male I ever felt a desire to kiss.

Those doctors who were trained in the Southern medical schools preferred to use chloroform and usually gave it with a high degree of skill, but I was always frightened when it was being used. I saw one fine young schoolteacher die from degeneration of the liver following chloroform anesthesia. After this, I refused to permit its use. This girl haunts me still. Chloroform had another distinct disadvantage at night. This drug, when the vapors are exposed to the flame of the kerosene lamp, disintegrates and produces a terribly irritating gas. I once battled with a perforated ulcer of the duodenum under these conditions for an hour and it was only by the exercise of all the will power I possessed that I was able to finish the operation, because of the irritation produced in my bronchial tubes by this gas. I carried away a bronchitis that lasted for many months.

Ether usually was unskillfully given and relaxation in abdominal operations was the exception. To remove a tumor with tense abdominal walls presented the same problem as stealing a watermelon through a fence, a procedure in which youthful experience came in good stead. It was not unusual for the anesthetist to require an hour or more to render the patient reasonably asleep, all the while being encouraged by the restless surgeon to pour on more ether. This was particularly the case after the "drop method" came to be advocated. This is like many other things in medicine—if you take them literally they do not work. The "drop method" as now employed does not differ in the least from the old Allis inhaler or a newspaper and a towel. It all depends on who is giving the ether.

The lack of assistants was the least of one's trials. If I ever deliberately commit murder I shall select an inattentive and awkward assistant as my victim. As Grade A I select one who has assisted enough to delude himself into thinking he could himself do the work better than the surgeon who is operating. This usually reaches the high point at about the third week of an interne's experiences. The chief activity of an incompetent assistant is to try to do the operation. Instead of handing a clamp to the operator he attempts to catch the vessel himself. Of course, he tries to catch it endwise and if he is particularly skillful he can cause the vessel to spurt into the surgeon's face. This is the very acme of assistant skill. I once had a resident who had one pet aptitude. As the surgeon prepared to make the incision he took time off from looking at the nurses to pull the skin of the abdomen sharply toward himself. The result was that the lower end of the incision ended at the northeast corner of the patient's abdomen.

Another way for the assistant to annoy a surgeon is to make a wild dab with a sponge just as he is ready to grasp a needle already passed through tissue into a deep part of the wound. The needle may thus be neatly upset, so that the surgeon must remove the needle and start all over again. Not quite so good is to take a poke with scissors just as the surgeon has finished the first loop of a ligature knot before he has had time to place the second. Making several wild jabs with the scissors before locating the ligature is ritual. If he can stick the surgeon's hands with the scissors in some of these passes, that is the height of technic. That will get a rise out of the most phlegmatic operator. Taking the clamp off of an important vessel just as the surgeon begins to tie the knot of the ligature is a real masterpiece. For this stunt I suggest the renal vessels or the inferior thyroid veins.

Nowadays it is beneath the dignity of an assistant to hand the surgeon an instrument he is going to use next. The difficulty here is twofold: first, he hasn't any idea what instrument is going to be used next and, second, it would be an indication of subservience to lend a hand. Of course, it is all right to offer him one after he has reached for the needed instrument himself. This indicates that the assistant knows the next step of the operation without lessening his own dignity. If the surgeon reaches for a sponge, dab in quickly with another sponge. The rest the surgeon gets while the assistant is doing this will do him good. Where several assistants are present each will do his turn at dabbing. Dab, dab, dab, damn. That is the procedure. The rhythm may be learned by watching several workmen driving a circus tent peg. This gives the surgeon an extra period of rest.

When something is effectually covered, one sometimes compares it to the efficiency of an old hen on a nest of eggs. Those who use this simile have never seen how effectively an assistant can cover a lot of instruments with his elbow. The position of his elbow at least has the advantage indicating to the operator in a general way where the instruments are located. The surgeon knows that somewhere beneath that elbow is the needed tool and all he has to do is to remove the assistant—and behold, there it is. Some day I am going to invent an operating table without any contraptions beneath. Then one can kick the assistant on the shins and in this way awaken him. Kitchen tables are made that way.

Of course no assistant would ever think of practicing the technic he is required to perform, notably the deft handling of a pair of scissors, in the seclusion of his room. He thinks baseball players get that way by just playing in regular games after they reach a major league. There should be bush leagues for surgical assistants.

I have interpolated the preceding in order to show that kitchen surgery had many advantages. Even the modest, intelligent well meaning assistant can make of himself a nuisance. Only one person can work at a time and while an assistant is doing something the operator is idle—that is his hands are, but his mind is thinking horrible thoughts. On the other hand if one operates alone in a kitchen his instruments are just where he placed them. One kept the instruments in the dishpan, took them out when needed, and put them back in again when he had finished with their use. They were always to be found in an area of a foot and a half, the diameter of the dishpan. There was no nurse to grab them, rub off real or imaginary blood and then place them somewhere else.

The assisting general practitioner usually was too timid to do anything on his own account—one could give him a forceps to hold and he was as contented and inoffensive as a child with a rattle, at least theoretically. But the local doctor could be a greater nuisance than even the greenest intern. For the making of a real unmitigated nuisance the assistant should be what is professionally called an occasional operator, one that removes tonsils, faucial pillars and uvulas, or makes Jews out of Christians. He is a surgeon. I once had two of these simultaneously assist me at a difficult goiter operation. Their fists bespoke their recent graduation from a wheelbarrow gang. Their arms were strong, and thyroid vessels are fragile. Yes indeed, it was the accessories during the act, as the lawyers say, that gave the kitchen surgeon his greatest grief.

The country assistant at each operation presented a new problem, because usually one had never met him before, and one had to devise new schemes for each case. After rubber gloves came into use I pretended to forget about his gloves and as the operation was about to start I would tell him to put on his gloves. This, like getting into a dress shirt and tie, is no simple procedure when tried for the first time and I usually had the operation done before he had finished this ordeal.

An operation in a neighborhood was more or less of a public event. The local newssheet would announce that the local doctor assisted by so and so successfully operated on Mrs. X. This having appeared in the weekly, the procedure could be said to be completed. Of course, sometimes one had an assistant who had had some experience. Some doctors, too, were just naturally good assistants. And, eureka!—sometimes I had a trained nurse to assist me. There are no better assistants than nurses. Their only thought is to assist the surgeon. This implies, of course, that there were no young doctors about.

The long trips on the road gave one time to speculate on what one would likely find at the journey's end. If one knew his doctor, that helped some. Some of the best diagnosticians I have ever met were located in small towns. Some of these men could be depended upon to have examined the patient carefully and in consequence have arrived at the proper diagnosis. Others did well if they located the disease on the proper side of the diaphragm. Many did not; the commonest mistake was to diagnose appendicitis when the trouble was pneumonia. I have made quite a number of long, weary, useless trips because of this error. Strange doctors allowed the widest speculations. It was a suspense, something like an opponent's shuffling of a deck of cards, except one hoped he would not draw a joker. These jokers were of varying sizes. The supreme joker was to be called to do an operation when there was nothing wrong with the patient, surgical or otherwise. Of course, then one could not operate. This made the local doctor mad and one got nothing for his trip, except the execrations of the said local doctor, and, I am pleased to note, usually the eternal gratitude of the patient. The hand for this sort of doctor to play when I refused to operate was to call a surgeon who would operate on anyone who would consent. The local doctor and the new consultant would, after the operation, make loud exclamations setting forth my ignorance and stupidity, and how they had rescued the patient from certain death. In most instances the patients backed up my judgment and refused to be operated on by, to them, a too willing surgeon. But such practices many times had a repercussion. The patient, if operated on, would not be relieved of her complaints, usually of a nervous nature, and often they were made worse by the ill-advised operation. In these cases they then remembered the advice of the surgeon who did not operate. I am still drawing revenue for my stubbornness. Patients are like that. If they believe you tried to do the right thing they are for you from now on. If you were right or not is of secondary moment.

In retrospect kitchen surgery does not seem so bad. Many of my best operations, figured in end results, were done under the most adverse conditions. There was something exhilarating in the battling with the elements to reach the patient which the surgeon misses when James drives him to the hospital and all he has to do is to dust off the cigarette ashes and change his pants to be ready for the operation. Nothing stimulating in that. The average individual requires some stimulus to bring out his best, a thing that athletic directors understand. We shall soon see what Stubblebeard can do with the City of Churches gang of goofy ball players.

Kitchen surgery offered variety; each operation was its own problem and had all the interest of a new show. It was always a thrill to get into a kitchen where one could give orders instead of peremptorily being ordered out. It was akin to the sensation a henpecked man apparently gets in rigging himself up with Lodge regalia and finding himself addressed as Most Worshipful High Goof. To be able to go into a kitchen and say, "Get me thus and so," and receive the answer, "Yes, doctor," and then have it done! Contrast the modern operating room. One look at the superintendent and one gets tongue-tied. The only big talk in the modern hospital is heard in the staffroom. Here all are equally brave and, it may be added, equally skillful.

The kitchen lacked one chief value of the modern hospital: the inexperienced operator had no one to blame. It is never the surgeon's fault if infection follows an operation done in a modern hospital—never. The technic of the operating room is blamed. In such cases the alleged dereliction is met by adding another sterile sheet over the patient, or someone else, or by adding another assistant. The latest stunt is to pin a sterile towel on the back of the surgeon. I'll bite—what is it for? I have never seen a surgeon sit on a wound, chances are they do not intend to sit on the wound, but there is nothing like being prepared for all possible contingencies.

If the surgeon becomes agitated over some anatomic anomaly, he can call for more instruments, a change in the position of the table, or call for more lights, to compensate for the light that comes only from experience. An anatomic anomaly, I may explain, is a condition wherein a surgeon finds something which he does not recognize. Thus a dodo bird would be an anomaly to an inexperienced or amateur ornithologist, he never having heard of one before. It's things like these that make surgery difficult. An anomaly never bothers a surgeon trained in the dissecting room.

The first thing the kitchen surgeon had to do was to diagnose the lesion, if any, for which he was called to operate. The surgeon was unacquainted with his patient and had only the diagnosis of the family doctor to guide him. His opinion may be of high order or worse than useless, depending on the individual. Even though he had confidence in the ability of the local doctor, the surgeon still had to make his own diagnosis in order to plan his operative procedures. The appreciation of this fact led Senn to define a surgeon as "a physician who operates." The surgeon's chief reliance in making a diagnosis had to be placed on a carefully obtained history and the physical examination. Though I carried at all times a folding microscope and accessories, this was rarely of use in the diagnosis of surgical cases. Of course, a blood count could be made but this was at best only confirmatory. Sometimes the diagnosis was possible at a glance. Sometimes an hour or more was required to come to a reasonable basis for an operative procedure, and sometimes it was not so very reasonable at that, as measured in the light of subsequent disclosures.

Be it remembered, kitchen surgery was not confined to acute lesions but for any disease under the sun. As a matter of fact, most patients could have journeyed to a hospital, if there had been such and they had been disposed to do so. Even if one was available they preferred to stay at home. Hospitals spelled flowers and slow music to them.

In that early day most operations were too long delayed, because the patient resisted advice to go to the hospital and the mortality consequently was high. This instilled a general fear of hospitals and it produced a vicious circle. This high death rate frightened the patients; the more they were frightened, the longer they delayed operation, the higher the death rate. Patients accepted operations at home more readily, and as they were operated on earlier, the mortality was less. This made kitchen surgeon popular.

As a matter of fact, fear is too little regarded as an adverse influence in the outcome of an operation. It matters but little to what the fear may be due. The average groom, when being led to the altar, is in no condition to undergo a major operation, particularly if he has been there before. Even today, I refuse to operate on a frightened patient. I have seen, too often, patients who stated that they would not recover, who proceeded to make good their prediction. Some of these cases did not show the cause of death, even at autopsy. I believe they were actually and literally scared to death.

Each kitchen operation was a class of its own, depending on the nature of the trouble, the utensils available, and what assistance the local doctor could give. For instance, in the case of gall-bladder disease one drained where he might remove this organ if he were operating in a hospital. These limitations sometimes forced conservatism against generally adopted practices.

I PRACTICE KITCHEN SURGERY

Appendicial abscesses were drained. So forced to conservatism, finding the results better, I adopted it as a principle, a lesson most modern surgeons have forgotten.

After the examination had been made with sufficient detail to make a presumptive diagnosis the instruments were placed on the kitchen stove to boil. The surgeon then returned to the patient and completed the history and examination. That completed, if there was idle time, one visited with the patient and employed this opportunity to remove any fear he may have had of the operation in the beginning. One young lady played the piano while the instruments boiled. One lady even sang to me; I presume that was her idea of how to get even with the doctor. Sometimes a facetious patient would come with a whetstone and offer to sharpen the "tools." Occasionally his services were accepted. This was supposed to be the height of humor. I think so still.

In some cases it was necessary to first find the patient. I remember one instance of a candidate for the repair of a hernia. He was the local drayman and I was obliged to wait until he delivered a load of coal before preparations for the operation could be begun. In a few instances the victim escaped and there was no operation. Such things seem ludicrous now but they were taken as part of the day's work.

In the preparation for the operation two general conditions prevailed. The one when the operation was agreed on beforehand and preparation could be made in anticipation of the surgeon's coming. In cases of emergency, of course, there could be no previous preparation.

In the first instance a well-lighted room was selected. All furniture and pictures were removed, the floor and walls scrubbed. A sheet was nailed before the windows to keep the neighbors from peeping in during the course of the operation. This was considered particularly important in perineal work. Then the wash boiler was half filled with water, which was boiled for an hour or more. A teakettle or two also were similarly prepared. This preliminary boiling accomplished, the containers were removed from the stove and allowed to cool. All this was done the day before the anticipated operation. Some doctors even had folding operating tables which they took to the patient's home the day before the surgeon was expected.

These preliminary preparations were, of course, in imitation of the hospital operating room. The boiling of the water was ritual. Well water is safe to use in any operation. I have tested it in the laboratory and have used it in its raw state for the making of solutions of local anesthetic in many hundreds of operations without a particle of trouble. Removing the pictures and scrubbing the walls belong to the same category. It did no real good; perhaps it did harm by agitating dust that had long reposed on pictures and the like. At any rate, I felt just as secure operating in a room where nothing had been disturbed.

After the surgeon arrived active preparations were begun. The portable table was set up. The parlor table was divested of the Bible and photograph album and placed beside the operating table. Whenever possible I carried regular hospital linen so that the requisitioned parlor table could be converted into a very convenient instrument table by covering it with a sheet. There was also a sheet for the patient and gowns for the surgeon and his assistant. Sponges were available, and in later years gloves. After the instruments had boiled they were removed from the dishpan and placed on the table, which had already been prepared by covering it with a sheet. This done, the conveniences approached those of a hospital. And speaking of luxuries, after automobiles came into use one ran the car up to the window of the room in which the operating was to be done. The head lights were turned on and a looking glass, held by a friend, was used to deflect the light from the car on the site of operation. There is no better light than this. Of course, if this friend fainted one had to get another helper. Such inconveniences were obviated by getting a woman to hold it in the first place. Women rarely faint at the sight of blood, or anything else. They may feint but never faint.

In contrast with the preceding, many homes were pitifully devoid of even the most meager requirements. In emergencies, too, there was no time for any preliminary work. Often I had nothing but a few instruments and no linens, as when the need for an operation was not anticipated or when the linens I carried had been used at some previous operation on the trip.

In such situations, if an extension table was available this was spread apart and the middle boards were placed lengthwise. This made the midportion of the table narrow so that the midportion of the patient could be approached more closely by the surgeon and his assistant. This was very desirable if the surgeon had a good assistant. If the assistant was incompetent the farther he was kept from the site of operation the better. If the assistant was incompetent the operator could place the patient on his side of the table, the assistant on the other side where he could do little harm. If there was no table available a door could be removed from its hinges and placed on boxes for support. For one as tall as I barrels were the ideal support. The kitchen operating table made perineal operations difficult. To keep the thighs flexed with a sheet for the duration of such operations is an uncertain procedure. First one thigh slips out, then the other, or the patient rolls over. If the anesthetist neglected his task, in order to come round to witness the operation, the patient would awaken and extend the thighs in spite of the most carefully placed support. Nevertheless, I have done many perineal repairs with no other assistant than a poor anesthetist. I soon learned that these operations could be more conveniently done under local anesthesia and thereafter nearly all pelvic operations were done in this way.

The instruments were placed in the family dishpan and boiled. If no sterilized gauze was available towels were cut up in convenient size to be used as sponges and boiled with the instruments. Usually an intact towel was boiled to place about the site of operation. Then the patient was shaved if there was a razor available. In the early days whiskers were so generally worn that such an implement often was unknown. In that case, the hair was clipped with a pair of scissors and the stubs scrubbed with homemade lye soap. In some homes green soap was on hand but this applied to the perineal regions caused loud lamentations. This was not the attenuated green soap of the operating room but the greenish full-strength article guaranteed to remove anything except the protestations of the victim on whom it was being used.

Sometimes in emergencies the patient was only partly undressed. If the room was chilly one left the patient's pants on for protection. The pants usually were cleaner than the available bed covering and in many households there were only feather beds. A feather would be inconvenient to have about an operating table.

The arrangements could even be more simple. I have drained many appendicial and neck abscesses by simply pulling the patient to the edge of the bed and proceeding with the operation. This simplifies the procedure. Local anesthesia without any assistant or clean linen was the usual layout. The mortality under such conditions was no more than it is in the modern hospital with a surgeon painfully searching for the appendix, the while contaminating diverse and sundry areas of the uninfected peritoneum.

After the operation was completed came the question of dressing and aftercare. As I see the elaborate postoperative care now generally employed in hospitals I can but think how little the young men of today know about how well the patients do when just left alone. That injury can be done by all the things that are done for, or to, or with, the patient of course it would be sacrilegious to say. The old dictum to young doctors was,

I PRACTICE KITCHEN SURGERY

"When in doubt, give calomel." Now it seems to be, "When in doubt, transfuse." A liberal course in kitchen surgery would be a valuable experience to any embryo surgeon. They would learn how well patients get along if just left alone. With this knowledge they then could compare the procedures they institute in the modern hospital.

I once saw a hemorrhage after abortion; the patient had bled through the mattress and I found a pool of blood on the floor which measured five by seven feet. The floor was uneven and this pool stood in the corner of the room some distance from the bed. The patient was much whiter than the pillows on which her head rested and she was gasping for breath. I packed the uterus with the aid of a head mirror and a tallow candle. She recovered with no aid other than frequent small sips of water. Of course, now one would transfuse. Had she been transfused there would have been no question in anyone's mind but that the procedure had saved her life. I have seen a number of such cases but none quite so extreme as this. In fact, I have never seen death from external hemorrhage in a case where the blood flow was checked. I have seen deaths from internal hemorrhage of small amounts but here one must take into account the shocking effect of absorption of blood through the peritoneum.

A funny incident occurs to me. It shows how reputations are sometimes made. It was another patient with severe hemorrhage after a miscarriage. Same old tallow candle, same old head mirror. I removed the placenta, no fetus. I presumed, of course, that it had passed. I packed the uterus with gauze and when the gauze was removed the next day young Mr. Schmidt, three inches long, followed, much to my amazement. The bystanders noted the escape of the fetus and the word went out that the young doc made a great effort to save the child and nearly succeeded.

In dressing the wound after operation one had to evaluate the intelligence of those who were to care for the patient after the surgeon left. The most explicit instructions to leave the dressings undisturbed had little effect on many of the old doctors. In a few days after the operation, when the patient was fever-free, the delighted doctor would become curious to see what made the patient do so well and he would remove the dressings. These doctors usually dated back to the days of "laudable pus" when every well-behaved wound was supposed to suppurate. In several instances the patient complained of pain from the sutures, usually in twelve or twenty-four hours after the operation, and the doctor would obligingly remove them. Sometimes this meddling had a very serious consequence. In several instances the wound burst open and one had to scramble and put the intestines back. I found the best way to prevent such meddling was to cover the whole wound area shinglelike with adhesive—that is, if any adhesive was available—then when the family was assembled, loudly announce: "Of course, the dressing must not be disturbed for a week." Usually then someone would be present to protest the premature removal of the dressings if the doctor became overpowered by curiosity.

Be it emphasized that these experiences had to do with the profession of long ago when many of the practitioners had graduated from correspondence schools or had "read medicine" with an older practitioner.

When drainage was necessary this furnished an even more difficult problem. In the drainage of abscesses a rubber tube or a piece of gauze or both were used. Too often the drain was prematurely removed by the doctor because the patient was "doing all right." In one such instance when the gauze in an abscess of the brain was removed by a young doctor who should have known better, the patient died from the spread of the infection. On the contrary, sometimes the drain was allowed to remain in place literally for weeks. This was particularly likely to occur if the family selected the surgeon contrary to the wishes of the local doctor. If things turned out badly the local doctor could say that he had told the folks that the surgeon they selected was incompetent. Sometimes he left the drain in permanently and then it would serve as a basis for a malpractice suit. Fortunately, those of us who traveled hither and yon were not attractive propositions for the lawyers.

Nor was this all. One had to contend with the village clergy. One of these functionaries frequently knew of some doctor member of his church who was older than I, had longer whiskers and was hence more qualified, who should be called. It may be inferred that I was never noted for my piety, at least not the prescribed variety, and these experiences did not help to make me more so. I want to record here that priests invariably stand back of the doctor and encourage the patient. Often have I heard them say to the patient, "The doctor knows best"; and sometimes they were right, and what is more I redoubled my efforts to justify their generous estimates.

On the whole, I may say that the unfavorable environment and the paucity of equipment was the least of the trouble in doing kitchen surgery. It was the annoying associated conditions which supplied the most grief.

One of these annoying conditions may be mentioned. Often the local doctor would meet me at the train and deliver himself of the following: "I haven't said anything to the patient about an operation but I believe if you talk to him right he will consent." In some cases the patient was not informed that an operation was even contemplated. Some even pretended to the patient that the surgeon's visit was casual, as he just happened to be going through town, and they figured it a good time to have the operation done, cheap. The visiting surgeon was then supposed to persuade the patient to submit to the operation. I hope it is unnecessary to record that I never engaged in such practices.

The most exasperating conditions were in those instances in which the local physician would call the consultant. When I arrived the doctor would meet me at the train and cheer me with the information that while the patients were excellent people unfortunately they were without funds, but they might be able to pay the expenses of the trip. This patient attended to, the doctor would casually remark that inasmuch as it would be several hours before train time he had another patient whom he would like to have me see for his own satisfaction; the family had not asked for consultation. This patient would prove to be really sick and usually a member of an opulent family. This left the local man free to charge full fee for himself; the consultant got nothing. I have known as much as seven hundred dollars to be charged in such a case, a fact which I sometimes did not learn of for several years. Sometimes operative cases were managed in the same way. This variation was needed. The doctor would say that the patient was perfectly willing that he himself should do the operation, but since I was to be there anyway he had deferred the operation until my arrival. One of these even had the effrontery to imply that I might be much instructed by acting as his assistant, thereby adding to my knowledge. This was true in a way: I once saw a doctor in a hernia operation merely close the skin, paying no attention to other structures. It seems incredible as I think back on those days that I never made any fuss. I may say, however, that no doctor ever played these tricks on me more than once.

When the local doctor called one in consultation on the insistence of the patient when he preferred someone else, there were many trying things he could do. One particularly aggravating experience was the following. I removed the appendix of a young girl, an operation she did not need, I now know, but I was following the teachings of the time. The operation done, I returned home, a distance of two hundred miles. When I arrived home a message was awaiting me to return to the patient at once. I did so, and found the patient in perfect condition. The nurse could not tell me why the call. A group of anxious friends had gathered. I asked one of these the cause for the message. He replied that the family doctor had told him that I had so injured the bowel that the patient could not live. The doctor was just getting even with me for not giving him a part of the fee.

Some doctors were smarter. I was called to a neighboring state to remove a large tumor. The doctor wrote me that the patient's husband was destitute, but that a brother had agreed to pay my fee. The patient certainly was destitute. A two-room shack on a bleak prairie, nothing in sight but bunch grass and thistles and not many of these. The house contained an old stove, a table and a few boxes which were used as chairs. The tumor, a huge ovarian cyst, was removed without trouble. The doctor gave the anesthetic, and did it well, and I was the entire operative team. The operation completed, the doctor said to the brother of the patient's husband as follows: "The doctor has done his part. Now it is time to do your part." The brother made remark to the effect that the tumor being removed, I could not put it back. He intimated that I might, well, go to Kansas, the operation being done in Texas. This seemed to clear the local doctor of any evil intent. But it proved too funny for him to keep to himself. He told a friend of his that it was a put-up job. He and the brother divided the fee I was to get, seventy-five dollars for each. Time levels many things; they both have been gathered to their stepfathers long since. The railway fare, riding in the smoker, cost me twenty-nine dollars and nearly two days of time. But I relieved the patient of a tumor that soon would have killed her. Also, I had a specimen.

Such instances, quite aside from the matter of the operation, made kitchen surgery disagreeable. It is pleasing to relate that such annoyances were the exceptions and it is for this reason that they stick in one's memory. In the vast majority of instances the doctor was cooperative to the extent of his ability. The drawbacks were the fatigue of travel and the necessity of spending weary hours getting the kitchen and the equipment ready.

In one of my early visits in the country I learned a new principle. The patient had a perforated appendix and, as a result of the associated general peritonitis, was hugely distended. My experience, both as pathologist and as surgeon, had been that such patients all died after operation. I did not operate. Some three months later—I had not heard from the doctor in the meantime—the patient walked into my office and nonchalantly asked for his bill. "Nothing," I yelled at him; I took him to lunch and a ball game. He had taught me something, when not to operate. The distended intestines were doing their best to keep the infection localized. Had I operated on him I would have defeated nature's block.

The best piece of work I have ever done in hospitals or in the kitchen dates back to my youth in the old traveling days. I received a call from an old retired country doctor, as grand an old man as one ever could hope to meet. When I arrived he told me that he had sent for me because he understood I was fearless, that his daughter had been sick for nine months and unless someone did something she would surely die. Some months before he had taken the patient to a city where some of his friends, of national reputation, had observed her for three weeks. Nothing was found. All the history revealed was that she had had a premature labor at seven or eight months and following this a low fever. Nothing seemed wrong in the pelvis; the eminence of the previous consultants, in fact, precluded the likelihood of finding any trouble here. Examination revealed nothing except that under the tip of the shoulder blade there was an area which gave a sound like the chest of an asthmatic old man—hyperresonance, we doctors say. This likely had developed because the lung beneath was consolidated, I reasoned. I stayed at the house all night but did not sleep. As day began to break I half dozed for a moment and I awoke with a start—it was a lung abscess.

I told the doctor my diagnosis and he replied that I should do whatever I thought best and he would back me to the limit. The patient was emaciated to a skeleton, was restless and whiny as patients become who have long harbored a suppuration. Hence a general anesthetic seemed necessary in order to resect a part of a rib. A local doctor gave the anesthetic. He dropped ether for a solid hour. At the end of this time he announced that the patient was ready. She asked, "What did you say, doctor?" She had not even started to go to sleep. Another long period was required but finally, with my constant encouragement to pour on more ether, she became sufficiently etherized to permit the removal of a part of the rib. The lung was stitched to the hole I had made in the chest wall and then I passed a long needle toward the area where I pictured the abscess to be. A resistance to the needle showed that my reasoning was correct. There was a dense area in the middle of the lung. I had yet to prove that there was an abscess therein. The syringe which I attached to the needle failed to produce any free pus, only a little blood serum. I made a slide at once and inoculated a tube of culture media. The slide showed a short chain streptococcus and the tube gave, after a few days, a confirmatory growth. I left the patient with the agreement to go back in ten days and put in a drainage tube.

I returned and placed a tube in the region where the dense area of lung was located. I found no pus. Ten days later the doctor joyfully reported that the tube was draining pus freely. The diagnosis had been proved. A number of weeks later the drainage tube became disarranged and I had to return and replace it. After a period of months I visited her again, and concluding the abscess had healed I removed the tube. A year to a day after the first operation the patient visited me to allow me to see how well she was. Her health was perfect, save that the long confinement to bed had kept her feet extended so long that the function of her ankles had become impaired and walking was difficult. I traveled about a thousand miles in treating this patient. It was worth it, for it gave me confidence in myself—I had unquestionably rescued a patient passed up by two nationally known surgeons. All things considered, that is the best job I have ever done and certainly the boldest, tackling a job two surgeons of national reputation had refused. When I think of those early days I laugh aloud, for I had the reputation of being a modest kid. The answer is I kept my mouth shut, and I was an expert anatomist. A good anatomist has no need to be afraid of anything in the operative field. Sure, I was a good anatomist. Waldeyer said I was and that made it unanimous.

Another good job was as follows. At the end of a long ride in a blizzard, referred to elsewhere, I met the family doctor and we went out into the country. A cattleman had been unconscious for ten days. All that could be learned was that the patient had had an earache sometime before he became unconscious. He had not had a medical attendant. With this major clue, I proceeded to hunt for a brain abscess, and found it. The patient recovered.

One of my operations on the road approached the comic. I was called a long distance to see an asthmatic patient who was supposed to be in a serious condition. My faith in the diagnostic ability of the local doctor made me feel quite sure that the nature of the trouble was nonsurgical. I found a patient sitting up fighting for breath, but a glance showed that asthma was not the trouble. A cursory examination revealed a goiter all but entirely hidden in the chest cavity. The house was a one-room affair with no facilities whatever and the interior was not suitable for an operating room. Therefore, an operating table was erected in the yard under an apple tree. The kitchen door was removed and placed on two barrels. A box served as instrument table and another box as a stool for the operator. The operation proceeded under local anesthesia. After the goiter was exposed it was the shape and density of a baseball. I had only a few small artery forceps and I was unable to grasp the goiter with them. As I sat there pondering over the situation I recalled having read somewhere that sometimes the patient could cough such goiters out of the chest cavity. So I nudged my patient in the ribs with my elbow and instructed him to cough. The pressure from the goiter on his windpipe being somewhat relieved by the incision, he was able to take a deep breath. As his huge chest contracted the goiter shot so far out that it lay fully exposed in the wound of the neck. Automatically I grasped it with both hands in true short-stop style, for which I had had training in my boyhood. Then I sat holding that goiter in both hands while taking stock of the situation. After locating my instruments, I released one hand and with it clamped the lower vessels. The rest of the operation was easy. The patient recovered uneventfully. There were no birds in the tree.

Sometimes there were little side incidents that relieved otherwise prosaic situations. I was doing an operation for strangulated hernia; no one else was present but the wife and, what is almost unknown for a woman to do, she departed for parts unknown as soon as she learned that an operation would be necessary. So it was the patient and I for it. I had not anticipated an operation and I had only a few instruments, such as were contained in the pocket cases of the old days. There were no linens and I could find only a single towel. This I cut up for sponges and boiled with my instruments. There was nothing to place about the site of the operation and the patient lay as bare as the day he was born except for an astonishingly large beard. Being bewhiskered himself, there was no razor on the premises. I clipped the hair as well as I could and doped him with iodine. In fact, the application of iodine was unduly generous and he emitted some lamentations. The local anesthetic injected, the operation proceeded without incident. As I began to place the sutures he found a new place where the iodine had burned and he squirmed, throwing my knife, my only cutting instrument to the floor. How was I to cut the sutures? That was easy. I grasped the sutures close to the knot with one of my two artery forceps, caught the sutures a little higher with the other and twisted the catgut until it broke. Perfectly simple, but I did some heavy thinking for a moment. The wound healed promptly and perfectly. In my cocky days I rather enjoyed such situations, like a good batter with the bases loaded, and I have invented a number of operations as I stood beside the operating table, tissue in hand.

One experience I had on the road was unusual. It did not impress me at the time, but after relating it in a hospital staff-room several times I found it impressed the inexperienced. It had to do with a patient who had suffered profuse hemorrhages from a fibroid of the uterus. She was hours away from a hospital. Besides, she declared she would lie in bed until she died before she would go to a hospital. She said it with a finality that left no doubt. This indicates that she was a large woman. I found myself without any surgical equipment whatever. In taking an inventory of the old doctor's resources, it was found he had only one artery forceps and an ancient scalpel but he did have a few good needles and some good surgeon's silk. Not much equipment for removing a uterus. But there seemed to be no alternative, so I proceeded with the operation, I am afraid with a nice bit of bravado. The lone artery forceps, of course, I had to use as a needle holder. Vessels had to be ligated before they were cut and some double ligation was necessary. Any good anatomist can indicate just exactly where ligatures under such conditions must be placed. I was a good anatomist and I double-ligated before I cut and I proceeded without a bit of compunction. The doctor gave the anesthetic, chloroform, and did it well. The operation proceeded without a single untoward incident, and without an assistant. The patient recovered without incident.

A most impressive case had to do with a maiden lady forty-six years of age. She had not walked a step for eighteen years. She was lifted from her bed to a wheel chair several times a day by some member of the family during all that time. She busied herself with making the various things women like to make. She seemed to be perfectly normal mentally and exhibited no signs of nervousness.

I made no examination of her nervous system nor of the tone of the muscles of the legs but I observed that during the examination she could move her legs any way I directed and that the muscle tone was good.

She had a tumor of the uterus, just beginning to produce bleeding that would ultimately demand its removal. I explained to the patient that the cause of her inability to walk was due to the pressure on the nerves of that tumor and that its removal would relieve her of her difficulty. I explained at length just how tumors pressed on the nerves, how this changed the structure of the muscle and all that. I would not have the layman gather that when a doctor becomes fluent of speech he is lying. Volubility is a varying and personal factor.

The tumor was removed. I made no reference to her condition while she was convalescing from the operation. In fact, she saw me scarcely at all. After three weeks, when she had fully recovered from her operation, I went into her room with a sheet and abruptly announced that we were going for a walk. And we did and she has continued to walk since—lo, these many years.

The cause of the failure to walk, failure is the proper word—it was not a deliberate refusal—never was revealed. I did not inquire his name nor did I attempt to extract details as to the occurrence. To have done so likely would have excited consciously or unconsciously memories that likely would have defeated my purpose. It is said a good salesman knows when he has made a sale and pushes over the dotted line and hands over the pen. It is equally as important in the management of certain types of patients to know when one has learned enough. Such cases cannot be handled well in a clinic where all sorts of irrelevant things are entered into. Such cases are a one-man job. And if he is wise he will keep strictly his own council, reveal nothing to anyone. Even to such patients the the local doctor may drop inadvertent remarks which may spoil all one's labor. I have recorded such an example.

The recollection of one patient I operated on makes me want to paraphrase an old saw: young surgeons tiptoe in where older surgeons fear to tread. The occasion was as follows. A patient with a huge ovarian tumor consulted a surgeon of note. He declared it inoperable. True enough, she had a tumor weighing about fifty pounds; both chest cavities were filled with fluid and her legs were swollen. The patient had been unable to lie down to sleep for some months. Her doctor had a friend who knew a young doctor who would tackle anything. The prospect was not really attractive. The surgeon she had consulted told her that she had but a few months to live. She was an intelligent woman and related to me the bad prognosis the old surgeon had given her. She said if there was one chance in a thousand she wanted it, because she had five children who needed her. I told her the tumor was operable all right, but that her general condition was anything but inviting. After everything was discussed she remarked that she wanted me to go ahead, adding that if I failed she did not want me to feel badly about it. This was the agreement. I added that in such desperate cases I wanted everybody to know that I did not intend to charge a fee, no matter how satisfactory the result. I made this a principle from the beginning when considering operations of more than usual serious outlook. When this principle is adhered to in case the outcome is disastrous no one can say that the operator knew before the operation that it would prove fatal and only operated for the fee.

This patient was treated as follows. The fluid was aspirated from both chest cavities. Thus was lessened the swelling of the legs. The enlargement of the abdomen was such that she could not lie down on the operating table. So she sat up, legs hanging over the end of the folding table. I sat down between her thighs and began the operation under local anesthesia. The tumor was semisolid, made up of a jellylike mass. The top of the tumor was exposed for six inches and a wedge-shaped piece cut out. The tumor was shifted a bit and another piece cut off. This was continued until the entire tumor was removed. It required about two hours to complete the job. She declared at once that she was able to take a deep breath for the first time in several years. She could lie down with perfect comfort.

The astonishing part is that when I visited her the next day she was sitting up at a table calmly writing a letter. There was no nurse to restrain her. The recovery was uneventful. Just as I liked to drive in the country when no one else would venture forth, so I have always gotten a thrill out of doing operations no one else cared to attempt.

The biggest scare I ever got was while doing an operation for intestinal obstruction. The offending band had been found and removed, fortunately. Just as closure of the wound was about to begin the man holding the coal-oil lamp started to faint and dropped the lamp. Fortunately, he tilted it toward himself, knocking off the chimney and putting out the flame before dropping it on the floor. There was no other lamp in the house. Someone thought she knew where there was a tallow candle, but was not sure. In the dark I placed several artery forceps on either edge of the wound and by crossing them was able to hold the wound together. It would be about six hours until day light and that would be a long time to hold the forceps. Besides, the patient would be coming out from under the anesthetic, which would complicate the problem. While I was engaged in cogitation, the tallow candle was found and the closure of the wound proceeded. On one other occasion the same accident happened, but that time I had a flashlight in my overcoat pocket and, strange to relate, it worked—hence the delay was short.

The shortest trip I ever made to reach my patient may be mentioned, the trip being short because I was both patient and surgeon. Following one of my attacks of erysipelas I developed an abscess of the neck. One night about two o'clock the pain became unbearable. So I prepared a local anesthetic, a few instruments and placed a looking glass on the kitchen table and proceeded to hunt for the abscess. An incision behind the facial artery failed to locate the abscess, so I made another one in front of this vessel. I bored a dissecting scissors into the depth of my neck until the abscess was reached, then I hooked an index finger in each handle of the scissors and gave a violent jerk. This made an opening as wide as the blades of the scissors were spread. I put in a rubber tube. The problem was somewhat complicated by the fact that the eye on the side of the abscess was completely swollen shut and I had to work with one eye. Ever since that experience when I open an abscess I know that the patient is going to have immediate relief and a nice sleep. I had many a chuckle over this experience. The nerve of it was not in making the opening but in the viewpoint. I was but a kid but I knew anatomy better than anyone else available. Besides, it was in the small hours of the morning and I had endured that throbbing for days and that was enough. Enough to me always has been enough. I was generally regarded as a modest kid but I was plenty cocky under the skin.

One time I was completely deflated. I went away out into the short-grass country not knowing what I was going to encounter. I was led into a bedroom where a wonderful black-eyed girl lay. She met me with a wan little appealing look. She was the replica of my own little daughter. I saw at once that she had an enormously distended abdomen; her pulse was running and so was my own. I asked her age. "Nine," she replied— the age of my little girl. In order to compose myself I asked her name. "Agnes," came the reply. My daughter's name! I thought I would choke. The abdomen was so distended with gas that I knew if it was a general peritonitis operation would be worse than useless; if not, operation was urgently demanded at once. The risk had to be undertaken. I made the incision under local anesthesia on this nine-year-old girl. I explained every detail of the operation as I proceeded with the preparation. The moment my hand touched the instruments all agitation ceased and I am sure I never worked more expertly. The moment the peritoneum was incised there was a gush of pus and gas. It was a localized abscess. She made a prompt recovery. That was thirty-three years ago but I still can see every detail of that room and can see in my mind's eye every step of the operation. When it comes to operating on children I am a coward at heart. I want to run away, but I never have.

Sometimes I have been a better pathologist than surgeon. I had a little lesion on my forehead which developed following a slight injury from coming in contact with a broken weed in one of my buggy upsets. It seemed to me to be a waste of good material not to examine it microscopically. So it must be removed. I proceeded as before and though I had the use of two eyes the perplexities mounted. The lesion bled profusely: both eyes were inundated with blood so that I could see out of neither. Nothing remained to do but to control the bleeding by pressure. I discovered that by tilting my head sidewise I had the use of one eye; but this unnatural position, besides the reversed movements from looking into a looking glass, made the procedure a bit awkward. However, I got the specimen.

I recall one operation that had several elements. Which dominated depends on the point of view. A pugilist of some renown needed an operation, but he feared the hospital. A dining-room table was prepared as previously described. As the patient began to go under the anesthetic he began violently to agitate his very husky body. The table broke in the middle. The partially anesthetized patient fell to the floor but instantly sprang to his feet and assumed the attitude pugilists do when posing for the reporters. I was his imaginary opponent. I had other ideas. Behind me was a screened door leading to a porch with a railing around it. This exit looked inviting to me. The door was latched, so I just took it with me as a souvenir and I also took the porch railing along as a memento and landed with both feet on the ground some four feet below. An ether-drunk pugilist is a forbidding object. I have faced mad bulls in my day, but they look like nice bossies compared to that prize fighter. Believe it or not, the family doctor persuaded the patient, after he partly recovered from the ether, to lie down on the bed; he was re-etherized, and I performed the operation. Needless to say, I stood on the porch and just peeped in the door until the deep snoring of the patient assured me that he was in deep narcosis.

It is said the Fates are kind to the beginner. This was most certainly true in my case. I did operations on the road for conditions I would not think of doing even in a hospital now. This was particularly true of goiter operations. I operated on patients I had never seen before and, of course, they had no preparation of any sort. I did one very toxic lady who ever had a rise of temperature and was as wild as the proverbial March hare. One lady had a widely dilated heart and was so dropsical she could not lie down, so I operated on her sitting up. Both recovered.

The majority of the operations I did on the road were the usual operations done in any hospital. The various pelvic operations for tumors, as well as the repair of lacerations. Breast operations for cancer, and resection of cysts that had been mistaken for cancer. I drained four brain abscesses on the road, and did many mastoid operations, one with local anesthesia without re-moving the patient from the bed, a typhoid-fever patient. She recovered from both. In fact, I have done about every opera-tion known to surgery in the kitchen, from ingrowing toenails to Gasserian ganglions. I was not afraid then. I would not con-sider tackling such things under those circumstances now. It is a strange feeling. I never feared any operation and do not now, but somehow when confronted by a difficult operation I like to see my old time-tried assistant of more than twenty years at my side. I presume it is a sort of premonition that sometime I shall hand the scalpel permanently to those who will follow me.

I look back on those days of kitchen surgery with unadul-terated pleasure. No doubt about it, I saved many lives, and made many friendships which have endured. Most of the doc-tors who were associated with me in these experiences are now dead, and of course many of the patients, happily most of them from old age. Many of the trips were terribly arduous, even worse, but these things are soon forgotten after a full meal and a warm fire, and an interesting specimen. Those days are gone forever. The coming generation of surgeons will not have a like experience. They will have to accept the word of the old kitchen surgeons that all that is needed for a good operation is a good surgeon and a patient.

CHAPTER

10 _____

TIME WAS WHEN THE PRIVATE HOSPITAL, COLLECTIVELY SPEAK-
ing, in Kansas was quite an institution. There were more hospitals per capita—or, perhaps better stated, there were fewer
"caputs" per hospital—than in any other like area on earth.
The upgrowth of private hospitals was a veritable eruption. I
have asked a number of men who became so afflicted why they
started a hospital. None could make a sound.

It seems, therefore, that in an attempt to answer that question for myself I have a virgin field. One can approach this
problem from two angles.

There is the abstract or impersonal which forces one to recognize that all projects have somewhere a commercial basis, or
something which it is hoped will sometime have a happy end
as a commercial success. To the doctor the approach is not direct.
No hospital in itself pays overhead. The doctor must seek his
rewards through the increase in practice which is expected to
produce the emoluments which the hospital will most certainly
not do. Next to money, the most sought-after factor is glory.
The owner of a hospital sort of imagines a crown for himself.
Crowns, generally speaking, have thorns. So it was here, and it
was right because the activating forces were not noble; but
despite this, taken in the aggregate, a worth-while end was
achieved.

I BUILD A HOSPITAL

As far as I can now recall, the bare facts in my case were something like the following: I had a surgical education but I had to face the fact that a surgeon is not a surgeon if he has no patients. Are those who have never been tempted virtuous? How can one tell? It is an abstract proposition, and at best I was then a surgeon only in the abstract. I had done some operating in private houses, as described elsewhere. It seemed to me that if I had a hospital I could augment my surgical practice. At least many of my colleagues seemed to think so, as expressed by their activities in building hospitals. Certain it is I had no intention of building a considerable institution which would ultimately absorb most of my professional efforts for the rest of my life. It was to be a meal ticket, as I now recall, until I could build up a city practice. Nothing noble in such a motivating force, a meal ticket, yet most people spend the greater part of their lives in just such a pursuit. Therefore, I need not apologize, for in most cases any success is made up of an urgent need of making a living; this, if attached to something of a vision and pursued with stubborn tenacity, may lead to something worth while. Few can visualize the route they must travel when they start—nor the end, fortunately—or there would be nothing started, nothing builded.

Decisions hinge on funny things sometimes. The time came when obviously it would be necessary for me soon to decide between the city practice which I had developed and my country hospital. One night at a social function at which I was an innocent bystander I spied a friend of mine, also of agrarian origin, trying to dance, rigged out in a spike-tailed coat, white vest and gloves. The thought flashed into my mind—to the country, you, before you fall.

Also, one might conjure up an ideal purpose in the building of a hospital, and to those who may possibly sometime wish to write my obituary for the delectation of my great-grandchildren I might suggest something like the following: maybe I had the feeling that my skill, certainly visionary, should be made conveniently available to the great middle class, of which I am unquestionably one—middle in genesis, in the middle of Kansas. This would imply that I envisaged the finished product at the beginning and that I ultimately achieved my hopes. This is assuming a great deal, but my great-grandchildren are still quite in the distant future. After one is removed from his competitors for a time it is not difficult for the generous-minded to attribute almost anything to the motives of the late-lamented. The degree of alleged success may expand to geometric proportions without notable protest. Truth in obituaries receives about the same rough handling as it does in a divorce court. This is just a suggestion.

In the abstract approach of the subject as to why so many hospitals sprang up through the enterprise of individual doctors, being a part of this movement, I can offer no solution. Actual participants are never so well able to judge motives as the grandstand managers. Likely, several factors were active with the most of them. At any rate, almost simultaneously the idea of building a hospital, out where the patients originate, occurred to a number of doctors. Therefore, it must have been a sort of contagious itch, or something. Perhaps it was because some doctor in a neighboring town had one—itch, hospital or both. This, among those who did not participate, was called envy or something like that. At any rate, as the result of that something many small hospitals sprang up in small towns even when the distance from an established hospital was not great. Actual need, therefore, was not a very compelling factor. I know of one small town which had five hospitals, the number, curiously enough, being exactly equal to the number of doctors located there. As above noted, at one time Kansas had more "hospitals" per capita than any other state in the Union, even though the term had to be inclosed in quotation marks as "securities" are now by honest writers of finance. The quotation marks are more conservative than a question mark would be.

I BUILD A HOSPITAL

After the private hospitals became a sort of epidemic, many churches established hospitals: either by building a new one in opposition to the private hospital, or by taking over a private one and with this as a nucleus building a sizable institution. Of course the churches were actuated by a desire to serve suffering humanity, or because the church around the corner had recently been so inspired. Churches, I have noted, are made up of one or more individuals, consequently they may be inspired by variable and very human motives. Be this as it may, the most of us sooner or later found it convenient to hand over our squalling infants to some church organization. So too close inquiry would be out of place.

It may help to look at the hospitals which were in existence prior to the hospital-building epidemic which I am now seeking to explain or excuse. Fifty years ago, only the larger cities had hospitals. Only emergency work was done by the country doctor, and at that time only the emergencies due to accident were treated by him. The conveyances in that day were such that most country patients were a long way from a hospital. For instance, this place was thirty-five miles from one and that meant at least five hours of travel if the roads were good. If the roads were bad the distance was lengthened. By the time the family gathered and sat as a jury on the doctor's judgment that an operation was needed, many other precious hours elapsed. Because of the delay the mortality of operations, therefore, was necessarily very high. When fatalities occurred the hospital, being the last link of the chain became, at least subconsciously, the culprit—the ultimate cause of death.

As more diseases came within the range of the surgeon the need for more convenient hospitals became emphasized. This was the more laudable excuse for the establishment of the many small hospitals. Before that excuse becomes valid, of course, a hospital needs to have a surgeon capable of doing such operations. Surgeons, I may confide, do not recognize their limitations until they outgrow those limitations, if they ever do, and look backward to their beginnings. To be sure, those of us who built hospitals had no doubts on this point—at least not before the hospital was built. Afterward, no doubt, there were moments that harassed us.

Medical cases in that early day were nearly all treated at home. In fact, there was little occasion for nonsurgical patients to be taken to the hospital. The examinations known in those days could be done as well in the patient's home as in a hospital. The profusion of examinations now commonly done, notably chemical and X-ray examinations, were at that time, of course, unknown. Nor did the doctors of that day hesitate to make themselves the trouble of caring for the patient at his home. The value of expert nursing was not appreciated by either doctor or patient; even if it had been, none was available except in the cities. Most patients, as a matter of fact, could not have afforded hospitalization and, not being able to pay for service, it did not occur to them that it was possible to accept service for which they could not pay.

Moreover, most patients can be diagnosed with reasonable accuracy by a good doctor without elaborate laboratory examinations. Ray Lyman Wilbur once said a good doctor clothed only in B.V.D.'s should be able to diagnose eighty per cent of the cases, which is equivalent to saying that the doctor should be able to determine the nature of the ailment with his unaided five senses—really three senses, for the doctor rarely tastes his patient and when the sense of smell comes into play it is involuntary. This represents the proportionate number that can be adequately managed without resort to either clinic or hospital.

Even today, it may be here interpolated, often the chief reason for sending the majority of patients to the hospital is that it is more convenient for the doctor. It is less trouble for him to have as many as possible of his patients concentrated at one point. This is quite necessary for very busy men, because in most cases it is only the patients whose ailments are obscure that come to him. Likewise, sending the patient to the hospital relieves the family of much responsibility, a thing to be desired in these days of cocktails, movies and bridge. True, it is often cheaper to have the patient treated at a hospital, especially in cases where a private nurse is required. In most cases, however, it is a matter of election whether the patient shall be taken to a hospital or not.

Nowadays the modern hospital has its distinct advantage for the nonsurgical cases in, say, ten per cent, in which every possible means of diagnosis must be used. Such examinations usually require several days for their completion, especially in those cases where X-ray examinations and many laboratory tests are required. Unfortunately, it is a common practice to have all these examinations made before the doctor even attempts to make a provisional diagnosis. It sometimes seems that the doctor does not use his brains until, or if, it really becomes necessary; let the laboratory girls do the work. For patients who are bedfast, a double service is secured, hospital care is provided while the detailed investigation is being conducted and the doctor prepares to function.

There were other factors which require mention. One motivating force for the starting of the small hospital was that country doctors noted that when the patient went to the city the expenses there were such that their part of the fees were automatically blotted out. Later "fee splitting" was invented in order to equalize the injustice wherein the city surgeon got all the money and the country doctor who made the diagnosis, and likely went with the patient to the hospital, got nothing. I had my turn at that too. There was a measure of justice in this understanding between the city surgeon and the country doctor. Fee splitting, it scarcely needs be explained (certainly not in Kansas), is the practice wherein the surgeon collects the fee and gives the referring doctor part, unbeknown to the patient. This practice showed its evil side when incapable surgeons sought to deflect patients from capable men by hiking the ante to the country doctors who referred patients to him. When the old established surgeon found his young opponent making inroads on his practice by a more liberal division of fees, naturally he came to regard the practice as diabolical. He made a moral campaign against it. The final floration of this virtuous spasm is to be found in the regulation of the American College which forbids the practice among its members; it sounds more noble the way this institution put it, but I have forgotten how it was. Of course, nimble surgeons could, and some did, preach the doctrine of nonsplitting and still split on the side. Not all smartness is concentrated in the professional politicians.

Some particularly bright doctors, having learned the system from the city surgeon, applied it to their neighbors in order to boost their own business. He added the refinement, in that he invited the doctor referring the patient to wash his hands in the hospital washbowl and thereby become his assistant, and the fee handed him by the surgeon was in compensation for this "assistance." As a matter of fact, this procedure was designed to give respectability to the doctor's insistence that he be handed a part of the fee. The practice of medicine may become a very complicated procedure.

Furthermore, the private hospital had an advantage in that it gave the man with a "hospital" a certain prestige over his fellow practitioners of the neighborhood who had none, and consequently it served as a lure to patients normally belonging to less ambitious doctors. This had a measure of justification, because those who established a hospital really were men of ambition, as indicated by this very act, and their knowledge was supposed to be and sometimes actually was superior in a general way to the plain horse and buggy doctor.

Unfortunately, bread is buttered only on the top surface. Those who started hospitals paid aplenty for the advantages they obtained, or sought to obtain, by the establishment of a hospital of their own. Like all baby white elephants they grew in the course of years and their food consumption, technically classed as overhead, became a most distressing thing to contemplate. The most of us, as a matter of fact, had never seen an adult animal of this species. Like most moonlight dreams it was not the first cost, but the upkeep, that became the important matter.

Whatever the lure or motivating force that led to the establishment of the small hospitals by individual doctors, they did serve an important purpose in the history of medicine. They did furnish opportunity to the ambitious doctor to do better work and there did evolve from them many outstanding surgeons. The patient was thus, at least ultimately, enabled to secure expert service at home, near friends and at a minimum of cost, or no cost at all if they wished.

It cannot be too strongly insisted upon that one of the chief services of the hospital was that it broke the patients of hospital shyness. They learned to go to the hospital for relief of minor ailments and for the beginnings of the more serious ones. Patients were much more willing to go to a hospital at home near their friends, under the care of a doctor known to them, than to go long distances to a city to be placed under the charge of a strange doctor and in strange surroundings. As patients submitted to operation earlier the mortality lessened, which in turn served to decrease the fear of hospitals. This in many cases enabled the small-hospital doctor to operate with lower mortality than the city surgeon, for no doubt fear plays a role in the recovery of the patient. This also helped the local hospital.

Naturally, hospitals were as valuable to the community in which they were built as the surgeon was capable, or honest. Perish the thought, all doctors are honest but some have less of that which has been called sales resistance. That is to say, some saw indications for operations when others saw none. Somewhere along the line the so-called "chronic appendicitis," and the like was discovered or evolved, as the case may be. This is a very complicated problem and no layman can hope to comprehend it in all its ramifications: sometimes names are operated on instead of diseases.

So whatever it was that induced us doctors to sell our skins for our little hospitals it served a purpose even though they failed in the purpose for which they were built: that is, to produce revenue, experience or prestige. There is no need to hunt too diligently for motives. It isn't generally done in any walk of life. Most heads which are crowned are so decorated because the individual had no idea where he was going when he started out and succeeded because he did not have sense enough to quit. Everyone knows that this is true in war and love, and it is equally true of us who established hospitals. Most monuments are erected long after the bones they represent have returned to dust. Most recipients of such honors died without ever having realized that they were heroes. Some of us old duffers who built hospitals are still trying to figure out if we were heroes or just plain stubborn fools. I cannot confide my own conclusions here, because I have not fully formulated them. The game is not yet played out. I am just stretching at the beginning of the seventh inning.

A hospital, it must be emphasized, is made up of two parts, the building and the spirit that actuates the conduction of it. Both may be good, both may be bad; one may be good, one bad. Anybody can see the building; only experts can see the other factor, or it would not be a spirit.

Physically, most of these small hospitals had for the greater part a like genesis. They had their beginnings, in most instances, in a private residence, ofttimes formerly belonging to a defunct or demised prominent citizen. Sometimes the doctor and his family lived downstairs and the wife did the cooking. The second-story rooms housed the patients. Some smart and handsome doctors married nurses, in which case the lady did the nursing and a cook was hired. I knew a number of instances in which the wife-nurse performed both functions.

Usually half a dozen or fewer hospital beds found available space in these houses. The operating room was usually the bedroom of the former cook, selected for this purpose because it was not a desirable room for a hospital bed. The kitchen stove usually supplied the heat for the sterilization of the instruments and dressings. This made it necessary for the doctor to eat an early breakfast, so that the stove could be available as a sterilizer when it came time to prepare for the operation. Operating in such hospitals was but slightly removed from the kitchen surgery of any private residence.

There are too many complicating factors involved in the building of a small-town hospital to permit of treatment in the abstract. Therefore, I shall give my experience with some detail, because it was, with some modification, a replica of others. Any bitter experience I shall not be able to suppress was not peculiar to my own experience but is applicable to any community which has harbored a struggling institution.

Those of us who began in towns too small to provide a private residence of sufficient size started with specially designed buildings which, because of expense, were wooden structures of about six or a dozen rooms. Such buildings could be more nearly adapted to the needs to which they were to be put than the old private residence. These small hospitals usually were fitted with a small sterilizing room and a more adequate operating room than their old residence contemporaries. Yet they were all equally primitive in every essential and all veritable firetraps. Even so, I have never known any of these buildings to burn down, probably owing to eternal vigilance, since the owner was on the job all hours of the day or night, either nursing patients or figuring "overhead" or nursing a headache.

It is enough to make one weep to think back on those early beginnings. These hospitals never paid their way and the hapless doctor had to use the earnings of the country drives and town calls to make up the deficit of the hospital. One of my friends, I have always felt, literally gave his life for his hospital.

Having demonstrated by the foregoing that an adequate excuse for establishing a hospital is at this late date not available, I may now proceed to describe the process. The beginning of my enterprise contemplated a building thirty-six by fifty feet; it was to contain five good rooms, suitable for surgical patients, and an equal number on the third floor, suitable for patients taken in for study only. It was constructed of wood, of course. It had a hot-air furnace put in by a local firm, and it never worked because of faulty construction. All the hot air emanated from the man who sold it to me. A reward for patronizing local industry.

There was a tank in the basement into which water was pumped by man power and which furnished pressure sufficient to force water to the operating room. Operating these hand pumps, I may explain, is something like playing golf, valuable for developing the muscles of the back and shoulders, and of course the vocabulary. At any rate, my hospital had hot and cold water for necessary scrubbing before operations.

The first floor contained, besides the operating room, the kitchen, dining room, bathroom and a bedroom or two. The operating room had a tile floor, a source of great pride to me. Other hospitals in the neighborhood were not so provided. A local mechanic laid the tile, using "hot air" instead of cement to hold the little hexagons in place. He had never even seen tile laid, but he knew he could do it. The result was that when one walked across the floor the loose tile rolled after him, so I had to import a man from the city to make the tile stay put. Another reward for patronizing local industry.

The floor of the operating room had a drain in the middle of it, just like the city hospitals had. The idea was that one could scrub the floor with a hose and the water could run out of the floor drain. That is, one could do this but one never did—just like a lot of other things about hospitals, things put in so one can do certain things, which one never does. Only those who know nothing about running hospitals can see the joke. It was too deep for us hospital people to fathom.

We had a low-pressure steam sterilizer costing sixty dollars and a pan made by a local tinsmith in which to boil the instruments and gloves, if any. This cost two dollars. That was the total equipment of the sterilizing room. Add up the figures, sixty-two dollars. Here is the point: the sterilization was perfect, equal to any built up to now. No laugh. Long on efficiency but woefully short on convenience.

A place was left for an elevator, a dream for future realization. In fact, most of the structure consisted of places for dreams for future realization. In the meantime, patients too sick to walk had to be carried upstairs—that turned out to be work and no dream.

My hospital was figured to cost four thousand dollars and it cost half as much again—close figuring for mechanics, as I learned later. Local merchants enthusiastically encouraged the building of the hospital. Not being a cow, I did not know the basic factor that gives these animals their social standing. I soon found out. After the lumber bill was paid the lumberman came to me and solemnly told me he had charged too little for his lumber by the sum of exactly five hundred dollars. I had the lumber figured by a brother then in the lumber business, and a profit of twenty per cent had already been collected. I let out a howl but to no purpose. I had to pay it. This shows, better than anything I can say, what a meek young yokel I was. Everything that was put into the building suffered the same fate. Half a dollar here, a dollar or two there; everybody was anxious to smell the pie even if he could not get an actual taste. In rural communities, I may explain, any sum over thirty cents is classed as big business.

One has to understand the psychology of small communities in order not to be annoyed by such practices. It is customary for all the citizens to encourage the development of a new enterprise. Collectively they are strong for it, because they confidently expect to collect. The joke is that while collectively the approbation is unanimous, they are also a unit in that everyone is for himself, trying to milk the critter while the misguided dupe who promotes the enterprise does all the feeding. If a cow objects to these numerous and miscellaneous milkings she just naturally loses social standing. She isn't a nice cow. I fulfilled all social requirements of being a nice meek bossie.

This capacity of the local businessmen to gouge hurt, and it hurt terribly. In retrospect, the little tiger engendered in me when I had my head injury still gnaws at my vitals. Of course, had I had any sense I would have moved away from such a situation at this early stage, but I have never bothered myself with the exercises of intelligence when a fight was a good substitute. I had started out to find out how cheaply first-class hospital service could be provided for middle-class people in a country town and I was going to find out. But what the cost would be I never dreamed and I cannot flatter myself by believing it would have made a particle of difference if I had. I am confessing, not boasting.

To those who did not live it, the personnel of my "hospital" in the beginning will seem amusing; but to those who lived it, it seems tragic. The trained nurse in charge received forty dollars a month, the most capable nurse I ever met. She has an oil well now, perhaps the gods are making deferred payment—long may she live and enjoy its bounty. Two girls, each receiving two dollars a week, did the cooking and the laundry. My assistant got fifty dollars a month and boarded himself. The janitor got half this amount for keeping the tank pumped full, carrying the groceries from the stores and in winter trying to induce the "furnace" to give up a little heat. I got my board. This service constituted the overhead. A personnel at a cost of one hundred and thirty-one dollars a month.

And so the building was built, a pitiable spectacle indeed. The big end was yet to come. I had only paid the county clerk the license fee. I had not even seen the bride in daylight, figuratively speaking of course. I had yet to build a plan of operation for the hospital—to formulate its spirit, if you wish. I resolved not to split fees, not with any high-sounding name back of it. I just figured it would not pay in the long run. I resolved to charge no more than four dollars a day for the patient's room and nursing, and no more than a hundred and fifty dollars for any operation. I resolved never to demand a fee in advance, never to inquire if they were or ever would be able to pay even a thin dime. That my plan was not universally followed is shown by the following incident. Some years ago an old friend came marching into my office and delivered himself of the following: "Arthur, I want to ask you a frank question and I would like to have an equally frank answer." "Shoot," I replied. "Why is it," he continued, "that you can run a hospital here alone while my entire church cannot run one in my town?" I continued that the explanation was very simple. That in order to run a hospital it was necessary to have at least one Christian on the job. He delivered himself of protestations of amazement. I inquired what was the first act his hospital performed when a patient sought relief. He had to admit it was to inquire who would pay the bill. I told him no Christian hospital would be guilty of such practices.

While my principles will cause any experienced hospital man to gasp, I maintain they are not so silly as they may seem. I had ridden the country roads and I knew my people. Our Kansas folks may do funny things politically, but they are men. Meet them man to man, look them square in the eye and they will not fail you. My faith has been vindicated to the fullest extent. I have told my patients, when they came with the announcement that they had no money, that I would do my best and all that I would ask was that they do the same. Very few have failed to honor this pact. I have continued this policy without equivocation.

Within the last few days one of these fine old men, a patient of forty years back, came into my office and announced that today he was eighty years old. He scorned government aid, no money earned by other hands ever insulted the palm of his hand. Your Kansan may fear God but he fears neither man nor the devil; neither grasshoppers nor drought, bond salesmen nor politicians, burglars nor bandits. Such as he, together with his equally courageous wife beside him, have made it possible for me to follow my plan even to this hour. This hospital is theirs because they built it.

But the struggle was long, difficult, heartbreaking. Naturally, at first only the most difficult cases, which established surgeons did not want, came to the new institution. Necessarily, the results were not always good. This, of course, works its vicious circle. What I still regard as my major disaster occurred in this period. It was then the practice, and still is in many hospitals, to make it a nurse's duty to count the sponges at the conclusion of the operation to assure the surgeon that none was left in the wound. One day the sponge count was correct, made by a capable nurse, now long since dead. But despite the perfect count one sponge was left in the wound. Never since have I depended on a sponge count, or even permitted one to be made. If a sponge is left in, I am the guilty party—that has been my policy ever since. And none ever has been left in.

Human nature being what it is, if anyone does something that sticks his head above his environment he invites the inevitable brickbat. I have suffered every vituperation active imaginations could conceive from my professional brethren. One must understand the psychology of local doctors. If they have a case which they are incapable of handling, it is their policy to send the patient as far away from home as possible, even though it is necessary to send them to lesser men in so doing. The idea is that if they send their difficult problems to a readily accessible consultant other less serious cases, which they deem themselves capable of handling, might automatically gravitate to the place to which they referred their more serious problems. Of course, whenever such patient goes to a distant hospital it is more or less a reflection on the local institution. The newspapers are most useful agents in aiding this aspersion. If a patient is sent to a distant clinic the local sheet headlines it. If the patient recovers it is good for a two-column headline. No matter if such cases are successfully managed several times a day at the local hospitals, the papers do not hear of it. And that is the truth—they do not hear of it. The local hospital may feel the injustice of it but never a sound emanates from it. They are and remain ethical. I am pleased to say all this is history. My professional neighbors now are my friends.

So we bumped along for several years. The financial complications were bad enough, but there were far worse complications in store for me. The afflictions Job had to bear were trivial and insignificant. My never vigorous constitution suffered numerous ailments that had not yet been invented in his time. What happened to me, of course, also affected the hospital. I was the only cow in the lot. A few of the disasters may be mentioned. I developed a tumor of my left middle finger. I removed this myself, under local anesthesia. The tumor occupied the tendon sheath for an inch and a half. The slide showed tuberculosis. The formation of a new tendon sheath was a terribly painful experience. The slightest movement of the finger caused a lightninglike, agonizing pain. Following the removal of the tumor, injections of iodoform-glycerine were made into the finger every two weeks for twelve injections. Each injection meant a continuous walking about holding that hand for twenty-four hours. Milder sedatives availed nothing in easing the pain and I did not dare to use morphine. It took nine months for it to heal so that I could again work with two hands without pain. This affliction made it possible to operate for only those things I could do with one hand and the hospital income became almost nil.

In the midst of these treatments I was laid low with jaundice, proved to be catarrhal, but some of my friends regaled me by considering the possibility of a liver tuberculosis inasmuch as the finger trouble was of this nature. I can salvage one pleasant thought from this period: so long as the jaundice lasted I did not have a single attack of my usual weekly migraine.

During this attack of jaundice I placed a cot in a back room of my office so that I could lie down when not busy with patients. This cot was not immune from female eyes and a number of females joined in the caucus to voice their suspicions. A doctor emaciated from jaundice is a devil of a fellow with the ladies as anyone would know. I can almost regard this as a compliment. At this point an old bachelor friend of mine took me to his house in the country and fed me until I could work again. I was at least away from female eyes. His characterization of the females before mentioned was a gem. I am sorry I cannot quote. I so fully concur in all he said.

After recovering from this illness I worked some months, after which I was again incapacitated by the most devastating of all diseases, acute articular rheumatism. Of all terrible pains to which the flesh is heir, and I have tasted a lot of them, I nominate the first twenty-four hours of this disease for first place.

Then followed the most trying of my experiences. As I was unable to work, of course resources soon sank to the vanishing point, and at that it was not much of a sink. Therefore, I was required, when in the midst of this disease, to sign away the very small equity I had in the hospital. It was a contemptibly cruel thing to do, because my equity was so small that it meant very little to those financially interested in the hospital. I had given the community all I had for a number of years and the act clearly indicated that I was supposed to die.

But I did not die. I recovered from the rheumatism fighting mad, prepared to fight the hounds who pursued me to what they believed was my deathbed. Though all that was left of me was a wabbly bunch of skin and bones, I came back—came back to complete the task I had begun.

During these long weeks of battle with the rheumatism only my faithful nurse stayed by me, knowing full well if I lived pay would be uncertain and if I died there would be none. If there was a single Christian in the land, none was visible. What crime had I committed? Crime aplenty—I had neglected to feed the cow.

The rheumatism barely recovered from, it was discovered that I had tuberculosis of the left lung. One of my old teachers urged that I go permanently to the Southwest. To remain on the job most certainly would result fatally, was his opinion. All right, then let it result fatally. As before noted, I never allowed judgment to interfere with a good fight. I had never yet turned back to foe, microbic or otherwise, and I could not do it now; there was a black-eyed little girl carrying a scepter, beckoning onward.

In spite of opposition of nearly everybody, the old cow began to give milk again, my practice grew and in 1916 I was able to build a fireproof building properly designed. By the time this was finished it was already overfull and another new building had to be started at once. My star was rising; I had licked various and sundry diseases, and the devil's cohorts, my fellow citizens, and come up defiant. The tiger kitten in my brain had become a fullgrown cat.

The new building was designed to take care of sick folks of a typical prairie state. It must, first of all, be of fireproof construction. Nothing could be spared to lessen the safety of the patients. It must be so constructed as to easily be kept clean and require no repairs. This was achieved by a tile roof, stucco finish and the woodwork a natural oak finish. It must be as homelike as possible in order to help the patients forget that they were in a hospital. That was the idea.

These features embodied a departure from the usual hospital construction in several particulars. The floors were of terrazzo but the washboards of oak. The idea of building washboards of the same material as the floors, generally adopted in hospital construction, is that one can wash the room out with a hose, if he should wish to do so, which of course one never does. The doors, instead of being the usual slab, are of one panel; they are thirty-six inches wide, much narrower than the usual hospital doors. I wanted the doors to look like residence doors, homelike doors, not hospital doors. The idea of the wide doors, generally used in hospitals, is that one can wheel the bed, patient and all, out of the door, which also one rarely if ever does.

I soon discovered that my previous experiences as above noted were small change. A few of these may be recorded. I want to say right here that there are honest architects but Diogenes, the old mutt, selected an easy job. I consulted an architect on the advice of a friend—the architect's friend, I learned later. Having no response from him, I later consulted another. Then the first one sent in a bill without even drawing a line. He was an artist, as I understood it, and was entitled to time, as much as he chose to take. After all, that architect was a piker. The next was the real thing. He drew the plans, putting in all the things he could think of, estimated the probable building costs, figured his percentage, proceeded to collect through an attorney. My father believed one had better confess to anything short of murder before going to court, so I paid. Had I known courts and lawyers as well then as I do now, he would have had more trouble. There are moments in my life I would like to live over again. The plans were useless and had to be wholly redrawn. This same person consulted me professionally years later. He figured, evidently, that although he cheated me I would give him a square deal in return. He was right. I always felt this was a fine tribute to medical ethics. A friend of mine once found himself in a similar situation. He charged just what he had been held up for to the penny. The bill was promptly paid. I hope I shall never be tempted in like manner again.

Then I got a contractor. The cement he shipped in was wholly worthless, as tests proved, and he shipped it out again, fast. I had secured a keen kid as construction supervisor.

Then came the heating engineer, so called. After which I got a plain plumber who did a fair job.

After building the addition above noted, the old building was to be rebuilt. Architect's "estimate," eight thousand dollars; final cost, twenty-six thousand. Poor guess.

From then on things became better. I had had as patient a builder of parts. I went to him rather timidly with my problem. He was delighted to give me every service. He checked subsequent plans and gave invaluable advice. Never a cent of charge. Next I discovered in a near-by town a capable and honest architect; also, right at home, a most excellent contractor; and particularly imporatnt, also in a near-by town, a most capable and honest heating engineer. Whatever the hospital has come to be, too much credit cannot be given these men.

Furthermore, I did not operate on the wife of a millworks man. She had a tumor that recovered spontaneously. He saved me many thousand dollars. Also, a furniture man took a personal interest in the growing plant and was a great help, both in the advice he gave and the very moderate prices he made me. Think of it, the excuse these men had for favoring me was that they knew hospitals never paid overhead and they were glad for the chance to help the cause!

I learned, in my building experience, that for capable and honest service go to big men and big firms. They can't afford to be dishonest, else they would not be big.

Two other additions, and a nurses' home, were added, concluding a quadrangle which, if placed end to end, would measure 576 feet. The end result was a hospital of about two hundred beds and a dormitory for about one hundred nurses.

I have already indicated the general policy I outlined for the conduct of my hospital. It was fairly simple in the beginning.

With the rapid development of diagnostic methods the need of added hospital equipment became much more apparent. X-ray and chemical studies some patients require can only be done in a hospital with the means to do these things, naturally. Specialization has advanced at so rapid a rate that a complete examination requires the services of a number of men. This meant the development of a staff. It is a great convenience for patients to go to an institution where this service can be secured, rather than to visit the several specialists in different offices ofttimes located in different buildings. These groups are called clinics and may be either detached or associated with hospitals, or they may exist independently.

Beginning with a single assistant the staff was augmented from time to time to between a dozen and eighteen men, or women. Sometimes short-handed, sometimes long-handed, because young men on salary, if they see what seems to be greener pastures, or if Wifey has yearnings for other scenery, are apt to depart with little or no notice, sometimes between days. The permanent staff now consists of eight well-trained specialists and a number of more or less temporary residents and interns. My staff is my staff in a biblical sense, all eminently capable, and honest. It now deserves to be called a clinic.

As the building was designed differently from other hospitals, and the clinic is conducted differently from most clinics, the general plan of procedure may bear mention, because it suits one person: to wit, myself. That makes it unanimous. Patients too sick to walk, or stand the unavoidable delay incident to a clinic examination, are admitted directly into the hospital and are then subjected to the regular examinations common to all orthodox hospitals. Those less sick, yet who require hospitalization, are examined first in the clinic and then sent into the hospital for a more thorough examination and treatment. Those not requiring hospitalization are treated as ambulant patients. They are examined, given medicine or treatment and sent home, either to return for further examination or to report by letter. This procedure is much like the lone doctor working in his office, except that specialists in all lines are available.

In most clinics patients are subject to the entire regular routine, including laboratory and clinical examination, no matter what the ailment. This, in cases where the nature of the trouble is at once obvious, entails much labor on the part of the medical staff with consequent loss of time and added expense to the patient. For instance, a patient with a wart on his nose is not exposed in my clinic to routine Wassermann examination of the blood and spinal fluid, nor X-ray examination of his stomach. I, being the old family doctor of the clinic, see them before they are assigned to the specialists. If it is obvious that no general condition exists, attention is focused on the entering complaint. Routine examinations, aside from the objections above mentioned, are likely to lead to indifference on the part of those who make them. The simpler tests, however, are always made. Before any special examinations, such as serum tests or blood chemistry is done, there must be some reason for ordering such tests. When such tests are made and found to be positive, the general examination must back it up. A positive Wassermann, for instance, is in itself not a sufficient provocation for the institution of antisyphilitic treatment. There must be a clinical evidence, indicating the presence of an actual syphilitic lesion. Conversely, a negative laboratory result does not preclude antisyphilitic treatment if the clinical signs indicate the presence of this disease. It is one of my greatest joys to recognize a syphilitic lesion that has had a negative Wassermann. This is a common experience, particularly in bone lesions. It is no unusual experience to find a patient whose lesion has been diagnosed sarcoma which rapidly disappears under specific treatment. This is particularly impressive to the patient in cases where amputation of an extremity has been urged.

My many years' experience in the laboratory as pathologist has taught me the limitations of these tests. Consequently, we never lose sight of the fact that in the vast majority of cases the laboratory is but confirmatory, or otherwise, of the clinical findings. Of course, the proportion depends on the clinical experience of the observer. Those who have no firsthand experience either in the clinic or in the laboratory are likely to accept without question the findings of the clinical pathologist. This situation compels many laboratory men to make a positive report in doubtful reactions, whether the evidence warrants a definite conclusion or not. The laboratory man in most instances must work without benefit of the history of the disease or the physical findings, which can be appreciated only by an examination of the patient.

It may be interpolated here that the new idea of the reformers to require a Wassermann test before marriage license is issued is going to lead to much grief because of the false positives which are inevitable even in the most capable hands—and not all hands are capable. That this reaction is reliable is just another vision of the reformers who know nothing of practical medicine. What the result will be any old family doctor knows now. He has battled with the syphilophobia induced by a false positive. It means a ruined life.

Those who grow up in a laboratory atmosphere, with little clinical experience, naturally do not appreciate the lack of ability to interpret their reports on the clinical side. The value of many such tests naturally varies, depending on the clinical experience of the doctor for whom these tests are made. For instance, a leucocyte count may be of great importance to the beginner but of very little occasional value to one with an educated touch. The clinician must be able to say in a great measure whether or not the laboratory test is correct. In order for the clinical laboratory to perform its highest function the clinician and the laboratory man must work together. One must view the other at work as the patient is being examined.

The overdependence on the laboratory is not only a waste of effort and expense but may actually be harmful in that it may lead away from a diagnosis apparent to one not overawed by laboratory reports. The laboratory is of great help to the clinician if the work done therein is reliable, but it is not a place where a diagnosis can be obtained just for the asking. Of course, the demand by the standardizers that every hospital have a pathologist has made it necessary for many hospitals to employ laboratory help of uncertain ability. Happily the standardizers are very liberal, for reasons that are obvious, and if a hospital will just designate someone as pathologist they are satisfied, small matter whether such persons have had three months or thirty years of experience. Therefore, to evaluate a laboratory report one must know who made the examination, even though it may have the stamp of approval of the standardizers.

The result of selective examinations which we follow here, as above indicated—a thorough examination for some, a simple inspection for others—is that we give outpatients the necessary examinations, including special ones, for a fee that would be impossible if the entire routine were followed. Of course, those examinations which involve the use of expensive apparatus and require much time such as cystoscopic, bronchoscopic or X-ray, naturally entail a greater expense. For those who require hospitalization, the time required is greater and subject to great variation.

Naturally these conditions require a considerable turnover, say fifty or one hundred patients a day. The object of this arrangement is to make it possible for almost any patient to avail himself of expert opinion in the shortest time and at a minimum cost. Herein lies the value of a clinic.

The city specialist working alone finds this unfair competition and his complaints are justifiable. Obviously, the solution is for us to stay in the country with patients of moderate means or less, giving service to those unable to go to the city, and allow the city specialist to charge his fees to the city dwellers who are able to pay for them. This country is too large to permit any one community to dictate the conduct of the whole.

As already noted in the beginning, I figured out a fee schedule which I deemed right for all concerned. It still seems to be as low a fee as it is possible to make and give first-class service. I am told a hospital in a large Eastern city, desiring to build a wing suitable for middle-class people, after careful investigation, reached the identical figure which I had reached thirty years before. Out here we are all middle-class people, both in finance and in thinking. Unfortunately, from my way of thinking, even hospitals which know in the beginning that they will be dependent on middle-class folks build as though there would be no patients except those able to pay a large fee. This results in the much-discussed high cost of hospital care. At least a part of the hospitals, even in cities, should have the man of moderate means in mind.

Country hospitals have suffered much annoyance from the various inspections to which they have been exposed in recent years. These self-appointed "slummers," a genus Chicagoiensis, species of pestis pestiferous, have sought to make us all accept the ideas of large opulent centers where abundant wealth can compensate for studied economy in both structure and maintenance. No thought is given to determine how or if the increased expenses they ask us to incur would reflect to the advantage or disadvantage of our patients. It is an annoyance only, because no one pays any attention to their recommendations and their refusal to recognize us is wholly ignored by the patronizing public.

The inspectors, so far as my observation goes, are, without exception, men who know nothing about the operation of hospitals, either economically or professionally, and whether they are amusing or annoying depends largely on the state of one's mind. For instance, some years ago we had just put in a new X-ray machine of the latest design. The inspector reported that our equipment was inadequate. The chief "standardizer" wrote us that we must put in a new machine. I wrote the company who had put in the machine, in a feigned enthusiastically angry tone. The president of this company wrote the chief standardizer and told him a lot and sent me a copy of the letter. This was in conformity with my general rule not to do anything when I can get someone else to do it as well. Since then, inspectors have pronounced us Grade A, just as they brand milk and cheese.

In the hospital field, standardization has sought to compel us, of the typical prairie states, to adopt the ideas of the more wealthy areas. The extravagant architecture naturally has resulted in vastly increased costs of hospital care, which in recent years has so vastly concerned those who have brought it on themselves. They should have thought of that before they started their building program. If one lives in a palace when he is well naturally he feels that he must be sick in one. Those of the common herd who think marble is used only for gravestones do not miss it when they go to a hospital.

It all depends on the viewpoint. If a few of the presidents of automobile industries manufacturing the higher-priced cars were asked to "standardize" an automobile it is conceivable that they would demand that a standard machine should weigh at least two tons and a half and that everything else be in proportion, including a radio. All other cars thereby being automatically branded as inferior and undesirable. This done, everybody would sit on his haunches and wail about the high cost of transportation, and wonder why. A Grade A automobile is one that provides transportation to where you are going. A Grade A hospital is one that provides adequate care of you when you are sick. Cost is only an incidental and not a determining factor. Those who can afford luxuries certainly are at liberty to indulge themselves, be it in automobiles or hospitals, but those of us unable to afford such luxuries should be allowed to go our simpler way. The Model T and the small country hospital served their day and generation well, and it is a question if their passing did not occur all too soon.

Why can't the standardizers leave us alone? If we are satisfied with our simpler institutions it is our affair. Being impecunious and dumb causes us no pain, certainly not so much pain as those who come about telling us that we are underprivileged. Their tears are uncalled for and unappreciated.

In another direction the standardization of hospitals has led to a misconception. It has not been pointed out that grading is based wholly on physical equipment. Naturally, those who do not know better are led to believe that the professional work done in Grade A hospitals also is superior. True, most high-class hospitals give a general supervision over the professional service rendered the patient. The standardizers have become much more liberal in recent years, I am pleased to note, but at best the essential factor in a hospital cannot be standardized: namely, the professional services rendered, the spirit of the hospital.

There is one feature in hospital building that has brought me only joy, the nurses. I had seen nurses abused in my medical-school days and I then resolved that if any ever came under my jurisdiction they would be protected. After my training school was established, when hiring a new superintendent I always gave her to understand that the pupil nurses were to be treated as though they were my daughters. Under no circumstances should they be scolded when on duty or before others. If or when correction was required it was a matter to be done in her own private office. No music has been finer to me than to have patients remark how obliging and cheerful my nurses are and I have heard this many, many times. I have always done as much as I could to furnish my nurses diversion, and it is with deep regret when I remember how little this has been. I ate the same food they ate; they were housed as well as I. I have heard so many nurses in other hospitals complain of always being hungry. Girls raised in better homes do not know how to live on beans and wienies. I was young and growing once, and had to go hungry. I hope none of my nurses has ever been in a like situation. Some of my old nurses are grandmothers now, but they are just old girls to me, loyal still. It is they who were my inspiration throughout the trying years.

It is a never-ending delight to see a bunch of girls, more or less timid, enter the hospital and at the end of three years go out magnificent, confident young women. I somewhat shamefully admit I never venture on the rostrum at Commencement, anymore.

I have seen some of the most contemptible things done by superintendents of nurses. Just two instances: one young girl was given leave to visit her home in a distant part of the city. She was to return at ten o'clock. She returned at ten-fifteen with the story that she had started in plenty of time but there was a streetcar wreck which had delayed her. The girl's reports from streetcar officials, setting forth the events of the wreck, were laid before that superintendent. She replied that evidently the girl was not at fault but her expulsion would stand because it would be a nice example for the rest of the nurses. Such a person is not fit to boss a bunch of track laborers, much less— infinitely much less—a fine bunch of Kansas girls. Another, a young doctor, took a nurse car riding, against the rule, and she was expelled within three months of her graduation. The doctor was retained on the staff. Both these instances occurred in so-called Christian hospitals.

It has always been of interest to me to note that the public is willing to spend a lot of money for the support of a high school. When a hospital educates a bunch of women who will be an asset to any community in which they may live the public accepts it as a matter of course. Some communities even tax hospitals for performing this public good. I hasten to note that my hospital has always been exempt from taxation, because I was able to show that I did a greater percentage of charity work than the charity hospitals in the neighborhood, which are automatically tax free.

After conducting the hospital for some thirty-odd years, the impossibility of securing efficient help for conducting it, together with the inability to convince the income-tax man that there are people in the world dumb enough to actually do things for which no pay was expected, I determined to get out from under the load. This I did, most happily by selling it to the Sisters of St. Joseph for a dollar: that is, it *was* a dollar. I am told it is only sixty-nine cents now, but I still have it.

The hospital was conveyed to the Sisters free from debt, the coalbin full, the storerooms up to standard, everything in shape. I state this proudly. I did not have to sell. I just got tired of being milked, tired of being a cow. It was a wise move, showing that almost anyone may do a sensible thing sometime in his life. The Sisters have given and are giving an efficient service which money would not buy. Their ministrations in a measure revive my faith, long dead, in the validity of the Golden Rule. My patients furnished the money with which to build my hospital; may it, through the instrumentality of the Sisters, serve them throughout the years. My patients paid for it, no one gave me even a thin dime. There it is, begun as a lofty idea, accomplished through innate, tragic stubbornness.

Happily the private hospital is a thing of the past. It has

served its purpose. The public is hospital-minded. They have learned the value of hospitals and contribute to their construction and support. They go to the hospital when they are sick, in full confidence.

I view the construction of my hospital with a mixture of pride, satisfaction and humiliation. Pride, because it has served many and has made both me and my hospital a host of devoted friends. Satisfaction, because within its walls I have been able to test out the applicability of an ideal. With humiliation, because I was dumb enough to persist in the face of so much opposition. Had I gone to other communities where other agencies had built hospitals, I might have escaped most of the tragedies of life. Were it not for the memory of the fine nurses who call the hospital their alma mater, I should unhesitatingly say that the price was too much.

Will Rogers once said that all there is to life is to go away satisfied. Happily, to be satisfied is entirely a personal matter, requiring no proof, no vote of the populace. I accomplished what I set out to do: to show that in a small community a small hospital can be developed without the rigid commercial methods generally practiced. But to do this one must have Kansans and the Kansas spirit. Yet, withal, there remains a bitterness—the old tiger only sleeps. There is always this consolation: one does not need to travel life's road again.

As I look at the building when it is all lighted up at night, 576 feet long if it were stretched out, conscious that it contains everything one could wish for in personnel and equipment, as I contemplate the streams of satisfied patients that pass through it, I cannot suppress the feeling that it has cost me too much. There is one consolation, no fool doctor will ever repeat it, the politicians will see to it that no doctor will ever again be able to hide enough money to build one.

CHAPTER

11 _____

IN A PREVIOUS CHAPTER I DISCUSSED THE PATIENT AS THE DOC-
tor meets him in the office. In that relationship doctors act
much the same, meeting conditions in like manner. Of course,
there are individual variations, dependent on the skill and viewpoint of the individual doctor. There is a yet more intimate
relationship between doctor and patient, a relationship undreamed of by our cloistered full-time professors, and it is as
variable as human nature itself.

It has been my privilege, or misfortune, during my lifetime
to have seen human beings under a great variety of conditions.
As I have intimated elsewhere, viewed in a broad way, the
difficulty lies largely in the attempt of the human animal to
act civilized. It is a constant conflict with the animal within us
to make us behave according to the rules. We simplify matters
by denying its existence.

It is so easy to see only the things we wish to see. We prate
about happiness, the more abundant life, and a lot of other things
nonexistent or beyond our ken. Money will not buy any of
these things, nor will striving achieve them. So far as I can see,
the best we can do is to escape pain, chiefly mental, and we do
this by keeping eternally busy—so busy that we have no time
to either hope or fear. Fear must have hope. The whole phi-

losophy of hope is engendered by fear. Fear not and one has no need for hope.

The advances in medicine are changing the entire aspect not only of disease but of life in general. Problems are not solved until we attack them as intelligent beings. We suffer in our attempt to escape this obvious fact. Wailing about diphtheria for centuries got us nowhere. Robert Koch began to grow bacteria on his wife's kitchen stove. The end was diphtheria antitoxin, and diphtheria has been practically wiped off the face of the earth. Perhaps that was the answer to centuries of prayer. My father, a very devout man, believed a striving to the limit in a worthy cause constituted the most eloquent form of prayer. Perhaps like measures will cure our social ills, but it is going to be necessary to look at cold facts.

The more intimate relations between doctor and patient have never before been discussed in print but I am going to come nearer doing it than has yet been done. Only an old doctor who has lived with people knows this relationship and only one who has cussed and discussed man for half a century would dare do it. The more nearly the doctor's experience of life has paralleled the patient's before him the better is he able to understand that patient. The tragedies of literature are silly things; they must be made simple and obvious or they will not be understood. Shakespeare wrote tragedies out of his imagination, not from experience. They are foolish, because he had not seen life in the raw. Tragedies cannot be written. They are inarticulate. They cannot be acted on the stage.

For obvious reasons, the tragedies of life as the doctor sees them cannot be adequately recorded because they are not nice things to talk about, but much more can be told than has ever been done. The time is coming when the truth can be disclosed but that time has not yet arrived. Because my relations with my patients have covered a range few men have experienced I am emboldened to present an outline, hoping that some idea may be conveyed of what we doctors could tell if it were possible to do so. This is but a preview of what some doctor is going to tell, say in a thousand years from now.

The changes that have taken place in the past fifty years, changes in which I have played my part, are in a measure parallel with the advancement of medicine but quite as much these fifty years present changes in the general attitude of people toward the fundamental problems of life. The conquering of disease has eliminated fear. This bare statement gives but little hint of what I mean, else I should not write it. The idea is that those who may understand can read it between the lines, those who cannot—well, it will save them a lot of trouble.

No doctor as a doctor can have any creed. If he has one it is a private affair quite apart from the practice of his profession. Creed is more or less a fixed state and the problems of medicine are shifting, as variable as the individual with whom he deals and the time of the contact. It is not for him to say whether or not he likes the trends in human affairs or not. It is obvious that none care whether the doctor likes what they do or not. His only concern is to understand them to the extent that he may do what he can toward the mitigation of human suffering, be it due to organic disease or to mental distress. No good doctor is afraid of anything, else he would not be a good doctor.

To the doctor the human being is primarily an animal actuated by the fundamental urges common to all animals. To these are added those elements which are due to the superior intellectual state which the human is alleged to have reached. These qualities are not at once obvious so that each doctor must find them for himself according to his own bent. This is why the more intimate relations of doctor to patient must be written by each doctor for himself. The fundamental factor one must realize is that the human being is seeking to harmonize these biological instincts with the teaching of Christian ethics. The result is that we have a queer mixture of characteristics which it is the doctor's business to unravel and bring to the individual's understanding. Obviously, to the doctor at least, some people battle the fundamental tendencies of the plain animal instincts; others offer no resistance and the plane is not drawn just where one might think. Shutting our eyes to facts, as other professions have done, has not cleared the atmosphere.

Many of these factors are matters quite apart from the organic diseases with which the individual may become afflicted although, of course, there may be more or less of an interrelation. In clinical parlance, it is sometimes difficult to determine whether the patient is sick in the organic sense or is struggling with these several tendencies. Too often the modern doctor, when confronted with an organic disease, fails to inquire whether or not there may be nonorganic conditions which distress the patient. In that event no matter how skillfully the organic ailment may be managed the patient may still retain the chief causes of suffering.

Though the emotional states of most persons are a mixture of all the elements of which the human is capable, a general division in fundamental states is possible. These are fear, hate and grief. They probably rise in nature in something like this order. Therefore, the doctor when he is confronted with complaints of a patient, not explained by the organic lesion present, must speculate whether or not one or more of these elemental emotions is active. These factors may first be discussed in the abstract and later clarified by the presentation of concrete examples in so far as this may seem expedient.

The fears, in so far as they are personal, may be divided into two great groups: fear of disease and fear of conditions or states not classifiable as disease.

Fear of disease, of course, applies to both sexes. These may have their basis in unrecognized symptoms of organic disease, or fears due wholly to imaginary ills. The fears based on symptoms may be illustrated by slight stomach disorders which the patient at once magnifies into symptoms of ulcer or cancer. Very commonly the stomach distress is wholly secondary to a nervous state. On the other hand, the digestive disorder may be due to persistent errors of diet or just plain overeating. Here the doctor must unravel the complaints in order to determine what is fear and what organic disease, which is sometimes by no means a simple task. The doctor may dispense conversation or drugs as the case may seem to indicate; generally, he does both. A cough may be translated into symptoms of tuberculosis. The fear of venereal disease presents the doctor with a very frequent and perplexing set of problems. The fear the patient has is very often much augmented, even engendered by a false diagnosis from a previous examination. Ill-advised laboratory reports have sent many a patient away with a persistent syphilophobia that may require years to dislodge from his mind, a state which he need not have reached had his first doctor fully evaluated all the evidence in the first examination. Of course, the charlatan designedly plays on these tendencies of certain patients who prefer to believe the worst. Add to an incorrect diagnosis a guilty conscience, and the doctor has a real problem.

The doctor may start with the fundamental probability that if the patient has a fear of a disease he has it not. Queer fact, this, but often true, nor is it confined to fear of organic disease. A patient with a cancer of the stomach rarely is possessed of any fear. If he has it he accepts the verdict without emotion. When death knocks on the door no one is frightened. The smartest observation ever made was when Shakespeare said there is no need to fear death. It will come when it will come, and then, it may be added, it will be without fear. It is often the fear of death that sends patients to the doctor, it is true; but most often it is an undefined subconscious fear.

The man who comes in and blurts out, "Doc, I got a cancer in my stomach"—this is Kansas lingo for "Doctor, I very much fear that I am afflicted with a gastric carcinoma"—never once in my experience has been so afflicted. Curious but true. A patient who has a tuberculous lesion is usually amazingly indifferent as to his state. He is always hopeful of ultimately conquering the disease. Those who come with the declared fear of tuberculosis have it not. These patients are usually young single women, all virtuous. This is a subconscious fear. They fix on tuberculosis as the preferred ailment because it is eminently respectable in that their repertoire of diseases is limited. The doctor understands. His business is to tell them they do not have tuberculosis. Curiously enough most of these patients give as their employment "at home." Any doctor should of his own accord be able to write the rest of the history.

The most common fear which harasses patients today must be for the most part left for the next doctor who writes on this subject to discuss. No prudent doctor would discuss it now. Yet who is better fitted to discuss it than the doctor who has lived long with his patients and has noted the trend? This is the fear most difficult to elicit, usually impossible to elicit by direct questioning, and must be inferred usually from the general trend of complaints. I have already denied responsibility for human nature as it is, but as a doctor I must recognize causes of human suffering even though nothing can be done about it. At least, one can refrain from operating on lesions which are nonexistent or have no real relation to the conditions which actually distress the patient. This is a very diplomatic statement, designed not to convey a single idea except, of course, to those who understand. Yet at the same time one need not be overly apologetic, because everyone recognizes the tendency even though it be contrary to civil and ecclesiastic laws. All laws change as people change, although they are sometimes a long way behind. My place here as a doctor is wholly one of diagnosis: that is, accuracy in diagnosis. What the relief measures will ultimately be, time alone must decide. That statement is, of course, designedly inaccurate. Time is an intangible something that one can credit or blame with relative impunity.

I have not the remotest intention of brushing against the legal or ecclesiastical phases of the question. Old "tempus" is working on that, and as he "fugits" changes occur. That is not a doctor's worry. Hitching a mite closer to what everybody knows, I may say that I was born into a denomination which believed that an unlimited production of offspring was a religious duty. I need not point out that I write only with a doctor's vocabulary and this must be interpreted as such. I recall as a child attending a wedding ceremony in which an aunt was among those present and my grandfather officiated. He made the admonition "Go forth and be fruitful" with such emphasis that my small mind wandered to the farmyard where there were a number of animals confined which seemed to be like-minded. I was filled with disgust as my aunt blushed in mortification, possibly in anticipation.

My further observations as a boy among our people revealed that in a number of instances a pair begot six or ten children. Then the mother, exhausted, died of puerperal infection or hemorrhage usually, sometimes of tuberculosis. The bereaved Papa overcame his grief in from ten days to three weeks and then started out to find a new wife with the same frankness as one goes out to buy a cow. Grandfather seemed to have a list of available widows or neglected spinsters, so that he was able to aid the bereaved, and the procession was resumed. This added to my childish disgust.

As so often in the progress of civilization, circumstances alter belief. In that ancient day a child was a commercial asset from his sixth to his twenty-first year. He toiled for the general good of the family as Father added farm after farm to his holdings. The more successful men were able to start their children with a farm. The children of those not so possessed sought to begin a career elsewhere. That is to say, they got a job.

ME AND MY PATIENT

Nowadays the trend divides. Some still regard their children only as contributing agents to the family assets. On the other hand, today most parents seek to place their children on what they regard as a higher plane than they enjoyed—by way of an education. The assumption is that they will be better off if they are placed in a position where toil is reduced to a minimum. That is, they seek to transform a congenital agriculturist or bricklayer into, say, a doctor of medicine. They must be credited with a good intent. In other words, the child has become an obligation and is no longer an asset. In that fundamental change in viewpoint is found most of our difficulties today.

With such families the child is an economic debt so long as he remains a member of the family. If the son is self-sustaining at twenty-five he is a bright boy—yet not too bright, else he would not be successful. The same applies to the daughter if she elects to make her own way. If she marries Father will be very fortunate if she ever becomes self-sustaining. The chances are about equal that he will have a crop of grandchildren to foster. This circumlocution, I trust the reader will recognize, is for the purpose of indicating how it has come about that mathematics first comes to play a part—yes, where mathematics first came to play a part.

Fortunately, in this country the urge for large families merely to serve as cannon fodder is not a factor. All the added population contributes is votes and taxes. Happily, no politician has been bold enough to propose this as an encouragement of larger families; not in a country where women vote.

At any rate, somewhere, somehow, a new attitude toward children has come to play the dominant part. One lives one's life for one's children, instead of the children living for Papa. The invariable result is that early in life Father, and Mother too, begin to figure the expenses of education per head of off-spring. There is a family conference at which Father's earning capacity is carefully calculated. Here enters a new factor which, if one will look about him with a scientific mind, will show that the renewed sense of responsibility toward children displaces eccleciastic ideals.

It is a very simple proposition, like it or not. Don't blame us doctors. All that concerns us is that in the transformation, or transition if you please, Mother has developed a fear. What concerns us is that if mother has a backache or is sleepless we must ask ourselves, "Has she a fear or does she require a surgical operation?" Still more perplexing if an operation is obviously needed, if Mother also suffers a fear she will still have a fear when she recovers from the operation. If she does retain the old complaints because of fear the various ladies' clubs will say, "Doctor So and So operated on such and such a person and she is no better." The result is that if one of the sitters in these conclaves becomes afflicted with a serious organic disease she defers operation because of the failure to cure the first lady. That is where the doctors' headache begins. Serves him right too—he should have considered the patient as well as the disease.

All this change has occurred in my lifetime and I have endeavored to find the motivating cause without result. One must seek the cause in the natural affection for offspring, after all the noblest sentiment in all biology. But why should it clamor for solution at this age and generation? Machine age, I reckon. Few families can afford ten or fifteen automobiles.

The public does not know what the doctor has in mind. The fundamental problem is biologic. When a state proposes to sterilize convicts and derelicts, at once a howl goes up from the general public about personal liberties. Noble cry for the public to set up? One must know history from its dawn to understand this. It is exactly this that actuates the wail of the tomcat sitting up on the back fence. Just as noble as the human, every bit of it. Does the tomcat want more kittens to love and cherish? Not exactly. If he gets a chance he will kill them just as certainly as the genus homo who sets up the same howl will neglect his offspring, producing criminals, morons, but voters, in this land of the free and the home of the brave. If there is anything more disgusting and contemptible than this attitude it has eluded my observations.

Of all the contemptible concepts of which I know is the one that parenthood as such is noble. One cannot glance at a newspaper without being confronted, and affronted, by a page of pictures of allegedly blushing brides or bathing beauties. Why fool ourselves into believing—nay, not believing, but lying about the nobility of it all? If anywhere in biology the exercise of a little intelligence is needed it is here. There is nothing fundamentally noble in marriage. To be noble it must be made so. How to accomplish this?—we old doctors know the answer but we would be chased into the creek if we told all we know. Unfortunately, our efforts must be expended in making repairs when it is too late. Generally speaking, these things concern the social reformers and others not confronted by actualities. These people mean well but they are ignorant of the actual facts. Domestic-relation courts bear about the same relation to the actual conditions as operating on general peritonitis when the patient's hands are already cooling in death. The surgeon may be doing his very best but defeat runs ahead of him. The first belly pain should have been recognized —that was the time to operate. We must cease to idealize a state that may presage disaster. This is an age of legs, if we can believe that many newspapers are right in estimating what the people want. We doctors have the laugh. We get paid for looking at legs, and we earn our money.

Nothing causes a doctor so many heartaches as the problem of the neglected child as it comes to him. Comes to him because it is neglected, undernourished, starved and thereby condemned to mediocrity and a lifetime of suffering, and receptive to a life of crime. The longer I live the more highly I regard tomcats. They are frank.

These problems—legs, parenthood, backaches—in one form or another provide the greatest perplexities which face the doctor today. The public is struggling, but they must do this unaided. But there is a handwriting on the wall. Don't blame us doctors. We did not do the writing. If we had, someone would facetiously remark that nobody except a druggist could read it.

Anger as a disturber of health is a less potent factor than fear, but as such is often overlooked. It is often suffused with fear—fear, say, of the blonde secretary. Grief? Grief, nothing, it is anger that upsets the digestion and gives a headache. The chief factor of interest to the doctor is that in the beginning it usually is a medical problem, a problem which I so deftly avoided mentioning before. Allowed to fully bloom, it ends in the divorce court. I have seen hundreds of such cases. Why don't people ask the doctor? That poor mutt's hands are tied, so he can't even open his mouth or unleash his pen. Given a chance, we doctors could become the social reformer's, broadly speaking, most valuable allies. Allies nothing, we would make the social reformer's job unnecessary. Unhappily doctors must face facts. We dare not construct ideals.

Fear and anger are easy to recognize—they are so articulate. Of the two there is only a difference in tempo and crescendo. Grief, on the other hand, one cannot determine by listening. It can be approached only by human understanding. Grief is inarticulate. No one can understand it who has not felt it. It has been truly said that in the deepest grief there is no weeping and, it may be added, no complaining. It is a strange fact recognized by all doctors that it is the grief of the father for his daughter, the mother for her son, that is profound and everlasting. This is a fact all doctors recognize, but it is too subtle for our understanding. From the medical point of view the widower is more profoundly affected than the widow by the loss of his mate. Of course, it may be countered that the reason is that he has a more worthwhile reason to mourn. This problem reaches to the very depths of human relationships and emotions. No one has yet dared to attempt an explanation. The difference between the mourning of the tomcat type of papa and the bereaved mate are as wide as human emotions.

The relations here vary with age. Grief for the mate is greater after the family has grown up and set up for themselves and the couple has once more found themselves alone. During the time the children are growing each has an interest aside from his mate but each is engaged in the same end—the children. The children gone, they are brought together more closely again. An old person dies of something and in a short time the mate just dies too. Here is something that transcends the laws of biology. If we could just understand this we would have a basis for a new philosophy, undoubtedly an understanding of the struggle to achieve Christian ethics. Tomcats will never solve this relationship.

When the doctor's problem is complicated by organic disease associated with a state of grief and operative procedure is indicated, a desire to die, to follow the mate, undoubtedly plays a part in recovery. I have seen so much that when an old person combats even an obviously necessary lifesaving operation, I do not urge it. There is that golden rule no one dare ignore.

The most reliable indication that grief lies at the basis of the patient's suffering is sleeplessnes. In any complaint associated with marked sleeplessness in the absence of physical pain, the element of grief must be considered. Here the doctor can, in complete ignorance of the true state of things, render an altruistic service. Nothing in all the range of human complaints excites my sympathy so much as sleeplessness. The eternal night. He who conquers this for his patient, more than in any other situation, has contributed to the alleviation of human suffering. Tomcats are sleepless enough, as everybody knows, but it is not grief that causes it.

One quizzes readily enough to determine the cause of complaints in most instances. But sleeplessness from grief is something different. Here one has the feeling that a curtain is drawn between the doctor and his patient. Behind it is something sacred, something beyond human understanding.

As an example I may mention an instance. A fine mother who had previously been my patient, learning that her son was to march off to war, that war to end wars, became at once sleepless. In due time her son was buried in France. She never mentioned this calamity but the sleeplessness continued. After some years I had to tell her that she was afflicted with a fatal disease. A peculiar look of joy lighted her eyes. Neither of us said one word. I anticipated the effect of the verdict, else I should not have told her so bluntly.

It is a peculiar thing that, no matter what one's ideas may be in general, when one's loved one has gone before, there is a lurking hope that somewhere, somehow there will be a meeting again. Even the noted agnostic, Bob Ingersoll, in the funeral oration over his brother expressed this hope. One has no more appreciative patients than these who feel that the doctor understands without asking questions, the answering of which would tear wider an unhealing wound. Here, also, biologic science fails us.

From the foregoing it is evident that in the management of such patients one is dealing with an individual. That is to say, the doctor and his patient are quite a different thing from doctors and their patients. In the former the doctor must act without any science to guide him. In the latter there are generally recognized methods of procedure. The former admits—nay, demands—of much more intimate contact and adjustment than the latter. Some doctors, just because of their personality, are able to manage certain types of patients with which other doctors, equally learned, face certain failure. The personality of each doctor differs. It certainly cannot be taught, and it is a question in how far it can be learned. One must begin with an inherent aptitude, even though experience may expand it. Naturally, if the doctor's background and experiences somewhat parallel that of the patient, as previously noted, he will be more receptive to the patient's state than will those doctors whose lives have always been tranquil, or as we say now, those who have always received the more abundant life. It is a cheap joke, often made, that the writers of books on the management of children have never had a closer contact with children than the ownership of a dachshund. That is not funny. It is tragic.

Though there are many things in the relations between doctor and patient that transcend understanding and forbid approach, there are many situations which the cautious doctor may unravel and in so doing place himself in position to help his patient.

The doctor most generally successful in this sort of endeavor is he who can evaluate his patients from all angles and anticipate factors the patient himself, or more commonly herself, cannot formulate. This is not the specialist's job. This intimate understanding is difficult to express in words. As a matter of fact, the doctor would not dare to do so even if he could. That word "understanding" has a wide application. The patient who finds some subconscious attraction is very much more likely to feel that her doctor understands her. These things must be recognized by the doctor because very often if he does not anticipate possible events he may find himself skating on very thin ice. This is particularly likely to be the case if the hapless doctor has a better half who regards herself as not fully appreciated.

Unfortunately the problems that so deeply concern a large part of the human race do not bear frank discussion. It is against the law, all laws except the laws of Nature. Perhaps

I may approach these subtle problems by reviewing some concrete cases. Here comedy and tragedy follow hard on each other. Unoccupied ladies are very likely to get some sort of complaint. They may develop aches and pains common to their particular club. For instance, literary-club members are likely to specialize in headaches; bridge-club members, in indigestion. This type of patient may respond to understanding, never to sympathy because they are already taking home treatment. The doctor with a detective type of mind sometimes has need to exercise his powers. One may pretend not to know all that he does. Or he may ask questions for which there are several answers. To make her see herself in the true light may be the first step toward a new life which is tantamount to a cure. The doctor may make an enemy of his patient, but if he succeeds in gaining for her a new outlook on life other members of the family may appreciate the doctor's self-sacrificing service.

A case in point: a childless woman, aged forty-five, who complained of everything in the book but who specialized in stomach trouble. She was a leader in clubs, one of the pseudo-intellectual type. I explained to her in detail that nervousness in many cases is not a disease but a state and one must learn to live with one's self, that much of the great work of the world was done by nervous people—and much more in this vein. She petulantly remarked, "I don't see why I can't have good health like other women." "Madam," I replied, "there has never been a method discovered whereby one can repaint a Model T and make a Packard out of it." The very gruffness of my reply so shocked her that it made quite a new woman out of her. Of course, she became angry with me and has remained so; but her husband is my ardent friend. This type of patient need cause us no deep emotions. The basis of their complaint is just plain selfishness. I could repeat like instances a hundredfold, but in doing so it would not be possible to suppress a certain glee which would be very unbecoming for a doctor. Most people laugh when a fat man steps on a banana peel but, of course, a doctor never does.

These cases are not suited for group practice and they yield nothing that can be examined in the laboratory; but, as noted above, the laboratory may give a false and disastrous lead. Furthermore, group practice is unsuited to the discovery of these intimate details. The patient likely will come in contact with a number of members of the staff all bent on the object of finding an organic lesion which will explain the symptoms of which the patient complains.

Too often the specialist is prone, in the absence of demonstrable lesion, to declare that nothing is wrong. This is but a natural result of their training, for young men are taught that all diseases have an organic basis and when such a basis is not demonstrable they suspect deceit. Much needless grief is often caused by such unwarranted interpretation. The saddest instance that has come to my experience involved a schoolteacher twenty-two years of age. Without known cause she suddenly became unable to swallow. For ten days she had taken only a little water and had emaciated markedly. I introduced against her protest a stomach tube of large dimensions. I told the patient that I was quite sure that my treatment would result in a cure; if not, it would need to be repeated. It was a complete cure and the patient ate normally. At the end of two weeks the father of the patient expressed his delight to the local doctor who had called me in consultation. The doctor replied that there was nothing wrong with her in the first place, that it was all in her head. The father, envisioning the twenty-five dollars he had paid me for my twenty-hour ride with team and buggy, stalked home and berated the daughter for making him the needless expense. The daughter at once relapsed into her depressive condition with a result I shall not record. I later learned the name of the faithless lover.

Some of my most regrettable errors have been the result of not spending sufficient time to find out the real cause of the patient's suffering. A case in point: I once treated a patient for twenty years without finding out the real trouble, and I knew it. Not until her husband became my patient did the real facts become clear. Tomcat.

Generally speaking, men are much more easily analyzed than women. This is particularly true of men of affairs who are used to dealing with facts and can, therefore, understand what the doctor is trying to do when he questions them. He credits the doctor with knowing more than he himself does. It is only the ignorant who know more than their doctor. Even the most intelligent patients sometimes, unconsciously I am sure, elude our most cautious interrogations.

One patient who did not respond to the usual treatment for nervous indigestion was sent to the neurologist because of a suspicion of early disease of the spinal cord. None was found. One day after he had gone through the clinic and received his medicine as usual, he came cautiously into my office and inquired, "Is that portrait in the lobby your daughter?" I knew then that the case was about to break, as the detectives say. "Then you will be able to understand me," he continued. "I have never mentioned it to anyone because I felt none would understand. I, too, once had a black-eyed daughter. We used to have the grandest times, rolling over the floor like a couple of pups. When I was not in the office we were constantly together. One day she went away. At first I attended to my business in a dazed sort of way. My unemotional state caused some to remark that my grief seemed inconsiderable. Suddenly, one day the truth dawned on me: she would never come back; she was gone forever. Since then I have walked the street vaguely hunting for a black-eyed little girl, looking over groups of children to find a counterpart. My business declined; I sometimes remained intoxicated for weeks at a time. Everywhere I looked I saw my black-eyed little girl. She was on the paper when I would try to write a contract. I saw her in my dreams, but when I tried to touch her she had vanished. My sister told me time softens all things, but it has not."

I have never listened to a more poignant story, calmly and simply spoken. In consolation I told him that my father believed that those who go before still see what those they leave behind are doing and rejoice and sorrow with them. "Perhaps," I continued, "that black-eyed little girl is on a 'beautiful isle of somewhere' and claps her little hands when Daddy makes a good deal or performs a kind act." He gazed at me long and steadily, the tears running down his strong face, and said as he arose to leave, "An understanding heart is worth more than all the medicine in the world." It was the portrait of my own daughter that had made us brothers. From then on he improved. I do not know what these sympathetic contacts are. They are not science, at least not within the range of our present understanding.

In the recent past I had a patient who turned out to be something quite different than we expected. A business man of parts, of cancer age, came in and related that he had completely lost his appetite and had lost considerable weight. He suspected something of a serious nature and the symptoms he related suggested early cancer of the stomach. However, careful examination failed to demonstrate the presence of a cancer, nor anything else in fact. Continued study failed to show anything of an organic nature.

I told him we could find nothing organically wrong and I was at a loss what to do or even what question to put to him next, that I hoped he would give me a lead as to the nature of the cause that was putting him on a tension. "Yes," he replied, "there is, and I have wanted to talk to you alone. I have felt you would understand." Then the story. He had concluded that he had a cancer—really hoped so, in fact. He related that he had a daughter much devoted to him and that she had been his guiding star for many years. She had married a worthless boy, much against her father's wishes, but he had hoped for the best. He had made his daughter financially independent. Whereupon her husband, in exultation at the new-found wealth, became unfaithful to his wife, wholly indolent and resorted to drink. His daughter came to believe that her father was trying to separate her from her husband, a thing wholly untrue, and in consequence she repudiated him; it nearly broke his heart, since he realized his daughter was gone for good.

I could only reply that I fully sympathized with him but as long as the game laws protect sons-in-law there was nothing he could do. I could only offer him the consolation that evidently he would find his daughter all he believed her to be, because among the higher type of woman, the more profound a scoundrel her husband is, the tighter she sticks to him.

I explained to him in studied detail that his sufferings were due to a wrong, even a selfish, view of life. All animals, once they attain physical independence, leave those who have nourished them. The human animal does the same thing. I told him that, if my memory was correct, it is recorded somewhere that this has full moral sanction. The honor a child is supposed to bear his father and mother ceases after they establish their own homes. One need not despair at this. It may be because the honor to father and mother may be exercised as well, perhaps better in many cases, *in absentia*. It is best that it be so. To want it otherwise is pure selfishness on the part of the parent.

I admonished him not to entertain a too pessimistic view, that sometimes these children in after-years come to recognize their mistaken conclusions and the former fine relations are resumed. But I added a quotation from Omar Khayyám's Rubaiyat: "Thou must not hope, thou needst not then despair." I told him that the most happy days that come to any man are when he walks the daisied fields with his daughter's hand in his, but biological laws decree that these are but temporary. That the fates have provided that as one grows older memory for past events becomes dominant and we again in memory walk the daisied fields together, though we walk alone.

The basis of one's grief, I explained, may be selfish, as I have seen exemplified by elderly women who cling to their sons, denying them the right to establish homes of their own during the mothers' lifetime; by then the son has passed the age when the finer things in life are irretrievably past. That is not love, not devotion to her son, but her own pure unadulterated selfishness. Had she unselfish love for her son, she would bid him go and establish his own home even as she had done. My patient remembered several such instances that had come into his range of observation. I drew him out to relating these instances to me, the object being that he might exercise his own mind in that way of thinking.

It is pleasing to note that pride in his daughter for her noble conflict is replacing his own sense of personal loss. It is a never-ending source of interest to me to see how much a mere change of viewpoint may act in relieving suffering. Self-pity is often the basis of grief, or at least intensifies it.

The most curious thing I know is the faithfulness with which a woman will cling to a drunken husband or a crippled or mentally deficient child, not much difference between the two. As I mentioned in a previous chapter, drunken doctors were fine if you could find them sober, so a drunken husband is a wonderful man when sober. Both abstractions because neither ever was sober. The reason women assume this attitude to a worthless spouse is that it appeals to the finest traits of womanhood, sympathy—sympathy as distinguished from pity. It has seemed to me that it is the noblest women who draw such derelicts in the great drama of life, or it may be that in adversity the finest traits in all of us are developed. Talk as we will, it is intensive labor coupled with grief that builds character. Opulence, the more abundant life, handed on a platter, tends to destroy it. We doctors know many of such conditions which never reach the public which proves this rather melancholy conclusion. It is our business to know if it is a private grief or a physical defect that ails our patient.

The point I am striving to make is that when a patient has a private grief it is the business of the doctor to make him see that his grief is nothing unique but that many kindred spirits are all about him. One must keep the patient from unconsciously lapsing into a kind of self-pity. In his mind he is the only one so afflicted by the fates. Once he is made to see that he is but one of a vast horde the personal element vanishes. And then give him hypnotics enough to make him sleep. One patient gave me the gun with which he had planned to commit suicide. All I did was to make him understand that no one who had ever buried a child ever doubted deep in his soul some sort of immortality, that there was yet service one had to render for the departed one. "Learn to labor and to wait" is the best medicine for the grieved and distressed. Such cases to my mind represent the very highest type of specialized medicine.

I mention these cases because they have to do with men of parts who are usually thought of as not influenced by the sentimental things of life. This one recognized his state and but needed a sympathetic soul to whom he could pour out his grief just as much as do the lesser persons.

I must interpolate here a conversation I had with one of America's greatest physicians some years before his death. Said he: "I am a philosopher and I know one cannot know anything for sure about a future life, but after I listen to the radio awhile and then go out on the porch and look at the stars, all I have to say is that anyone who says there is no God is a goddam fool."

Sometimes such close contacts are not possible. I recall a man who came to me to have a cancer of his stomach examined. He had been told he was afflicted with cancer. He had a worried look and not the peculiar color that goes with malignant disease. I sent him to the hospital, he was impatient to go and my attempt to inquire into his condition brought only angry replies. If I did not want to remove his stomach someone else would do so. The next day a son came to town, so far as he knew, to be with his father at the time of operation. I asked the son to tell me the facts, told him that his father did not have cancer. I learned then that his mother had died three months before and since then his father had eaten practically nothing. We visited the father's room together and explained that there would be no operation. I told the son to take his father to the Harvey House and get him the biggest steak he could find. With this I left the room. Just what happened between father and son I do not know but the following day the two visited my office. The father had the look on his face of the tiger in the cartoon after he had eaten the lady. I did not inquire if he had eaten the steak. There was no need of it. Whether the father ever learned that the son had told me the real facts in the case or not I do not know. Sad to relate, though he seemed perfectly well for three years, having regained the lost forty pounds, he ultimately died in an asylum.

Not all such cases are tragic; in fact, some are actually funny. An example. It will be necessary to quote this patient because it is his direct statements that make the story funny. An old railway engineer came at once into my office, without the formality of registering. "Say, Doc," he said, "I've been to the big town." "So?" from me. "Yep, the doc down the road said I had a cancer and sent me to the chief surgeon. You know how the wind blowed March twenty-first?" I assented. "Well,

I was a pullin' the Golden State and it was that dusty I couldn't see the names on depots nor numbers on posts and I just pushed that engine sometimes to seventy miles into that dust bank. When I got to the end of the run I was just that done up, my fireman had to help me out of the cab. I couldn't eat no supper because my stomach was the size of your fist and right under my Adam's apple. Result was I lost fifteen pounds in ten days. The local surgeon said, 'Age sixty-six, loss of fifteen pounds means cancer,' and he sent me to the chief surgeon. He sent me to the hospital where a bunch of fellers stood me up in the dark without my shirt on and took pictures of me, twenty-four of them. At the end of a week the doctors held a consultation, eight of them. They was divided into three bunches, one bunch said I had cancer, another one said I didn't and the third bunch wanted to cut in to see which of the others was right. I said to my wife, " 'We're going home,' so I'm here."

He continued: "I knowed all the time what was wrong with me. It was that dust storm, but I couldn't make them docs listen." He had a good laugh and after three weeks he was back on the job.

For the most diabolical incident in print or out I submit the following incident. A young woman was brought to us in an advanced stage of Bright's disease. From this she died two weeks later. The story in brief. She had been teaching school when she came home, with swollen legs, declaring she was too sick to work. Her father declared that if she was going to stay at home he would compel her to work in the field. He did. Because of the state of her eyes, due to the Bright's disease, she was unable to do the work to his liking, so he whipped her. I mean to record here that he whipped her, a girl old enough to teach school. She collapsed at this treatment and she was brought to us with the result as above noted. Date A. D. 1935. Yet some people do not believe in capital punishment for murder. If that father were condemned to be hanged the clergy would convert him and he would go to the gallows blubbering faith in salvation. Nobody ever thought of that phase of capital punishment before. That just goes to show how smart we doctors are. Just think of allowing a rapist murderer of a child to be given life imprisonment and allowed to go to hell—save his soul and hang him. Funny, I thought it was that kind hell was made for.

My father used to tell of one instance alleged to have occurred in his boyhood. An old time revival was in full swing and all and sundry were gathered in the fold, all that is except an old soak. He just refused to see the light. In order to help his vision it was decided to take him to the river and hold him under water until he was ready to repent. This done he blubberingly admitted that he had confessed his sins, while under water. The delighted minister, standing on the bank, joyfully shouted, "Keep him under, he is saved. If he comes out and gets dried off, he will get drunk and backslide."

The purpose of this digression is to indicate purposely in a vague way that patients present two sides, the obvious and the less obvious. It is the latter that the doctor must guess. The perfectly respectable citizen may have worries induced by the other phase of his life. In other words he may be scared of being caught. Also members of their families may become our patients as we have noted.

The reaction to bereavement may make a very interesting phase. It is a very common occurrence to note in the history taken by a resident that the patient's indisposition dates from the illness of her husband, and it is often added that the care of him entailed much physical labor. If the labor expended was in behalf of a son it is not mentioned, and usually even not the bereavement. Such instances are interesting, because it gives a clue to the domestic relations. It reminds one of the statement of a recently bereaved when offered condolence by a friend: "Well, Emmy was a good wife, a good housekeeper and cared well for the children, but I never liked her." There are a lot of poor Emmys. Two different kinds of peas in the same pod. We doctors understand.

Sometimes our investigations bring surprises. A young woman complained of digestive troubles, loss of sleep and some pelvic trouble—sufficient, by the way, to justify operation had that been the only trouble. It required tact and patience to induce her to tell us that her real trouble was due to the fact that her husband was in a penitentiary and that she worked long hours in a restaurant in order to keep her little daughters until her husband would be released, years away. This is just another example of a high-minded woman giving her all to an altogether worthless spouse. I have thought much as to the basic cause for such devotion. I have concluded that it is to keep a father for the children.

It is a tragic thing that in the eyes of a woman any sort of a derelict seems to her better than none as a father to her children. These are basic factors and the workings of a woman's heart are strange. I know one such who lived with a drunken husband for forty years for the sake of the children. From an outside viewpoint this motive seems questionable. Often in these cases the question is one of finance, the woman being unable either to support her children or to think of seeing them taken from her. We have societies for immoral women but for these moral widows there is no succor, no care because no one takes heed. No one has suggested, as far as I know, that we are also our sister's keeper. If any man suggested it the ladies' societies would give a shriek of delight. It would smell of scandal.

In many cases some organic disease is simulated in the history given to the doctor. The real cause of the symptoms of which the patient complains lies hidden in some tragedy of the past, the influence of which the patient does not suspect or cannot tell even to his doctor. Sometimes it is the loss of a little baby; often, too, it is the mourning for a baby that never came; perhaps it is a galloping Lothario that never appeared. There is nothing in the books to help one solve these cases, and solved there is no remedy.

Such examples as this show the difficulty the surgeon has to avoid operating on lesions that have nothing to do with the real cause of the patient's complaints, and the performance of which is destined to be wholly impotent to relieve the patient of her suffering. Perhaps a group of women will sometime form a missionary society to save their sisters from the despair of a broken heart. The heathen Chinese would not notice the defection of their efforts.

One of the finest services the country doctor renders his fellow man is in the management of the complaints of the aged. All one can do for them is to make them comfortable. If they have bad habits, let them keep them. The press recently carried a squib relative to the causes of longevity. It had to do with twins, nonagenarians. One attributed his long life to the constant use of tobacco since childhood; the other was quite as certain that he could attribute his long life to the fact that he had never used the filthy weed.

The most common complaints in the aged are pain or cough. One can control each of these simply and efficiently. If they have high blood pressure or low blood pressure, all right they have high or low blood pressure and there is no use making them miserable either mentally or physically by trying to do what just can't be done. If they get pneumonia or a brain hemorrhage you know a kind Providence has not forgotten them.

Not so long ago a fine old friend of mine came to me because he could not sleep. He was sent into the hospital. His examining physician found numerous organic diseases and set about to cure them, but neglected to secure the sleep which he so much desired. He left the hospital angry with me because I did not see to it that he secured the wanted sleep. Thus a friendship of more than forty years was broken. I regret it terribly but it was all my fault. He came to me as an old friend asking understanding. I turned him over to science. The only excuse I have to offer is no excuse at all—I was too busy with patients with curable diseases.

One sweet old lady once told me that she had no desire to live because her children had already done all their mourning at her passing, but she did not like to suffer. Would I just relieve her pain, needn't bother with trying to prolong her life. We had some fine half hours together. Her children were irretrievably gone out of her life and she liked to hear about the doings of mine. A picture of my kiddies which I brought her delighted her greatly and this picture, of children she had never seen, decorated her little table at her dying day. I used to bring her a quail now and then; I didn't bother much to look up a calendar to see if the season was off or on. The light these birds brought to her eye would have been worth the price of a fine, had I had to pay it, which I never did. This little lady taught me more about the care of the aged than all the books in the world, just by her gracious appreciation of the little things I did for her.

A young doctor is likely to feel a bit sheepish in showing a sentimental side to the aged. The young doctor is likely to feel embarrassed in the doing of the little things, but he learns that it is a doctor's business to relieve suffering no matter what is required to do it. These old people are perfectly safe. Even a doctor's wife does not get jealous if he shows these people a little attention: that is, if the patient is more than eighty years old.

There is yet another field of usefulness. Nowadays the doctor more or less ignores the bedside of the dying. The night nurse attends to these things. In the hospital, of course, the patient's relatives go out after visiting hours, whether they wish it or not, and come back in the morning to see if their patient is still alive, and the doctor does likewise, an hour or two later.

But in the family doctor's practice, in the home it is different. There the family gather about the bedside. The doctor personally sees that the last hours are passed without suffering. If a quarter of a grain of morphine does not do it, perhaps a grain or five or six will. Not given subcutaneously under the cooling skin but into a vein. I ask only, for the reward of my labors in behalf of others, to be accorded this attention in my last hours.

The doctor must be able to understand the feelings of those about the bedside. An old person is seldom much mourned. Their passing has been too long anticipated. If they have property their passing has been, so to say, anticipated. I have long noticed with interest the greenest graves in our cemeteries are of those who have never done much for their children's welfare. To insure oneself peace in his grave he needs but to give his all to those about him. This is, of course, speaking in the abstract; the exceptions are many and notable.

The grief caused by the passing of a child is another matter. Here it is the living that suffer and the doctor who can tactfully secure them some sleep serves them in a very definite way. The surviving parents may be dry-eyed, apparently stunned beyond the comprehension of the events that have just transpired. The most contemptible gossips are those who attend funerals just to see how the family "carry on." If they are dry-eyed the word goes out that the deceased was not much mourned. Contemptible fools, that "in the greatest griefs there is no weeping" has never penetrated their dull brains. Happily the public funeral is almost a thing of the past. In no time in life has one so great a need to be alone as when he takes the last look at a loved one.

There are a number of things that come to the family doctor which may be difficult to fathom because the source of their information is obscure. Quite often a patient will mispronounce a medical term. One knows at once that the patient has been reading about his ailments. The sources of his knowledge are either the family paper or pamphlets sent out by quacks who come into contact with the family by the aid of the aforesaid sheets of enlightenment.

The quack can buy space in many newspapers proclaiming the efficiency of such remedies; thus the two are partners to the steal. Of course, newspapers go on the theory that the public wants to be humbugged and that it is their business to give people what they want as news: to wit, the address where they can receive the hocus in largest original packages. I infer that those newspapers publish these things gratuitously. Certainly, they would not knowingly injure their readers for money at so much per inch of space. Be this as it may, we doctors see distressing examples of the cruel things wrought by the coalition of quacks and newspapers but we make no attempt to do anything about it.

It is cheering to note that more and more newspapers are refusing to accept advertisements of persons whose purpose is to delude and rob their patrons. I believe that whenever a doctor meets an instance when a patient has been so deluded, if he would frankly write the editor the practice would soon cease. Why we do not do so is a mystery. Just recently a dying patient paid a large sum to a quack. Did I write the editor who carried the advertisement that brought sufferer and quack together? I did not. The next time I encounter such an instance that editor is going to get an express package. What I shall write will be too hot for the mails.

The intimate contact between doctor and patient as here set forth is passing. The sphere of influence of the family doctor is being wiped out by regimenting medical practice as we find it in the hospitals and clinics. It is wholly obliterated by contract practice and politically controlled institutions. It is possible to regiment organic disease, perhaps, but the more intimate touch between doctor and patient cannot be so controlled. That is a growth of years. It is as impossible as to have our intimate friends selected by proclamation.

ME AND MY PATIENT

Certain kinds of suffering react better to a doctor whom the patient knows and respects. This is particularly true of those cases where grief and bereavement enter the picture. These patients will tell their family doctor intimate things, where they would be mute before a hospital interne. This is true in all complaints of nervous origin, or that have a strong nervous element except, of course, in the case of those neurotics who specialize in complaints and enjoy ill health. That the personality of the doctor is an important element is proved by the fact that medicines prescribed by a young assistant may produce no favorable result but the same medicine, prescribed in a slightly different form, by a long-known doctor may produce happy results. Silly, perhaps, but people are like that.

A problem which the doctor often must face is whether or not the patient should be told the facts when a cure is extremely unlikely. I was repeatedly informed by ministers in my early days that the sinners at least should be told when faced by a fatal disease so that they could be prepared to meet their God. The average doctor, I believe, is disposed to agree with a statement of Ruskin. "There is but one place where a man may wisely be thoughtless, his deathbed. No thinking should be left to be done there."

The doctor, by the nature of things, focuses on the problem of keeping his patient on this mundane sphere as long as possible and any act calculated to influence this unfavorably is resisted by him. This applies particularly to diseases which frighten the patient, notably heart disease; with proper management "heart" patients may have many years of usefulness before them. Therefore they should not be informed that their condition is serious, certainly not that it is more serious than it really is. The most disastrous results may follow a tactless warning of even the true conditions. The family, or one member of it, may, as a matter of protection to the doctor, be given the true statement of the facts. One must use caution in the selection of the confidant, lest the information be blabbed to the patient, not through viciousness but just through the habit of telling all they know, plus imagination. Patients with goiter hearts particularly are likely to be unfavorably influenced by injudicious remarks as to the seriousness of their condition.

Some patients tell the doctor that they wish to know the truth, and by their bearing convince him that they mean it. I once had a patient of this type, a huge mountain of a man, a noted sheriff of the Southwest for thirty years. His opening remark was: "I am told you tell the truth. I want to know if I have a cancer and if you can do anything for it." I told him he had a cancer and that it was inoperable. After he had dressed, he remarked, "I thank you. What are the charges?" "Nothing," I replied. "Don't do business that way." With this he laid a ten-dollar bill on the table and walked majestically down the hall, head up, shoulders back. He had faced bandits and death many times in his career and he did not fear death from cancer. His magnificent personality lives with me still. He was a man.

Hope springs eternal. Some people refuse to recognize the fact when presented to them by the course of the disease. It is pitiable in the extreme to see some people struggling with the inevitable. I once had as a patient an old man who had a well-advanced carcinoma of the stomach. He wanted to know the worst and I told him. I gave him medicines to control his distress. He wrote me repeatedly, joyously stating that my diagnosis was wrong because he was rapidly recovering. A return visit showed him to have emaciated rapidly, and in a few weeks he was dead.

I once saw in consultation a very intelligent woman in the advanced stages of cancer of the breast. As I looked at the huge ulcerating mass she mildly remarked: "You think you see a tumor, but you are wrong. There is none there; I am going to get well." She denied that she suffered pain, though her face showed unmistakable evidence of prolonged and intense suffering, which obviously the disease must have caused for a long period of months. Yet she was so steadfast in her assertions that she suffered no pain that she refused what little aid medicine had to offer, the relief of suffering. She finally accepted the proffer of alleviation and her looks expressed her gratitude, though those about her kept repeating that she had no pain, and when euphoria was obtained by narcotic drugs they declared that the relief from pain was the reward of her faith, that the medicine had nothing to do with it. Her relief was due to my faith, not hers, faith in morphine to relieve the terminal sufferings of cancer patients.

Sometimes the situations take on other forms. I once had a fine old gentleman with a cancer of the stomach. I told him that all I could do was to relieve, in a measure, his pain. He expressed the wish that his suffering would terminate quickly. He said Christ died to save the world; he only asked to die to relieve his old wife and his daughter the care of him throughout the months to which my prognosis condemned him. Though he would leave them moderately comfortable financially, yet he had not enough to bear the expense of prolonged care. It would mean that they would need to suffer even after his passing. Within a few minutes after I left his bedside he drank carbolic acid, with which, unknown to me, he had provided himself before he called me for my last visit. His was a high type of mind considered from every angle. He was actuated by the highest motives. He was not "temporarily insane" as many tried to indicate in order to excuse his act and he died as he had lived, unafraid, actuated by the desire to extend to his family the final measure of devotion. I am recording a fact.

I learn by the papers that if one has anything unpleasant to say the best time to say it is when one is leaving for the office. I am confronted by just such a situation.

We hear much of the moral aspects of divorce. We doctors know that the fundamental causes are physical. So long as the public makes of marriage, *per se*, something exalted, the problem is not going to be solved. It is very much a biologic state and in great measure solvable as such if we would just put aside general concepts which everyone knows are not true and take a look at the underlying factors. Many married states are wrecked in the beginning. Rape committed in the holy bonds of wedlock is not only legal but moral. If anyone remembers the experiences of Napoleon and the Austrian princess he will know what I mean. If not, it is quite as well, for in the present state of social thinking such things do not exist. Hell on this earth is ignored. Had I the pen of a Milton, and the courage to do it, I could shock the nation. I have listened to too many stories not to know full well the suffering and anguish that can be crowded into a lifetime. One would think our Christian philosophy was written by tomcats.

The triangle which the dear public loves so much to hear about is related to the cause of domestic trouble just as closely as the death rattle is in the patient moribund from pneumonia. It is a terminal symptom. I have seen a lot in my day. Before kicking Papa in the face and then throwing him out go see your doctor and tell him the truth. If he survives the shock he may be able to help.

When I began practice both members of the domestic team worked hard. There was no time nor opportunity for anybody to get into devilment. When one member of the team works hard and the other loafs, there lies the germ for divorce. Nothing mysterious about it at all. Don't fight, lay your troubles before the doctor. He may not be able to help but he can present the facts and that may help. It will at least exonerate the blonde stenographer and that will help. If the stream of difference is too wide, recognize it. Nothing is gained by blackguarding and scandal. Just ask the old doc, but don't ask him unless you want to hear the facts. The old bird is just about fed up with pretense and high-sounding terms indicating the high moral standing of somebody.

ME AND MY PATIENT

Some vulgar person has said that when the wife is kept barefooted and pregnant there are no divorces. Bad as this sounds, it is so because it is so near the truth; but it does not fit into our growing notion of what constitutes civilized society.

Next to biological misfits plain selfishness enters as a potent factor. These seldom come to the doctor. These are economic and belong to the lawyer. It is not a medical problem. We doctors have only contempt for the gold diggers. May the gods deliver us from them. Some people regard the redlight districts as representing the lowest form of life. Honesty gets no credit. I like dogs; they are honest. A wise judge once said in my hearing that the commonest cause for domestic discord in his experience is the difference between the gross and net income. That is to say, friend wife thinks the gross income should be available for spending.

But economic and social factors now are such that the old precepts are categorically rejected. The people of all religious views, or none at all, do reject them. No doubt about it. They do it badly. We doctors know what to do but there are legal and ecclesiastic restrictions, though they are giving way. Facts are facts and are not made less so by denying them. Those who deal with moral problems in the abstract may close their eyes to truth. We doctors who deal with individuals dare not.

Just remember this: it was the medical profession which controlled the infectious diseases. They were in my childhood regarded as an ecclesiastic problem. We doctors are fundamentally biologists trained to look facts in the face whether we like it or not. When in trouble ask your doctor. He saved your child from diphtheria and he can save you from scandal, unless you are just plain cussed. He isn't afraid of anything, not even of the truth.

I regret more than I can say that now there is not the leisure for such intimate contacts except in exceptional cases. One cannot approach such patients if he is surrounded by a bunch of assistants. It is a personal matter, personal to each doctor, and personal in his own way. Yet it is a part of his professional duty, to relieve suffering. To die is painless, to live may be terrible, defying our science, eluding our test tubes and our microscopes.

CHAPTER

12 _____

THE ADVANCEMENT OF THE SCIENCE AND ART OF MEDICINE IN the last fifty years may be judged from the preceding chapters, but a final summary is needed to indicate more clearly the position in which we find ourselves today.

Generally speaking, so far as the public is concerned the advancement has taken place in two directions: the education of the profession in general—that is to say, everybody's doctor; and the general advance in the science and art of medicine.

The general advance in medical education finds expression in the preliminary education demanded for entrance to the medical school, the length of study demanded by all schools as already set forth and, it must be added, the many additional years of apprentice work elected by many. One reason for the lengthened term is that we have more knowledge to impart. In fact, there is vastly more offered in the intellectual menu than any student can digest. It follows that outstanding men acquire more of the knowledge offered than is possible for the average man. But even the poorest student must have knowledge far above the dream of any student of even twenty years ago.

The advance in medical education is a source of pride to the medical men, because it has come from within the profession. The public has not demanded it. The standards of medical practice, for that matter, always have been higher than the public has required or was willing to accept. In fact, when the public has become articulate it has been to criticize the action of the medical profession or obstruct its advancement. There has been a constant conflict between the medical profession, the press and the clergy but the contest is drawing to a close. This progress is due to the public. We are helpless to lessen the opposition, except as we acquire the help of the laity.

What has been the motive for the improvement in medical education? One does not need to assume a crown in order to answer it. It is all very human. Doctors, like the great run of human beings, wish to escape pain, defeat, failure. All words no one likes to use when applied to himself. What does the death of a patient mean to the doctor? All three of these. On the other hand, what does advancement mean—the conquering of a disease? It spells achievement, new power over our common enemy—disease, suffering, death.

Consider for a moment the distance we have traveled. From the "two courses of lectures of five months each," as was called for in the medical-school catalogue I read in 1886, it is a long road to the present requirement of four years of nine months each in medical school. To this must be added at least a year of internship. This is the minimum requirement.

From the "reading knowledge of the English language" of that distant day at least two, in many schools four, years of college work is required for admission. The result is that the student as you meet him in medical schools today, in contrast with the student of my day, is a cultured gentleman. They are of rather uniform age and, generally speaking, of like achievements. The rowdyism of the old days is gone. Gone also is the wild enthusiasm. The poor student and those without capacity are now not permitted to enter, or if they do gain entrance they are soon eliminated by the dean in collaboration with the instructors. The student who survives the first year is sure to be of good capacity and have some knowledge of how to study.

The general outline of the modern medical course may be of interest. The first two years are devoted to the fundamental scientific branches, chiefly anatomy, physiology, chemistry and pathology. Each of these branches requires much laboratory study, so that the use of the hands is constantly necessary. This use of the hands is a very important factor in the first two years of medical study, in that it bears directly on the practice of the art of medicine. No matter what the future course the student may elect, he will need to know how to use his hands. Those who lack this capacity become reformers and spend their days telling the rest of us what to do while shedding tears for those who lack medical care—old maids orating on the pains of childbirth and the raising of children—back seat drivers who somehow manage to get their feet on the brakes.

It is only the period following the scientific years that the student is directly occupied with the care of the sick. From then on he studies patients in the dispensary and hospital for the remainder of his school days. The student for the first time has a chance to learn that the subjects of the first two years have some use. The facts they learn in the scientific years are applied to concrete cases. The dispensary is, in fact, a replica of the general practitioner's office. Those patients well enough to go to a doctor are able to go to a dispensary. Those too sick to go to the dispensary represent the type of patient whom the doctor visits in the home or whom he sends into the hospital. The student walks with wabbly pins the devious path of medical practice under the guidance of the instructor. In the intern years he continues this imitation of practice entirely in the confines of the hospital.

By the time the student has finished his medical course and his internship and enters a practice the public is assured that the young man is a competent practitioner. As diagnosticians they are capable far beyond the dreams of the best doctors of half a century ago. They have learned much of scientific treatment. The art of medicine must be acquired by harmonizing the science he has learned with the vagaries of the human animal.

After the internship is completed instead of entering practice on their own account many seek an assistantship with some established general practitioner or specialist. This added period usually extends from two to five years. The student after the first year is classed as a resident. His job usually is to take charge of the patient after the intern has taken a preliminary history, in order to prepare him more fully for the final examination of the chief. Thus step by step the art of diagnosis is acquired.

Having traced thus briefly the metamorphosis of the young doctor of today, it is in order to catalogue the achievements of medical science in the past half century. One might answer this by a wave of the arm and say that all those dreadful things which were recounted in the first chapter have been practically eliminated and all the successful therapeutic means now available have been discovered or invented within the last fifty years. This would be very near the truth. However, there are communities in which infectious diseases still occur—diphtheria, smallpox, typhoid fever—but these are matters of election. When they appear someone has been remiss in his duty. Only eternal vigilance gains freedom from them. The government health service, the state board of health, the county health officer—all are constantly active trying to mitigate the fool things the public insists on doing. Remove these agencies and the devastation by disease of the centuries past would return. The public is prone to forget that it is not only the achievements of the regular profession of the past but the constant vigilance of the profession today that is securing immunity from all the dreadful diseases of the past. It is the regular profession, let it be noted, who have done these things and are doing them; no cult, no faith, no wailing and gnashing of teeth brings protection.

Control of preventable disease is no more remarkable than the management of other diseases. Operations undreamed of fifty years ago are performed today. Nonmalignant tumors of the abdomen are easily removed and in large proportion the malignant ones are now permanently cured. Even tumors of the brain are being successfully attacked. Diabetes is controlled; the causes of most cases of asthma are discovered and eliminated— in fact, few diseases defy the modern doctor. It is the modern M.D. who does these things.

Unfortunately availability of service is not enough. We have examples aplenty today of the penalties paid for the neglect of the means now available for the prevention of disease. It need not be a surprise that the immunity from disease is dependent on the intelligence of the community. Puerperal fever, for instance, is practically unknown in Kansas, yet it is not rare in the cities where eminent specialists reign, even hail. Diphtheria is extremely rare here; yet there were fifty thousand cases in the United States in 1935, the most of which occurred in the large cities. Smallpox is rarely observed here, while it is nearly constantly present in the large cities. It is estimated that sixty-five per cent of the country population are protected from smallpox by vaccination, as contrasted with forty per cent in the cities. Modesty forbids me to extol further the superiority of Kansas. The government health reports may be consulted by the skeptical.

Public service in large measure is able to protect the public from infectious disease whether it wishes it or not. The cure of individual disease is much more difficult to force on the patient.

The difficulty, therefore, lies not in the availability of adequate medical service but in the intelligence of the patient to use it. The term intelligence must be given a broad application.

Education has only a general relationship to intelligence. The last diphtheria death in this community occurred nearly thirty-five years ago in a child whose father was a doctor of philosophy —an import, not a native Kansan, needless to say. The willingness to avail oneself of adequate medical service seems, therefore, not so much a matter of abstract intelligence as just plain horse sense.

It is a curious fact that it is many of the educated who are most refractory to the acceptance of fact. They have learned to believe things that are not true. It is very obvious that anyone may believe anything he wishes with impunity. But disease brooks no trifling. If you have a ruptured appendix and you choose to believe there is none or that by rubbing the back of the neck the spreading peritonitis will be halted, it is just too bad. The relationship of intelligent people to the laws governing disease is really very complicated. The point is that this is allegedly a free country and if a person sees fit to reject the aid of scientific medicine, no one can say him nay. Perhaps it is Fate's way of eliminating the unfit.

We hear that there are a lot of tears shed nowadays because one-third of this great "American People" are without adequate medical care. I wonder where these persons live. I know this country from the Father of Waters west and they are not here. So this is temporarily no worry to an old Kansas doctor who knows his people. This line of conversation seems to emanate from the same Fount of Wisdom that urged us Kansans to plow up our pasture and sow wheat, and that now advises us to put the grass back and plant shade trees and then give the land back to the Indians and buffaloes. Really, it does seem that a good deal of grief could be spared if people would confine their vociferations to things they know something about or at least to regions where their ignorance is not so conspicuous. Why fools are endowed by nature with voices so much louder than sensible folks possess is a mystery. It is a fact emphasized throughout history.

Certainly, thousands of people do not have adequate medical care, but it is not because it is not accessible to them. They are people who think they can think. The regular medical practice does not sound logical to them. They are the same people who were running up and down the land a few years ago urging other peoples' sons to "fight for democracy," "making war to end war." Anyone with the slightest knowledge of history of human nature could even then see at a glance the pitiable silliness of it all.

Those without medical care are so because they elect to do without it. Stubborn dumbness stands in their way. Who judges whether or not there is adequate medical care? It is wrong assumptions here that are leading to disastrous conclusions. Those who are able to judge come to no such conclusion. Some would say that a person with a wart on his nose who is treated without a preliminary Wassermann did not receive adequate examination. This presupposes that the examiner does not know a wart when he sees one and also that everyone must be suspected of having syphilis. Now this country of ours is quite a large patch of ground and both these possibilities may exist in some regions; but in Kansas doctors who do not know a wart are rare, and syphilis is a rare disease here. Of course, this statement will be received with incredulity by many. All right, let everybody speak for his own country. I am speaking for Kansas and I have hundreds of thousands of case records beside me to prove the truth of my statement. The people of Kansas do have adequate medical care, if they wish it, whether they have even a thin dime or not. That this is the truth, the whole truth and nothing but the truth there is not a shadow of a doubt.

The regular profession, of course, would agree that those who are treated by cultists and quacks do not receive adequate medical care. It is because they do not desire it. Those who deny the existence of a perfectly obvious lesion are beyond the pale of reason as are those who believe an impingement on a nerve, even granted such a condition existed, could produce a neoplastic proliferation, or any organic change, in fact, are not a problem for the medical profession.

Even including all these, this part would hardly amount to one-third of the population. Examining the statement that one-third of the population do not receive adequate medical care reveals that it lacks definiteness. Do they mean one-third of all sick people? Many seeking treatment are not sick, at least not physically sick. What these people need is tactful and sympathetic entertainment, where they can exercise their great reasoning powers unhindered. Social and biologic misfits make up a large part of this class. These are proper subjects for all sorts of pretenders. These do not need and do not want adequate medical service. Why should anyone shed tears over them? They're having a perfectly lovely time and if or when they get sick they hunt up your friend the M.D.

A great difficulty still confronts doctors and concerns vitally the patients. The science of medicine has made advances almost or quite beyond conception. The science becomes an art when applied to the treatment of the sick. Artists differ in capacity. The medical art available to any one person depends on the capacity of the one practicing the art. That is the task now, to assure the greatest capacity of the individual practitioner. Certainly the ultimate will not be achieved if either the boss of the factory or a political boss is allowed to select the doctor. Efficiency can be hoped for only if the patient is allowed to select his own doctor. The science of medicine is abstract, the relation of doctor and patient is something else.

In times past it is true people were frequently imposed on by the pseudo specialist. He decided to be one—and lo, he was such. Now, however, the various specialists have separated the trained specialist from the pseudo specialists. Any prospective patient can secure such lists by appealing to any secretary of a medical society, local or state.

We hear much of the high cost of medical care. The poor may resort to free hospitals, the wealthy are able to go to first-class hospitals. The middle-class people too proud to avail themselves of the former are in many instances unable to meet the cost of the latter. Two difficulties are apparent here. Many people make no provision for a rainy day and when sickness overtakes them they are unprepared to meet the situation. Efforts are being made so that these people may secure insurance which will provide for these emergencies. There are many who reject even this means of security. People so improvident should not slam the free institutions. A major difficulty lies in the high charges of the city hospitals. Palaces are built accessible only for the rich. Lay people and architects play a large part in the building of dream palaces. The chief culprits are the standardizers who though allegedly medical men have no knowledge of the requirements of a hospital. I believe the hospitals were the first to suffer from what is generally known as braintrusters. These are the people who are to blame for the high cost of hospital care. What shall we do with these? Nothing. They never learn anything and it is against the law to shoot them. This statement may be regarded essentially correct for I have given both possibilities careful thought for many years.

I do insist that these standardizing individuals restrict their vociferations to those regions where the conditions which they seek to wash away with crocodile tears exist. There are no such problems in Kansas.

In summary let it be emphasized that the freedom from disease that the public now enjoys is the result of the labor of the regular profession. It is all right for those with minor ailments, or with none at all, to consort with the cultists. It is all right to do fool things if someone is standing by able to protect us from the fruits of our folly. But, let it be emphasized, if the cultists

Inherited the earth the epidemic diseases would be upon us with their original pristine terribleness. After more than sixty years I can still hear the eloquent prayers that filled the countryside when epidemics of diphtheria appeared. One tube of antitoxin will do more good than all of these. I have seen all of these things. A doctor, an M.D., must think the truth. Perhaps it would be better if he sometimes proclaimed it.